Rickey & Robinson

Also By Roger Kahn:

Into My Own, 2006
Beyond the Boys of Summer, 2005
October Men, 2003
The Head Game, 2000
A Flame of Pure Fire, 1999
Memories of Summer, 1997
The Era, 1993
Games We Used to Play, 1992
Joe and Marilyn, 1986
Good Enough to Dream, 1985
The Seventh Game, 1982
But Not to Keep, 1978
A Season in the Sun, 1977
How the Weather Was, 1973
The Boys of Summer, 1972
The Battle for Morningside Heights, 1970
The Passionate People, 1968

Rickey & Robinson

The True, Untold Story of the Integration of Baseball

Roger Kahn

RODALE

Mention of specific companies, organizations, or authorities in this book does not imply endorsement by the author or publisher, nor does mention of specific companies, organizations, or authorities imply that they endorse this book, its author, or the publisher.

Internet addresses and telephone numbers given in this book were accurate at the time it went to press.

Ballpark capacities verified by Gary Gillette

Rodale books may be purchased for business or promotional use or for special sales. For information, please write to: Special Markets Department, Rodale, Inc., 733 Third Avenue, New York, NY 10017

Printed in the United States of America

Rodale Inc. makes every effort to use acid-free ♾, recycled paper ♲.

Book design by Elizabeth Neal

Library of Congress Cataloging-in-Publication Data is on file with the publisher

ISBN: 978-1-62336-297-3 hardcover

Distributed to the trade by Macmillan

2 4 6 8 10 9 7 5 3 1 hardcover

RODALE

We inspire and enable people to improve their lives and the world around them.
rodalebooks.com

For the incomparable Katharine
Who somehow suffers writers.
Or anyway one writer,
Gladly.

CONTENTS

FOREWORD

"Adventure . . . All adventure"

IN 1903, WHEN BRANCH RICKEY WAS STARRING AS A catcher for the Ohio Wesleyan baseball team and coaching the squad though still a student, an incident erupted in South Bend, Indiana, that would change his life and, in time, change the country. The manager of the Oliver Hotel on West Washington Street said that Charles Thomas, Rickey's black catcher who doubled as a first baseman, would not be permitted to register because "we don't let in nigras." That was one persistent and corrosive side of American life in 1903. Bigotry.

Rickey shouted down the hotel manager and dragged a cot into his own ground-floor room. Thomas would stay with him. Startled by Rickey's intensity, the manager backed off. "But you gotta keep the colored boy downstairs," he said. "He can't go nowhere else. He can't ride the elevators. And he sure as hell can't eat with the white folks in our dining hall." For emphasis the man slammed a fist on the counter.

Rickey turned away and took Thomas by an arm. "After we got into my room and I closed the door," Rickey told me years later, "tears welled in Charles's large eyes. His shoulders heaved convulsively and he rubbed one great hand over another with all the strength and power of his body. He was muttering, 'Black skin . . . black skin. If only I could make my black skin white.'"

Rickey's sense of drama was extraordinary. He paused to let Thomas's words and pain impact me. "Looking at Tommy that day," Rickey said finally, "I resolved that somehow I was going to open baseball and all the rest of America to Negroes." Large, assertive eyebrows moved closer together. Rickey bit his cigar and puffed a thundercloud of smoke. "It took me many decades, but I did it."

"Forty-four years later," I said. "When you signed Jackie Robinson, did you know how good a ballplayer he was going to be?" Many suggest that Rickey was the greatest talent scout in all of baseball history.

He made a rumbling laugh. "Adventure," he said. "Adventure. Show me a ballplayer with a sense of adventure and I'll show you a great one. Adventure, all adventure . . . that was the Jackie Robinson I signed."

The implications of that signing and indeed the significance of Branch Rickey's long life and of Jackie Robinson's life, which was all too brief, transcend the game and the business of baseball. But wasn't integration coming to America anyway? Wasn't integration an irresistible wave of the American future, as women's suffrage once had been? Possibly so. Perhaps even probably so. But before Rickey–Robinson, America's movement toward integration was so slow as to be barely discernible.

Marian Anderson, the great black contralto, was barred from singing at the Metropolitan Opera until she was almost 60 years old. Paul Robeson, the matchless bass baritone, was hounded to death by right-wingers citing Robeson's defiant, leftist politics. Arrant bigotry played a major role in the persecution of Robeson, who had also been one of the first blacks to play in the National Football League. Turning on Joe Louis, the hammering heavyweight champion, functionaries at the Internal Revenue Service demanded enormous payments in

Louis's later years. They flatly refused to give him credit for the hundreds of thousands of dollars he had donated to Army and Navy family relief during World War II. Louis was careless with money, but government bigotry was a major reason that the Brown Bomber died broke and broken.

As Robinson told me on many occasions, "When you think about it, my demand was modest enough. I wasn't asking to move into your neighborhood, or send my kids to school with your kids, and I certainly was not proposing to join your golf club. All I wanted was the right to make the kind of living that my abilities warranted."

Obviously Rickey–Robinson could not and did not categorically end American bigotry, but they significantly diminished it. At the very least, they played a clear white light into corners that had been crawling and ugly. I used to say, "No Jackie Robinson, no Martin Luther King." I expand that statement today. Without the foresight and the high moral purpose of Branch Rickey, and without the radiant courage of Jackie Robinson, Barack Obama could not have been elected president of the United States.

A nice touch to this rousing saga is the element of unpredictability. Close as I was to Jackie, intimate as I was with Branch, all the time I thought that the first minority American president would be a Jew.

—Roger Kahn

STONE RIDGE, NEW YORK

ONE

CONTRADICTIONS

LIKE MOST OF US WHO TAKE WRITING AND BASEball seriously, Walter Wellesley "Red" Smith retained a soft spot in his portable typewriter and a valentine in his heart for Wesley Branch Rickey. *Mister* Rickey, as generations of ballplayers were required to call him, was the game's greatest orator, a clubhouse Churchill, its preeminent theoretical thinker, its talent scout beyond compare and, most important in America's social history, its noble integrator. Rickey's polysyllabic eloquence made the craft of baseball writing easier. Quote him accurately and the eloquence edged into your own prose. That may be what inspired Smith when he created this enthusiastic and extraordinary paragraph.

> Branch Rickey was a player, manager, executive, lawyer, preacher, horse-trader, spellbinder, innovator, husband and father and grandfather, farmer, logician, obscurantist, reformer, financier, sociologist, crusader, father confessor, checker shark, friend and fighter. Judas Priest, what a character.

Well aware of Rickey's merits, a college professor named Judith Anne Testa, who wrote an excellent biography of the intimidating pitcher Sal Maglie (whom she called "baseball's demon barber"), raised an interesting question. "How," Judy Testa asked when I was working on this book, "are you going to write something consistently interesting when one of your principal characters has no vice worse than smoking cigars?" It is true that Rickey neither drank nor caroused. He was unfailingly faithful to his wife, Jane, and to the Christian religion as he perceived it. He was a doting father to his diabetic son, Branch Rickey Jr., who in later years became, for whatever reasons, a heavy drinker. (Branch Jr. died at the age of 47.)

But there existed another side to the Mahatma. Rickey was a greed-driven man, obsessed across the nine decades of a remarkable life with amassing and guarding a personal fortune. He never once went to a ballpark on Sunday, citing a promise made to his mother always to observe the Christian Sabbath. That oath, however solemn, did not prevent him from banking the gate receipts of Sunday games.

His penury became legendary, notably among the men who played for him. "Mr. Rickey," Enos Slaughter remarked to me one day at Cooperstown, "likes ballplayers. And he likes money. What he don't like is the two of them getting together."

A journeyman outfielder named Gene Hermanski hit 15 homers and batted .290 for the 1947 Dodgers. The following winter he strode into the team's Brooklyn offices, where Bob Cooke of the *New York Herald Tribune* was loitering in search of a story. "This time," Hermanski said to Cooke, "I'm gonna get the raise I deserve." Half an hour later Hermanski emerged from Rickey's presence smiling.

"You got the raise?" Cooke asked.

"No," Hermanski said, "but he didn't cut me."

After the star-crossed pitcher, Ralph Branca, appeared in 16 games for the wartime Dodgers of 1945, Rickey offered him a 1946 contract calling for a salary of $3,500, which, on an annual basis, comes out to about $67 a week. Branca was only 20 years old, but locally prominent. He had been a two-sport (baseball and basketball) star at New

York University and possessed a good fastball and a snapping curve. He consulted with his older brother, John, himself a pretty fair pitcher and later a New York state assemblyman. John thought his kid brother deserved $5,000 and Ralph returned the contract unsigned with what he recalls as a courteous letter "to Mr. Rickey" requesting an additional $1,500.

The response was silence. After a bit, Ralph telephoned the Dodger offices. Rickey would not take his call. When the 1946 Dodgers assembled for spring training in Florida, Branca still had heard nothing. Further, he was not invited to the camp. He borrowed money from his brother and drove a battered car to Vero Beach. There, alone and unhappy, he checked into a motel he recalls as being both ugly and dirty. "I was worried," he says, "that my big-league career might be over before it really began."

Following two weeks of increasingly frantic telephone calls—the borrowed money was running out—Ralph reached a secretary, who said, "Mr. Rickey will see you at nine o'clock tomorrow morning."

When Branca appeared, Rickey produced the $3,500 contract. "Sign this immediately," he ordered.

Branca did. "You may now check with the equipment man about your uniform," Rickey said. He paused and fixed Branca with a gelid stare. "And Branca, one more thing. Don't you ever hold out on me again!"

For the record, Branca, at $67 a week, went out and won 21 games for the Dodgers in 1947, when he was 21 years old. But he seldom seemed happy as a ballplayer, and a few years after Branca threw the notorious home run ball to Bobby Thomson, his career tanked and he went into the insurance business. Before reaching his 30th birthday, Branca, the pitcher, was finished. He had the good sense and good fortune to marry a wealthy woman, but even half a century later, when I see Branca, I sense a man with a battered and unrecovered psyche.

Would a gentler, less parsimonious Branch Rickey have given the large, sensitive Branca the confidence he lacked? Would a confident Branca then have gone on from his 20-game season and etched out a career that brought him into the Baseball Hall of Fame—not as a sometime guest, but as a member?

Perhaps.

"The love of money," St. Paul wrote in an epistle to his disciple, Timothy, "is the root of all evil." Not, as in the common misinterpretation, money, but the love of it—the sheer, unbridled, salivating lust for lucre—is what Paul insisted causes disaster. Few have read the King James version of the Bible as studiously as the devoutly Methodist Branch Rickey. Few, considering cupidity, have paid the words of St. Paul so little heed.

When Rickey was signing star athletes out of the Negro Leagues—Roy Campanella and Don Newcombe followed soon after Robinson—he refused to pay Negro League owners for their contracts. These owners, Rickey maintained, setting an unofficial record for sporting rationalization, were shady characters. Therefore they did not deserve to be paid.

But compared to Rickey's greatest accomplishment, integration, parsimony becomes a minor shortcoming. Under close scrutiny no figure remains flawless. Even as Thomas Jefferson wrote "all men are created equal," he kept slaves. While Abraham Lincoln was composing the Emancipation Proclamation, his family finances were in shambles. "No man," Montaigne supposedly has written, "is a hero to his valet."

Nor is any man necessarily a hero to his wallet.

In Rickey's halcyon years, running the St. Louis Cardinals and the Brooklyn Dodgers, he demanded and got a percentage of receipts from the sale of ballplayers' contracts to other major-league clubs. The costs of developing baseball players—paying managers and coaches, building and maintaining fields, buying uniforms, bats, baseballs, clubhouse hamburgers and all the rest—were paid by the organization at large. (Professional ballplayers must purchase only their spikes—now cleats—and gloves, although some finesse these costs with endorsement deals.) Presiding with care and penury, Rickey supervised expenditures from an executive suite, and often did hands-on coaching and evaluating around home plate. Or even in his office.

Carl Erskine, late of the Dodgers, who set a World Series record by striking out 14 Yankees on a cool October afternoon in 1953, remembers one of Rickey's unique tests. He directed a pitcher to hold a baseball with his palm inward, facing his nose. Now bend the elbow as deeply inward as possible until the ball touches the shoulder. From that position throw the baseball as far as you can. (That will not be a very great distance.) "Mr. Rickey," Erskine says, "could tell from that little toss just what kind of an overhand curve a pitcher would have." Mister Erskine's overhand curve was good enough for him to throw two no-hitters during a relatively brief but glorious Dodger career, mostly as a teammate of Robinson.

Rickey justified his percentage of player sales as fair compensation for his expertise. But the unusual arrangement raised at least one troubling question. Wasn't it tempting for Rickey to sign more young ballplayers than his own major-league team could possibly use? Surplus athletes would mean more player sales and more cash in Rickey's personal percentage piggy bank. Rickey never acknowledged that this issue might represent a conflict of interest. When he died in 1965, he left an estate of roughly $1.5 million. It would have been considerably greater had his personal avarice not antagonized other executives. Sam Breadon, the Cardinals' president, who forced Rickey out of St. Louis in 1943, subsequently sold the team for $4 million. After Walter Francis O'Malley, Rickey's fierce Brooklyn rival, died at the Mayo Clinic in 1979, the O'Malley estate amounted to an estimated $350 million. Baseball is a game for small boys and flinty businessmen.

Rickey's covetous acquisition of young talent became so extreme that Kenesaw Mountain Landis, the commissioner of baseball from 1921 until his death in 1944, released 91 St. Louis Cardinal farmhands in March 1938. That is to say, Landis overruled what was then baseball's prime directive, the reserve clause, and made these young players free agents, suddenly able to sell their services to the highest bidder. This was a revolutionary act, coming as it did during baseball's feudal years. The total number of players "Czar" Landis released was more than enough to stock four full teams. Landis's decree cost the Cards a lot of talent and might well have been a deathblow for Rickey's baseball career, seven years before Rickey signed Jackie Robinson.

But Rickey survived. He was not only eloquent, but shrewd and tough. Besides, his great idea, the baseball farm system, worked. It worked so well that it became the wave of the future. Fighting against it—an idea whose time had come—Landis learned what Nicholas II of Russia discovered earlier when he went up against Vladimir Ilyich Lenin. Even the power of a czar has limitations.

In the pattern of a Rickey farm system, the major-league team controlled scores of minor-league rosters through what were then called working agreements and are now known as PDCs, player development contracts. Essentially, ballplayers throughout the minor leagues function under contracts that are owned or controlled by teams in the major leagues. A major-league "farm director" distributes talent among the big club's affiliated minor-league franchises, which are classified from Triple A (the best) down to rookie leagues. The big-league team pays the players' salaries and may also pick up other expenses for the minor-league operation, such as the cost of bats and balls and chartered buses. The players advance, or are released, entirely at the discretion of the big-league team. The minor-league club owner runs ticket sales, plans promotions and determines the price of ballpark beer. Although his title is team president, he is in effect a combination doorman and barkeep. He is not allowed to make baseball decisions. The "independent" minor-league team, locally owned and locally controlled, was formerly a staple of organized baseball. It is now largely an anachronism.

Joe DiMaggio, a Bay Area youngster, broke in with the locally owned and controlled San Francisco Seals. Pee Wee Reese, a Kentucky native, first signed with the Louisville Colonels. Both minor-league teams eventually sold the contracts of these young stars for a significant profit. But that is not how things work today, in post-Rickey baseball. The actual talent in the minor leagues, the players—without whom, of course, there could be no games—are chattels of big-league teams, usually located a long way off. Some Massachusetts natives start playing pro ball in Oregon. Some Texans break in with teams in the Dakotas. "Our principal focus," one farm director tells me, "is not where the athlete comes from. In fact he may do better away from the pressures of his family and his hometown. Our focus is on consistency of instruction, creating, so to speak, a uniform product." I wonder if the McDonald's Corporation got the idea of franchising its uniform hamburger salons from the baseball world invented by Branch Rickey.

Curiously, or not so curiously, there was no hint of future integration in the Rickey farm system. His players were white, his managers were white, his coaches were white, and his scouts were white. If Rickey felt—he says he did—that a time for change was coming, he kept that to himself. Debates about the farm system were creating all the controversy he could tolerate.

In 1939 Rickey's St. Louis Cardinals had agreements with no fewer than 33 minor-league clubs. The Cardinals organization, which owned the baseball franchises in Rochester, Columbus and Houston, was an empire unto itself. One does best to think in terms of colonialism. In ordering the release of the 91 minor leaguers, Landis, who pined for fully empowered local ownership, provided what turned out to be only a hiccup in Rickey's grand career. (But among the players Landis liberated was the implausibly gifted Harold Patrick "Pistol Pete" Reiser, who helped the Brooklyn Dodgers beat Rickey's

Cardinals out of the 1941 National League pennant. As a 22-year-old Brooklyn rookie, Reiser batted .341, which led the league.)

For several years before 1939, Landis and his staff had been digging into the working agreements Rickey negotiated with a number of minor-league teams: Cedar Rapids of the Western League, Springfield of the Western Association, Crookston of the Northern League and Fayetteville in the Arkansas-Missouri League, among others. At length, when Landis reviewed the findings, he was appalled. The so-called working agreements, the commissioner told reporters in Chicago, "are being manipulated into arrangements for complete control of the lower classification clubs through secret understandings." Rickey himself saw nothing wrong with having a working agreement with two teams in the same league. Landis maintained that this sort of thing affected pennant races. The parent club, the Cardinals, could load one team with talent at the expense of another. Why might this happen? The parent club's first interest was in developing players, not in minor-league pennant races. You might want to stress speed on one club, strong-armed pitching on another or perhaps speed and pitching together. Landis, a lawyer and a former federal judge, decreed that "no [minor-league] club should contract away its right and obligation to get competitive playing strength as needed and whenever obtainable." In simple English: Play to Win.

Although Landis was an autocrat, he believed that minor-league club owners should be in complete control of their teams. Rickey, Landis charged, was "perverting working agreements with minor-league clubs so that he exercised complete control of various minor leagues."

Matters came to a head in 1939 during a hearing at Landis's office in Chicago. "You have agreements with two teams, Danville and Springfield, in the Three-I League so that you, in St. Louis, can influence the Three-I League pennant race," Landis told Rickey. Landis lowered his pointed chin and glowered. "The agreements are big as a house, aren't they?"

Rickey: "No, sir. Not as big as a house."

Landis: "They are as big as the universe."

Landis proceeded to lecture Rickey toward the point that pennant races in the Three-I League were "just as important as races in the National and American Leagues." Rickey's farm system, a baseball octopus, was strangling minor-league competition, Landis warned.

Despite Landis's threatening manner, Rickey continued developing his farm system, but now he became careful to work with only one minor-league team per league. Across the 1930s and 1940s as many as 59 minor leagues came to exist in America, from San Diego up through Maine, and Rickey's farm system and bank accounts flourished. Landis did not again intercede. "The general feeling in baseball back then," wrote J. G. Taylor Spink in an authoritative biography, *Judge Landis and Twenty-Five Years of Baseball*, "was that farm systems were here to stay and the Judge had simply cleared the air, promoting competitive pennant races throughout organized baseball."

Privately, Landis referred to Rickey as "that sanctimonious son of a bitch," and "that Protestant bastard masquerading in a minister's robe." I can neither find nor recall instances where Rickey spoke critically of Landis. It would have been destructive and pointless to badmouth baseball's historic czar.

In a decision handed down in 1922, the US Supreme Court issued a classic ruling. Writing for a unanimous court, Justice Oliver Wendell Holmes Jr. exempted organized baseball from antitrust laws and standard government business regulations, maintaining that baseball was "first and foremost, a sport and not a business." I played fast-pitch softball for many years alongside a shortstop named Charles "Cy" Rembar, who after-hours made a fortune practicing constitutional law. Rembar, a student of American legal history, wrote an authoritative book called *The Law of the Land*. Holmes's 1922 baseball ruling, Cy Rembar told me, was "the worst decision any great Supreme Court justice ever made."

In essence Holmes said that organized baseball could run itself any way it pleased. No minimum wage laws. No mandatory recognition of unions. No humane treatment of employees. No fair play to athletes. No fair employment. The men who ruled baseball were free to do anything they pleased, up to if not including assault and battery.

Rickey is hailed, and rightly so, for signing Jackie Robinson. But a hard-eyed look shows us also a Rickey who, more than anyone else, perpetuated baseball feudalism. Of course, contradictions in great leaders are not unusual, but seldom are they so dramatic. Branch Rickey, the Great Emancipator, was also a practicing feudal lord.

Aside from Landis, the baseball establishment generally came to accept the farm system as an efficient way of doing business. Quite simply, it worked. Only sportswriters made protest. Some called the farm systems "chain gangs," and one columnist, Jimmy Powers of the New York *Daily News,* almost drove Rickey out of baseball in 1950. Powers was a resolute reactionary and a closet anti-Semite—in short an unappetizing character—but he championed the salary rights of individual ballplayers with enduring passion. His ferocious clashes with Rickey came later, when Rickey was presiding over the Brooklyn Dodgers. These seemed to blind Powers to the nobility of Rickey's highest calling: integration. Thus Rickey's crusade in Brooklyn proceeded without the support of New York's most popular newspaper. For its part, the *New York Times* seemed embarrassed by the whole thing.

James Timothy McCarver, a major leaguer at the age of 18 and later a prominent baseball broadcaster, says candidly, "I don't have fond memories of Branch Rickey." Tim and I were lunching at a well-known French restaurant in Midtown Manhattan, and as we splurged on fabulous fish, McCarver went on. "In 1963, after the Army discharged me at Fort Knox, I headed to St. Petersburg to join the Cardinals at Al Lang Field." (That arena has since been renamed Progressive Energy Park.)

Most ballplayers in those days held winter jobs and did not work out year-round. Spring training began with endless hours spent swinging against pitching machines that threw only strikes. No batting gloves, either. You wanted to refocus your hitting eye and toughen your hands, bringing them from the blister phase to callus. Stan Musial says that for position players, not pitchers, spring training was mostly about developing calluses. Except for the pitchers and the publicity value, spring training then, and probably now, could be compressed into about 10 days.

Rickey, 81 years old at the time and a "senior consultant" in his second tour with the Cardinals, sat near the machines, chomping an unlit cigar and repeating the mantra "A good ball, a good ball, a good ball." He wanted the players to start saying the phrase themselves. If you repeat "a good ball" enough, he believed, you would be unlikely to swing at eye-high fastballs or curves bouncing into the dirt.

"Spring training was reentry," McCarver said, "and you were always making little adjustments with your feet and how and where you gripped the bat. I was holding mine a little higher than I should have. During the first week, Rickey called a team 'sit-down' to discuss aspects of what he had observed. Looking directly at me, Rickey said that one 'foolish' player, who will remain nameless, has been around long enough so that he ought to know how to hold a bat. Rickey continued to glare at me. Nameless? The whole team knew Rickey was talking about me.

"We had some solid veterans, [third baseman] Ken Boyer and [shortstop] Dick Groat, and I got some teasing about not knowing how to hold a bat. It was highly embarrassing for a young player, which I was."

"What did you hit that year?" I asked across a platter of flaky halibut.

"I believe .289," McCarver said. "I must have been holding the bat properly some of the time." He considered briefly. "Rickey's comment was humiliating and needless."

TWO

CIVIL WRONGS

BRANCH RICKEY'S SHORTCOMINGS ARE UNDENIABLE. Indeed, they caused recurring problems for him both with other baseball executives (notably Walter O'Malley) and with the working press (notably the New York *Daily News*). But his frugality, his sometime pomposity, his militant piousness and his intellectual elitism shrink in the balance when they are weighed against a monumental deed of moral courage performed during a hellacious time.

On August 6, 1945, a United States Air Force B-29 named *Enola Gay* dropped an atomic bomb called Little Boy on the Japanese city of Hiroshima. The explosion killed approximately 140,000 people. One Japanese radio announcer reported, "All living things, human and animal, were seared to death."

Three weeks later, on August 28, 1945, during a highly dramatic first meeting, Rickey agreed to sign Jackie Robinson to a minor-league contract in the Brooklyn Dodgers organization, ending so-called "organized" baseball's all-powerful, unwritten rule against employing black athletes. Major-league baseball had been rigidly segregated for 61 years. It is not entirely hyperbolic to suggest that signing Robinson in the year of Hiroshima was also a nuclear event, exploding in the white-washed corridors of big-time, big-money baseball. Hopefully this began the searing to death of American bigotry.

More than 40 years after Rickey's rich life came to an end in a hospital at Columbia, Missouri, the Rickey–Robinson adventure reverberates within baseball and beyond. Many, particularly young people, in the 21st century wonder how arrant prejudice could have persisted for so long in baseball. That is an underlying consideration of this book. Put briefly right here, if baseball was racist, and it was, so also was America. The game is an aspect of American life and mores, and a reflection of both. Like the moon, it simultaneously is a source of light and a reflector.

Baseball flowered as the segregated national pastime in the United States, the last major enlightened power on earth to renounce black slavery. As we all learned in grade school, the renunciation occurred in 1863 with Lincoln's Emancipation Proclamation. But—and we were not taught this in any classroom syllabus—segregation and bigotry persisted.

I remember my own grade school, a sedate Brooklyn prep called Froebel Academy, where each day began in chapel with the reading of a psalm and the singing of stirring Christian hymns.

Cast thy burden upon the Lord,
And he shall sustain thee.

There were no black faces in the chapel, nor on the faculty nor on the sporting fields behind the school building where we played ball. This was the 1930s. A rule, perhaps *the* rule, in privileged upper-class America was simple enough. Whites only. This approach extended far beyond the paneled walls of the Froebel chapel. In a variety of forms and manners, bigotry suffused the entire nation.

Occasional widely publicized exceptions appeared, mostly in college football. A great running back, Frederick Douglass "Fritz" Pollard, entered Brown University on a scholarship endowed by the

Rockefeller family and was named to Walter Camp's 1916 All-America team. Pollard later coached, played professionally, ran a variety of small businesses and lived to the great age of 92. Currently Brown and the Black Coaches and Administrators cosponsor an annual Fritz Pollard Award, given to the college or professional coach chosen by the BCA as coach of the year. Pollard was inducted into the College Football Hall of Fame in 1954 and the Pro Football Hall of Fame, posthumously, in 2005.

In 1917 Paul Robeson, later famous as a basso cantate, actor and political activist, made Camp's team as an end from Rutgers. "A Rutgers dean once called me in," Robeson told some friends, "and said his grandfather had traveled north from the same part of North Carolina where I had roots. He wondered if my grandfather had traveled the identical route. I told him no, my grandfather did travel from Carolina, but the dean was using the wrong verb. My grandfather didn't simply travel. He *escaped*." Robeson won 15 varsity letters at Rutgers in four sports. He also made Phi Beta Kappa and graduated from Columbia Law School. For a brief period he worked for a prominent law firm, but quit after a white secretary refused to take dictation from him. Subsequently he left the law and became an internationally acclaimed performer and later the most memorable Othello of the 20th century.

Splendid as these men were, they were splendid exceptions. They entered mainstream America through portals in the academic community, which was arguably more enlightened than the nation at large, at least in northern states. When Rickey brought a black man into organized baseball for the season of 1946, he did so against centuries of whites-only tradition that extended far beyond academia, and against wide and ferocious opposition.

After the chaotic Reconstruction era, no black had sat in the American Senate, no black had ever been appointed to the Supreme Court and neither major political party had even considered (heaven forfend) a black as candidate for the presidency of the United States.

American schools and colleges largely were segregated. American armed forces, so heroic in defeating the Nazis and the brutal Japanese military, were segregated. Most black soldiers in the Army served in segregated units. Blacks in the Navy were limited to menial work, such as waiting on tables reserved for white officers. It was not until 1943 that the Marine Corps accepted *any* black volunteers. Still, America's World War II experience chipped away at the wall of racism. Segregated or not, blacks (including Jackie Robinson) did serve in the armed forces, sometimes heroically. Many returned from military duty with a sense of legitimacy and worth that had not been there before.

Franklin D. Roosevelt, president from 1933 until his death in the spring of 1945, is rightly remembered as an enlightened liberal. But his actions against American racism were painfully deliberate. Meeting with A. Philip Randolph, the leader of the Brotherhood of Sleeping Car Porters, and Walter White, director of the NAACP, primarily to discuss the lynching of blacks, Roosevelt insisted that his hands were tied. He could not campaign for a federal antilynching law and his great make-work programs during the Depression, such as the Works Progress Administration and the Civilian Conservation Corps, had to remain as rigidly segregated as the military. "I did not choose the tools with which I must work," President Roosevelt told the black leaders. "Had I been permitted to choose, then I would have selected quite different ones. But I've got to get legislation passed by Congress to save America [from economic turmoil that could lead to socialism or even communism]. The segregationist Southerners, by reason of the seniority rule in Congress, are chairmen or occupy strategic places on most of the Senate and House committees. If I come out for the anti-lynching bill now, they will block every bill I ask Congress to pass to keep America from collapsing. I just can't take that risk."

Historians generally accept 1968, long after the reign of FDR and three years after Rickey died, as the time when wholesale lynching of blacks finally disappeared from the American scene. A song remains:

Southern trees bear strange fruit,
Blood on the leaves and blood at the root,
Black bodies swinging in the southern breeze,
Strange fruit hanging from the poplar trees.

Across the decades, more than one cross-burning Klansman would cheerfully and savagely have strung Branch Rickey from a tree.

Baseball swept into the American South during the 19th century and subsequently prejudices from the American South swept into baseball. Some historians claim to have found evidence that black slaves had begun playing ball as far back as the 1830s. But the records, if any survive at all, are skimpy. A few oral recollections exist, but no written accounts. Other researchers suggest that during the Civil War, Union soldiers between battles spread the game throughout southern red-clay fields and rural hollows. Whatever, it was after the Civil War, during the bitter Reconstruction period, that baseball boomed into the national sport. With that boom came baseball's hostility toward blacks.

As far as I can learn, the first formal statement of racism in baseball appeared just five years after the Emancipation Proclamation. "On the first day of January, in the year of our Lord one thousand eight hundred and sixty-three," Abraham Lincoln wrote, "all persons held as slaves within any State . . . shall be then, thenceforward, and forever free." When General Robert E. Lee signed terms of surrender in a private home at Appomattox, Virginia, in 1865, the death of legal American slavery became assured. But bigotry has had a vastly longer shelf life.

In 1868 the National Association of Base Ball Players publicly announced a ban on "any club including one or more colored persons."

Although a "national association of players" sounds like a union, actually it was a federation of club owners, a primitive major league.

Over the late 1860s and 1870s baseball evolved from an amateur activity, a club sport conducted broadly along the lines of English cricket, toward becoming predominantly professional. When the National Association splintered into competing organizations in 1871, professional teams no longer were restricted by the 1868 racist rule and for a short while—in 1878 and again in 1884—African Americans played in the major leagues. But abruptly, they were excluded in 1885. No written decree, much less a public statement, came to light back then, nor has any since. But black faces vanished, first from the major leagues and then, over about 15 more years, from the minor leagues as well. By the end of the 1898 season, when the minor leagues were finally and totally closed to blacks, the triumph of baseball bigotry became complete.

In 1884 two Negro brothers, catcher Moses Fleetwood Walker and outfielder Welday Wilberforce Walker, played part of a season for the Toledo Blue Stockings of the then major American Association. They are generally accepted as the first blacks in the major leagues. The Walkers came from an upper-middle-class background in Mount Pleasant, Ohio, the sons of Dr. Moses W. Walker, the first African American physician in Mount Pleasant. Fleet Walker, a man of keen intelligence, enrolled in Oberlin College in 1878 and played on the college's first varsity baseball team in 1881. He transferred to the University of Michigan law school the following fall and played varsity ball for Michigan in 1882. With the Toledo Blue Stockings two years later, Fleet Walker batted .263 in 42 games. His brother, Welday, played in five games and hit .222.

The numbers do not suggest great skills, but Hugh Fullerton, one of the ablest early baseball writers, offered a telling story. It came from Anthony John "Count" Mullane, a native of Cork, Ireland, who settled in the Midwest and became an early pitching wonder. Mullane was ambidextrous. He threw equally hard from either side and never used a glove. How, then, did he contend with line drives bashed through the box? Quite simply, as Count Mullane put it, "I got the hell out of the way."

Mullane signed with Toledo for 1884 and that season pitched 65 complete games. He won 35. "Toledo had a colored man [Fleet Walker] who was declared by many to be the greatest catcher of his time," Fullerton wrote in the *New York World,* "but Tony Mullane did not like being the battery partner of a Negro."

> "I had it in for him," Tony admitted years later. "He was the best catcher I ever worked with, but I disliked having a Negro catcher and whenever I had to pitch to him I used to pitch anything I wanted without looking at his signals. One day he signaled me for a curve and I shot a fastball at him. He caught it and walked down to me.
>
> "'Mr. Mullane,' he said. 'I'll catch you without signals, but I won't catch you if you are going to cross me when I do give you a signal.'
>
> "And all the rest of the season he caught me, and caught anything I pitched without knowing what was coming."

Toledo finished eighth in a 12-team league. Neither Walker was re-signed. Mullane kept pitching in the majors for another 10 years. He won 284 games and lived out most of his days in Chicago, working as a policeman. The ambidextrous cop, Count Tony Mullane, died at the age of 85 in 1944, the year before Jackie Robinson signed his first organized baseball contract in Branch Rickey's office above Montague Street in Brooklyn.

As I mentioned, no baseball blacklist was publicly announced in 1875. Blacklists seldom are proclaimed formally. Most often they are the stuff of backroom conspiracies. But within a few seasons such stars as Adrian "Cap" Anson, first baseman and later manager of the early Chicago Cubs, was telling anyone who cared to listen that he would never step on a field with a Negro as a teammate or even as a rival.

Anson drove that point home on July 14, 1887, when his Chicago club was scheduled to play an exhibition against the Newark Giants, a minor-league squad from the International League, which included two black players (Fleet Walker and George Stovey). Anson refused to let the game start until both black men exited the field. He would not countenance allowing either to play or even sit on the bench. Anson was a great star—he had batted .371 the previous season—and the Newark officials yielded without a protest. Soon thereafter, all the owners in the Triple A International League voted secretly to refuse future contracts to black players. Christy Mathewson quotes John McGraw as not wanting his New York Giants to mix with "a bunch of coffee-colored Cubans" even in spring exhibitions. I had probably better add in this dismaying chronicle that neither McGraw nor Anson hailed from the South. McGraw was born in the central New York State village of Truxton, Anson came from Marshalltown, Iowa. Like baseball, America south *and* north was something less than a temple of enlightenment in those days. Indeed, the Baseball Hall of Fame inducted both Anson and McGraw into its chambers in 1939. For many decades officials at the Hall prattled about the personal character of inductees, all the while closing their eyes to—and even endorsing—racial prejudice. (Of late, Hall officials, now frantic to be politically correct, have been overcompensating.)

After the major leagues banned Fleet Walker, he caught minor-league ball and semi-pro, struggling to make a living. Then one night outside a Syracuse bar called the Crouse Saloon, at the corner of Monroe and Orange streets, he got into a dispute with six whites. As they assaulted him, Walker reached for a knife and stabbed an ex-convict named Patrick "Curly" Murray in the groin. Walker then fled for dear life. Murray died in a Syracuse hospital.

Police arrested Walker and charged him with second-degree (unpremeditated) murder. After a tumultuous trial in Syracuse, he was acquitted on the grounds of self-defense. Walker quit baseball and became a supporter of a movement generally called black nationalism. In 1908 Walker published a 47-page pamphlet entitled *Our Home Colony: A Treatise on the Past, Present and Future of the Negro Race in America.* Here Walker recommended that African Americans migrate back to Africa. "The only practical and permanent solution of the present and future race troubles in the United States is entire separation by emigration of the Negro from America." Fleet Walker warned, "The Negro race will be [seen by whites as] a menace and the source of discontent as long as it remains in large numbers in the United States. The time is growing very near when the whites of the United States must either settle this problem by deportation, or else be willing to accept a reign of terror such as the world has never seen in a civilized country."

Mostly forgotten, Walker died on May 11, 1924, in Cleveland at the age of 67, when Jackie Robinson was 5 years old. There is no evidence to suggest that either Robinson or Branch Rickey knew the full story of a gifted American named Moses Fleetwood Walker. It is nothing less than a tragedy.

In signing Robinson, Rickey was moving against currents of tradition and proceeding under a battery of dangers. At the time of the signing it seemed possible that baseball's ruling powers would invalidate the Robinson contract and expel Rickey from the baseball business. "My grandfather knew the risks," says Branch B. Rickey, currently the president of the Pacific Coast League. "He had spoken at a meeting of club directors, 15 men besides himself, and every one said with iron resolve first that Negroes had no place in the national pastime and second that anyone who tried to bring in Negroes should be disbarred." Disbarring Rickey would have turned a lifetime career, decades of hard and often inspired work, into a handful of dust.

A few, such as George Weiss, functioning as general manager of the New York Yankees, argued that their sentiments were purely a matter of business. Black ballplayers would attract black fans, "offending our [affluent, white] box-seat customers from Westchester. They don't want to sit with Negroes and they'll stop coming to our games at the Stadium. To bring in Negroes is to court financial ruin." Others said that blacks already had their own leagues and that was how "the good Lord and the US Constitution meant for things to be." Indeed, on May 18, 1896, the Supreme Court had held by a vote of eight to one—in an infamous case called *Plessy v. Ferguson*—that racially separate facilities, if equal, did not violate the constitution. Thus, segregating blacks to their own leagues in no way compromised equality. After 1896, segregation reigned with the blessing of the Supreme Court's purblind vision. One recalls George Orwell's sardonic theme that "All men are equal, but some are more equal than others."

Fully 58 years passed before the Court got around to recognizing that separate facilities, if they existed at all, were not likely to be "equal." On May 17, 1954, seven years after Jackie Robinson made his debut with the Brooklyn Dodgers, the Court under Chief Justice Earl Warren unanimously held that black children had a right to attend—and integrate—all public schools. The new doctrine stated simply that segregated facilities were "inherently unequal." Theoretically at least, integration became the law of the land.

One summer night in 1952, while the Dodgers were defeating the Philadelphia Phillies, Benny Weinrig, the press box attendant at Ebbets Field, approached behind my station in the box and said in a soft, anxious tone, "Mr. O'Malley wants to see you." Walter O'Malley, who had wrested control of the Dodgers from Rickey following the 1950 season, presided from a private box suspended from the front of the upper deck directly behind home plate. A splendid seat, this was a level below the chirping portable typewriters of the working press who labored in a box suspended from the roof. A private bar and kitchen served both facilities so that neither the sportswriters nor O'Malley and his guests had to subsist during games on the bottled Schaefer beer and the Stahl-Meyer hot dogs that bellowing vendors hawked.

(Before O'Malley's Dodger days, Walter had been chairman of the board of trustees at Froebel Academy when I was a wafer-thin running back there. That old school tie probably is why O'Malley made himself so accessible to me. Buzzie Bavasi, the late Dodger general manager, told me long afterward, "Walter never let any other writer get close.")

An expansive and political man, O'Malley enjoyed entertaining dignitaries with gourmet food and fine whiskey in his prized private seats above home plate. One year Douglas MacArthur attended 13 Dodger games as O'Malley's guest, always guarded from the press and public by a sturdy, haughty aide, Major General Charles Willoughby, born Karl Weidenback in Imperial Germany. (According to a Dodger publicist, Irving Rudd, the Dodgers lost all of the games MacArthur attended.)

As I cleared a catwalk and entered O'Malley's box, he called my name heartily and said, "There's someone here I want you to meet." His guest was distinguished looking, bespectacled and white-haired. It was Earl Warren of California, stopping by for a ballgame on a trip home from a sightseeing tour of Europe. Warren ran for vice president under Thomas E. Dewey in 1948. They lost. Now, while still a prominent Republican politician, Warren was, as they say in the theater, between engagements.

I sat beside Warren, who had a drink, not his first, in hand. He said that while vacationing in Europe he found the international edition of the *Herald Tribune,* the so-called *Paris Herald,* "a perfectly splendid newspaper." I asked if I might mention his visit to Brooklyn in the *New York Herald Tribune.*

"That's a Republican paper, is it not?" Warren said.

"When last I checked, sir."

"Then assuredly you can mention my name and, you can add that I'm certainly enjoying this ballgame and Mr. O'Malley's Brooklyn hospitality."

Below us, on the green and brown and chalk geometry of the playing field, all the players were white men, except for one. Jackie Robinson had singled and he was now leading off first base, a threat to steal and a greater threat to shatter the composure of the Phillies' starting pitcher, the redoubtable Robin Roberts. The Dodger home uniforms were a vivid, almost luminescent white. Robinson's skin was very dark. "Uncompromising ebony," I once called it. So there under Earl Warren's gaze at Ebbets Field, 62 years ago, the fact of color, white and black, made a mighty statement.

Robinson's movements at first base were dramatic and unique. He balanced on the balls of his feet, crouching a bit, arms extended and making feints toward second base. He was always in motion, toward second or back to the safety of first or simply bobbing up and down. I have never seen anything quite like Jackie Robinson taking a lead. Neither had Earl Warren. While we talked lightly and amiably, Warren's eyes never left Robinson. Sometimes Warren sipped, but his eyes stayed on Jack. When at length Robinson stole second, the excitement of the moment brought Warren to his feet and wonder glazed his face. I like to think that the excitement Robinson generated, and the image of a gallant black, alone in white men's country, worked within Earl Warren two years later when he led the Supreme Court to its monumental verdict on school integration. Warren ruled on *Brown v. Board of Education of Topeka,* but first he had seen Robinson v. Philadelphia Phillies. The one fed the other, in a classic example—probably *the* classic example—of baseball as a force in American life, quite beyond the base paths.

So many theories surround Rickey's signing of Jackie Robinson that figuratively it takes a bulldozer to drive through the fluff and approach reality. I will here deal only with the leading propositions.

Rickey acted out of venality. He knew Robinson would become a fabulous drawing card. Largely false, at least as regards Rickey's primary motivation. In fact Robinson did become the greatest drawing card in baseball. Typically when the Dodgers played in Cincinnati during the late 1940s and early 1950s, black fans from as far away as Mobile, Alabama, chartered buses and journeyed to Crosley Field, roughly a 1,400-mile round trip. "I did not wholly anticipate that sort of occurrence," Rickey told me, "but when it developed, I certainly did not object." Visiting teams back then retained 25 percent of the gate receipts.

Robinson's effect on Dodger home attendance is more elusive. The all-white Dodgers of 1946 drew 1,796,824 paying customers to Ebbets Field. The integrated Dodgers of 1947 drew 1,807,525. The difference, roughly 11,000 tickets, is not significant. What these numbers say mostly is that Brooklyn, with its bandbox home field, was one hell of a baseball town.

Rickey saw the Negro Leagues as a prebuilt farm system, from which he could sign outstanding ballplayers at minimal expense. True to an extent. As I have noted, Rickey never paid Negro League owners for the athletes he signed, and we find here, in the midst of the noble work of integration, more evidence of Rickey's disconcerting cupidity. In time the late Effa Manley, who ran the Newark Eagles of the Negro National League, denounced Rickey as a "pirate." Mrs. Manley, who was white, tried to improve the condition of players throughout the league. She advocated better scheduling, higher pay and improved accommodations. Her athletes traveled in an air-conditioned Flxible Clipper bus. A gifted businessperson and a diligent worker in the civil rights movement, Manley was elected to the Baseball Hall of Fame in 2006, the first woman so honored. (Rickey had been elected in 1967, more than a generation earlier.)

Rickey acted out of a lofty moral sense, fulfilling an unwritten contract that he believed existed between baseball and America, black and white. Largely true. "Baseball should lead by example," he said once, "because it is a quasi-public institution . . . and, particularly in Brooklyn, I am not so sure about the quasi."

In considering all of Rickey's voluminous papers, stored in 131 boxes at the Library of Congress, I found no evidence that he systematically studied patterns of American racism. Rickey was constantly dictating memos, often to himself, on ballplayers, pennant races and characters that crossed his ken. But I found no memos on racism. By the time he enrolled at Ohio Wesleyan in 1900, as an 18-year-old scholar–athlete, he had developed a personal loathing for bigotry. The Rickey family, in Scioto County, a sweep of rolling land in southern Ohio reaching to within 30 miles of the Kentucky border, were devout Methodists. John Wesley, who founded the Methodist Church in 1874, called slavery "a complicated villainy." At least one early American Methodist bishop was excommunicated for keeping a slave. The issue of slavery eventually caused a schism in the American Methodist church, but the Rickey family remained staunchly in the abolitionist wing. The mainstream Methodist church similarly was opposed to alcohol, maintaining that abstinence is "a faithful witness to God's liberating and redeeming love for persons." Rickey's opposition to drinking came naturally out of his family and religious background. So too did his feeling on that complicated villainy, American racism.

On a light news day in the winter of 1954, I enlisted the *New York Herald Tribune*'s telephone recording room—usually used for overseas dispatches—to cut a 33⅓ LP disc while Branch Rickey, the closest thing baseball had to Winston Churchill, talked and answered questions that I tossed at him. I am setting down the story as it ran. What we get is a vivid sense of Rickey's command of the language. What we do not get, for reasons that will presently become clear, are his ardent views on racism.

"RICKEY ON THE RECORD"

New York Herald Tribune, February 14

The mystifying speech patterns of Branch Rickey, a man who generally prompts reporters to throw away their notebooks in despair, were captured yesterday on a record connected to a telephone recording machine. The record was not thrown away.

I reached Rickey in Fort Pierce, Florida, where he was awaiting the opening of the Pittsburgh Pirates spring camp. The Pirates have finished a distant last for the past two seasons and Rickey was questioned on prospects. Here, verbatim from the record, are the questions and Rickey's answers.

Q: Are the Pirates going to do better this year?

Rickey: I know a rosebush is going to bloom on the 18th of May and do it nearly every year. And it's all green today and three days later it's in full color. Well, I don't control a baseball club's development the way nature does a rosebush. But I know damn well—pardon me, very well—that these boys physically fit who can run and throw and have power are going to come to some kind of competitive excellence. And I don't know whether it's the 18th of May and I don't know when it's going to come, but it's my job to get it to come all at the same time. I've got to take all these darts of uncomplimentary remarks because of youth movement or an old man movement. I've got to take a lot of punishment but I guess I'm old enough to do it.

Q: When do you think the Pirates will move out of last place?

Rickey: I'm not too mindful about moving up in the second division. I have no desire to finish anywhere except first place. I would much rather finish in eighth place with a club I knew was going all the way, than I would in second place with a stand-patter. That's fact and I've been criticized for that viewpoint in Pittsburgh. But at my age I'm not interested in being in second place, but I know I have to pass second to get to first and, of course, I'm anxious to get out of the hole: I don't want to be in last place. I'd rather be in seventh or fifth. I don't mean to be ridiculous and say I'm not interested in being in fifth any more than I am in being eighth. I'd rather be in seventh with a team that's going to be in fifth.

Q: Oh, I see. Well, how long do you expect it to be before you do for Pittsburgh what you did for Brooklyn and St. Louis?

Rickey: I had a worse situation in Pittsburgh than I had in Brooklyn. We've been in last place on merit. The crowd I started with in Brooklyn, had [Arky] Vaughan, [Billy] Herman, Pee Wee Reese and Dixie Walker and three or four pretty good pitchers and twelve 10-year men were there. There was a nucleus to build around. And I had something in St. Louis. I had Rogers Hornsby, a great ballplayer. In Pittsburgh I didn't have a nucleus. It took me three or four years in Brooklyn. It took me six years in St. Louis and I've really had two here now because the first year we just had what we had. To tell you that it's going to be another year or two years, to put a dateline on it—I can't do it. I can't tell you. We're on a long-distance phone and you're paying the bill. You ought to stop me when I get talking.

Q: No, no. You're being quite eloquent.

Rickey: Heaven's sakes, no eloquence. I need help. If you know how to help a tail-end ball club, come down here. I'll pay you more than you're making. I don't care what it is.

Q: Why not start with another Jackie Robinson?

Rickey: Oh, well, goodness is relative. If I compare it with player X on the Brooklyn club and player Y on the Milwaukee club, why my boy might not be as good. But there are some instances where I wouldn't trade them, and I have a number of boys that I really like very much. The Army has hurt us more than it does Brooklyn or Milwaukee or any great team because the players I lose to the Army are men I could use. The men they lose to the Army are men that would be there for four years before they could use them. And I am hurt by that. But in spite of that I've got a number of boys that are reporting here that I think are good. We have half a dozen young catchers and we've got seven first basemen and our pitching, we have some good prospects there but they're young. They're too young. I like old pitchers. A lot of people think I want young players all the time. Why, heaven's sake, I want good men. I don't care how old they are if they can run and do things, the older the better.

Q: Are you interested in trading?

Rickey: Yes. But I don't anticipate any deals before the 15th of April. I want to look over everyone I have first and then, the other fellow doesn't come up with a sense of need until he has seen something of his team, too. You know, now, there are seven clubs in the National League who expect to win the pennant. I don't ever make any excuses on that myself. We've got an ideal training camp here for a unit camp—that is, for a one-club thing. It's not a Vero Beach. That, as an organizational camp, is in a class by itself. Last year we didn't play as many exhibition games as we do this year but, as a matter of fact, a great deal of good comes out of not playing games. The compensation of games, however, is overall good. Where you don't play games if your instructors are minded to do it, they can do a great deal of work in the field of teaching skills, techniques and individual improvements.

Q: Will the Pirates be improved?

Rickey: Yes, sir. In all departments. They're a year older and a year better. I've been frank with you. Very frank. Come see me any time. I do believe I'd like to have you to work for me.

The elapsed time of the conversation was 12 minutes. The telephone bill was $6.90. Even Vince Kellett, the chief editorial auditor at the *Herald Tribune* and a man of surpassing frugality, agreed that the money was well spent.

Myself, I wonder to this day why I didn't ask about Rickey's heroic journey toward integration. But then I recall a cold reality. Robert B. Cooke, a smooth and handsome Yale man who was sports editor at the *Tribune,* had told me over a drink that by hiring a Negro "Rickey has done more to damage baseball than any man who ever lived." Cooke developed his point with great intensity. He had been captain of the Yale hockey team in 1936, he said, and he drove his shots as hard as any New York Ranger. But the Rangers were staffed by Canadians who "had the legs to skate Americans clear off the ice."

In baseball, Cooke said, Negroes had the legs, too, and they would soon run every white man out of the game. These words were spoken with passion and, as Sartre wrote, you cannot argue away a passion. If I focused my recorded interview—a great novelty at the time—on racism and injustice, Cooke might have killed the entire piece. He had that power. I certainly could have argued, but I was not ready for a career crisis that February day. Given my friendship with Robinson, my admiration of Rickey and my own impassioned support of integration, a career crisis with Cooke was inevitable. But I didn't know that at the time.

And then, perhaps whimsically, suppose I had taken Rickey up on his offer to join him with the Pirates for more than the *Tribune* was paying me—at that time a less than overwhelming $6,240 a year. I might have evolved into a professional baseball man rather than an author. In short, I might never again have had to change a typewriter ribbon. But across the next four seasons, the Pirates finished seventh once and eighth three times. Roberto Clemente joined the team in 1955, but other Rickey seedlings were slow to grow.

Given that maturation rate, there was no job security in Pittsburgh, not even for Rickey himself, and had I accepted his offer I might also have ended up unemployed amid the steel mills and the coal towns of western Pennsylvania, telling my sorrows to the foam atop a mug of Rolling Rock beer.

"And you would have found," said Dick Young, of the New York *Daily News,* the king of caustic sportswriters, "that the real problem out there goes beyond baseball.

"In Pittsburgh, all the pretty women are pregnant."

THREE

COMING TO BROOKLYN

I FIRST ENCOUNTERED BRANCH RICKEY (IN THE flesh) at a wintertime assembly at Erasmus Hall, a venerable Brooklyn high school, where he came to speak. At the time Erasmus was sharply split into divisions. In the academic wing I studied Latin over four years, from grammar to Vergil's towering epic, *The Aeneid.* ("*Arma virumque cano. I sing of arms and the man . . .*") In nearby classrooms, young women entered in the "commercial" branch of Erasmus Hall learned shorthand and typing. The place, some 4,000 students strong, was half prep and half secretarial school.

A group of "Flat Bush gentlemen" founded Erasmus Hall in 1786 as a private academy affiliated with the Dutch Reformed Church. Tuition was a then formidable six guineas a year. The new school took its name from the Dutch renaissance scholar Desiderius Erasmus of Rotterdam (1466–1536), who prepared Greek and Latin editions of the New Testament and was sometimes described as Prince of the Humanists.

Later Erasmus Hall went public, but for many years the academic—as opposed to the commercial—division of Erasmus Hall retained a strong classical element. In my time there we were required to study the life and theology of Erasmus and I was able to complete my four years of Latin under a remarkable polymath, Dr. Harry Wedeck. In one of my few—very few—academic triumphs, Dr. Wedeck awarded me a gold medal as the premier Latin student in the class of 1944. To this day, thanks to Erasmus and Dr. Wedeck, I can quote lines from Caesar, Cicero and, as above, Vergil. More than 65 years after graduating, I find myself listed among the school's distinguished alums, along with Sid Luckman, Mae West, Mickey Spillane, Bernard Malamud, Barbara Stanwyck, Susan Hayward, Barbra Streisand and Moe Howard, one of the Three Stooges. Quite a gang.

When Rickey came to Brooklyn in 1943, first living in modest quarters in the Clinton Hill section, he plunged himself into community affairs. To his pleasure, he discovered that the borough consisted of a series of individual neighborhoods, some with a decided ethnic character, and many with distinctive names. Bay Ridge, Bedford Stuyvesant, Bensonhurst, Brownsville, Coney Island, Crown Heights, East New York, Flatbush, Fort Greene, Park Slope, Sheepshead Bay and Williamsburg were (and are) some subsections contained in the merry old borough of Brooklyn. "I like the mix of neighborhoods," Rickey said. "To my mind it is a microcosm of America at large."

At that winter assembly back in the wartime year of 1944, Rickey talked about the future of a world that would soon be at peace, while mentioning that Dodger season tickets were now on sale. Would the future belong to the scientists or to the artists? That was his topic. Few knew then of nuclear bombs or the Holocaust. As Rickey spoke he held a jar full of raisins and nuts, which he shook occasionally. At the end of the talk Rickey said, "Remember now, tell your parents to order their season tickets right away for the best choice of seats. And, oh yes, about the future; scientists or artists? Who can say? But if you observed closely, whenever I shook the jar you learned something useful. No matter how hard I shook that jar, the nuts always came out on top." (So much for Rickey as humorless.)

I found myself fascinated by Rickey, a pudgy sort with massive eyebrows, as I had been by only one other speaker at an Erasmus assembly. The great World War I fighter ace Eddie Rickenbacker (1890–1973) appeared and talked passionately about the ordeal that led to his book, *Seven Came Through.* On a secret military mission during World War II, Rickenbacker rode aboard a B-17 that had to ditch in a remote patch of the South Pacific. Quickly taking command, Rickenbacker got the eight survivors onto a raft, where, before being rescued, they drifted on an endless sea for 24 days. One man died. The others subsisted on rainwater and such food as they could find. Once, a seagull landed on Rickenbacker's head. The bird became dinner for seven. Rickenbacker told his story of courage, discipline and luck with magnificent gusto.

Dodger survival was a different matter, and I don't recall Rickey saying much about the team. The great ball club that I later called the Boys of Summer at this point was no more than a gleam in Rickey's eye. Pee Wee Reese, Carl Erskine and Duke Snider were in the Navy. Gil Hodges was serving in the Marine Corps. Carl Furillo and Billy Cox were in the Army. There wasn't much talent left to perform at Ebbets Field.

Dixie Walker, the popular right fielder, batted .357 and led the league, beating out Stan Musial by 10 points. But the pitching was dreary. Curt Davis, a lean side-arming right-hander and the best of the wartime staff, won 10 games. He lost 11. No Dodger starting pitcher finished above .500. The team dropped 91 games and finished in seventh place, just a game and a half ahead of the team sportswriters called the Phutile Phillies.

On one painful western swing, the Dodgers performed so poorly that Roscoe McGowen of the *New York Times* composed a parody of the wartime song "Bless 'Em All." McGowen's Dodger version went "Lose 'Em All." Rickey pretended to be unconcerned and constantly touted questionable prospects, particularly a young infielder from

New Jersey named Eddie Miksis. But Miksis couldn't hit much, even against wartime pitching, which moved McGowen to compose another bit of caustic doggerel. This one began:

Miksis
Will fix us,
Said Rickey, the boss . . .

Over nine big-league seasons, Eddie Miksis would bat .236, but not even a chain of dismaying Dodgers could depress me in 1944. Moving from poetry to hyperbole, Rickey promoted at least four other infielders as "the next Pee Wee Reese." Here are their names, the club to which Rickey sold their contracts and their lifetime big-league batting averages:

- Claude Corbitt, Cincinnati Reds, .243
- Tommy Brown, Philadelphia Phillies, .241
- Bob Ramazotti, Chicago Cubs, .230
- Bobby Morgan, Cubs, .233

Looking back, Rickey's hustling of pseudo Reeses may seem amusing, shipping inferior players to other teams, also inferior. But as I have mentioned Rickey pocketed 15 percent of each sale and to O'Malley that fiscal leak out of the Dodger bank account was a serious matter. O'Malley had advanced from Dodger club lawyer to part owner on stock he purchased with a loan from George V. McLaughlin, president of the Brooklyn Trust Company. O'Malley, called the Big Oom, quietly fumed at what he considered Rickey's unconscionable double-dipping. Sometime back then—there is no exact date—O'Malley began scheming to take over the Dodgers for himself.

As a young man I knew nothing of the byzantine Brooklyn front office. Youth is about hope, and I understood Rickey's history of building championship teams in St. Louis. So I hoped and trusted that given time he would bring a consistent winning team to my hometown, which up until then had zero history of consistent winners. While the New York ball clubs, the Yankees and the Giants, became ongoing powerhouses, success for the Dodgers had been rare and episodic. (The team was then known as the Robins after their portly, genial manager, Wilbert Robinson. The Dodger nickname became popular during the 1930s.) Only two pennants between 1900 and 1940, and after each a dismal loss in the World Series. In Game 2 of the 1916 Series, which the Boston Red Sox won in five games, a young Red Sox left-hander defeated the Dodgers, two to one, in 14 innings. His name was George Herman Ruth. During the 1920 Series, which Cleveland won handily, a Dodger pitcher named Clarence Mitchell hit into an unassisted triple play. Next time up Mitchell hit into a double play. "Two swings, five outs," my father remarked in his droll way. "Hard to do."

Rickey was always intensely serious about religion, and when he came to Brooklyn in 1943, he found his new house of worship within a few blocks of 215 Montague Street, the Dodger offices. That was the Plymouth Church of the Pilgrims, at 75 Hicks Street in Brooklyn Heights, a vibrant and historic Congregational institution founded in 1847.

Henry Ward Beecher, the most prominent American pastor of the 19th century, long presided at the Plymouth Church, which became a bastion of abolitionism. (His sister, Harriet Beecher Stowe, wrote *Uncle Tom's Cabin*.) Abraham Lincoln twice worshiped at the Plymouth Church. It is the only church in what is now New York City that Lincoln ever attended. Beecher invited a dazzling roster to speak from his pulpit: Clara Barton, Charles Dickens, Ralph Waldo Emerson, Horace Greeley, William Thackeray, Mark Twain and Walt Whitman. But across the years Beecher remained the star. Mark Twain described his preaching style like this: "Sawing his arms in the air, howling sarcasms this way and that, discharging rockets of poetry and exploding mines of eloquence, halting now and then to stamp his foot three times in succession to emphasize a point."

Beecher was also given to pomposity, which led Oliver Wendell Holmes Sr. to compose a witty limerick:

The Reverend Henry Ward Beecher
Called a hen a most elegant creature.
The hen, pleased with that,
Laid an egg in his hat,
And thus did the hen reward Beecher

Long after Beecher's sudden death in 1887, the pulpit of the Plymouth Church remained a podium for social reform and a prized spot for Congregational ministers. The Reverend Dr. L. (for Lawrence) Wendell Fifield, a tall, bespectacled and rather solemn theologian, became pastor at the Plymouth Church in 1941 and stayed through 1955, the year the Brooklyn Dodgers finally won the World Series. Fifield was 10 years younger than Rickey, but the men shared a Midwestern background: Fifield had graduated from Oberlin College, not far from Rickey's beloved Ohio Wesleyan. He rose to prominence as pastor of the Plymouth Congregational Church in Seattle where, among other activities, he presented weekly book reviews on Wednesday evenings, open to the public and widely attended. He headed a Red Cross emergency drive, served on a committee charged with handling the problems of servicemen and, in 1940, received an award from the King County Association of Realtors as "First Citizen of Seattle."

He and Rickey, successful, high-achieving, outspoken religious Christians, bonded when Rickey came to Brooklyn. The first person to learn of Rickey's momentous decision to sign Robinson was his wife, Jane Moulton Rickey. Walter "Red" Barber, a great sportscaster but a distressingly self-important man, long claimed that he was the first person outside the Rickey family to get the news. "Mr. Rickey took me to Joe's, a very fine restaurant on Fulton Street in downtown Brooklyn," Barber told me in 1972, "and outlined his daring plan. He wanted to know if I would come aboard. I can still see those strong catcher's hands of his, trembling with intensity as he began to break a hard roll."

Barber had a worshipful following in Brooklyn and his background in the segregationist South was widely known. "The Ol' Redhead," as he liked to call himself, spiced his broadcasts with phrases he had picked up in the rural South. A player doing well was "sittin' in the catbird seat." The Dodgers rallying late were "tearin' up the ol' pea patch." He spoke and of course broadcast with a refined but unmistakable Southern drawl.

From the start, Barber championed Robinson and the cause of baseball integration. Early in 1947, Robinson's rookie season in Brooklyn, Barber delivered a brief, powerful statement during an afternoon game. Turning away from the action, he said he found Robinson to be not only a fine ballplayer but beyond the diamond a fine human being. With great fervor, Barber concluded, "I hope he bats 1.000."

Robinson's signing was a lightning rod for controversy, and since Rickey's relations with the New York media were uneven, Barber's support was indispensable. But the Ol' Redhead was not the first person beyond family to hear about Rickey's grand design. Convinced that in signing Robinson he was following the path of righteousness, Rickey still grappled with concern and doubt and worried about his survival in the racist world of baseball. That led him to the study of the Plymouth Church and a memorable meeting with the Reverend Fifield.

June Fifield, the minister's wife, composed a description of the meeting for a book she hoped someday to write. As far as I know that book was never completed. The account that follows, written in 1965, has not previously been published.

Chapter Three

BRANCH RICKEY'S "DAY OF DECISION"

By June H. Fifield

News of the passing of Branch Rickey, a treasured friend of my late husband, Rev. Dr. L. Wendell Fifield, came to the world on the day that I sat writing an anecdote about a game we saw with him at Ebbets Field, for one of the chapters of a book based on my husband's life and works.

It was a strange, mystical experience to me to have been so surrounded by the spirit of Mr. Rickey that I should be writing about him at that time. It seemed, somehow, a sign that the time had come to tell a story I had long hesitated to write because it seemed privileged material. Dr. Fifield had shared the feeling that Jackie Robinson and the rest of the world should know the story but that it should not be told in Rickey's lifetime without his permission.

I had always felt that Mr. Rickey would be the first to approve, for his own life was so bound up in this young man, his affection so deep and his expectations so high. His affection, shared by his wife and "Auntie," the sister in her eighties who never missed a game and kept an impeccable box score, was evidenced to us many times. "Auntie" gave us her own witness once when we dined at the Rickeys' home. She said, "When we have the team over for refreshments, Jackie is the one who offers to lend a hand, and he unfailingly says a word of appreciation when he leaves. He has the best manners of the bunch!"

I write this in the spirit of a tribute and a plea: a tribute to Branch Rickey and L. Wendell Fifield—two men, strong of character, pastor and parishioner, whose rapport was a quick mutual outpouring of meaningful forces that drew them together inextricably as friends; a plea to Jackie Robinson to realize what went into the launching of his career—that someone cared enough to grope for wisdom beyond himself, to call upon God's guidance—and that the man who did this was, in common erroneous parlance, "white."

One day, as my husband sat working at his desk in the study of the church house, his secretary buzzed to say, "Mr. Rickey is here and asks to come in." No appointment was ever necessary for someone with an urgent problem, and my husband's "Certainly, show him in" carried with it more than casual interest. He was always warmed by the presence of this friend whose busy schedule of travel and activity allowed him little time for communication on a social level. In high hopes of a long chat, Dr. Fifield rose to greet him at the door.

"Sit down, Wendell," said Mr. Rickey. "Don't let me interrupt. I can't talk with you. Keep right on with your work. I just want to *be* here. Do you mind?"

Without another word, Branch Rickey began to pace the floor. He paced, and he paused, he paced and he paused. Occasionally he gazed out the window at the sooty gloom of Brooklyn Heights, slightly relieved by the church garden struggling for beauty below. Pace, pause, pace, pause; turn, gaze, pace, pause.

Once in a while my husband glanced up from his work, but he spoke no word. He knew that whatever brought Mr. Rickey to his presence was an extremely important and personal matter, and he gave him the privacy of his struggle. Mr. Rickey stood with eyes closed and seemed to draw his great frame up to a new height. Then he'd sag again and pace. As the pauses grew longer, my husband once caught a kind of glow about Mr. Rickey as he stood in silence. Then, back to the pacing and pausing—and silence.

Forty-five minutes of this can be a long, long walk. I believe, on the average, allowing for pauses, about three miles. It proved to be a mighty significant three-mile hike, in the equally significant atmosphere of a minister's study. At the end of the time, Branch Rickey, his face aglow under those famous outthrust eyebrows, bent over my husband's desk, his eyes piercing, and cried:

"I've got it!" He banged his huge fist on the desk, rattling everything from fountain pen to intercom. "I've got it!" he banged again, elated, transported.

It was too much for Dr. Fifield. He'd waited long enough to know what was going on in his own home base. "Got what, Branch? How much longer before I find out what you're up to—pacing around here and banging on my furniture and keeping the whole thing to yourself? Come on, out with it!"

Branch sank, exhausted, into the nearest chair, fortunately big and overstuffed, as he was himself in those days of generous teeming good health and vigor.

"Wendell," he said, "I've decided to sign Jackie Robinson!"

Moisture glistened in Mr. Rickey's eyes. He blew an emphatic blast of his famous big nose, while my husband awaited the rest of the story.

It scarcely need be pointed out to anyone who reads that, in 1945, Jackie Robinson was the first Negro major league basball player to be signed, a step in professional athletics that had worldwide repercussions and opened the way to careers for Negroes in virtually every phase of the sports world hitherto denied.

"Wendell," Branch said, when he regained his composure, "this was a decision so complex, so far-reaching, fraught with so many pitfalls but filled with so much good, if it was right, that I just had to work it out in this room with you. I had to talk to God about it and be sure what He wanted me to do. I hope you don't mind."

Remembering this, I understand better a remark a young friend made recently when I chided myself at still missing my husband so terribly 18 months after his passing. He said, "What can you expect of yourself? It was a great experience for anyone just to be in the same room with him. Of course you'll miss him—forever."

Mr. Rickey straightened his bow tie and reached for his old battered hat. "Bless you, Wendell," he said, and was off. He went from the study that day out into the fray where he

> loved to do battle, armed with a strength from his God whom he trusted. He revolutionized athletic practices and attitudes in this country and beyond, during that forty-five minute walk with God in the warmth of my husband's presence in the environment of the church study. He had humbled himself and sought to communicate with a Presence and a wisdom and a power beyond his own, for he knew that, alone, he was insufficient to the task of knowing right from wrong, as we all are.
>
> He went from that encounter in confidence and in faith. In the certainty of God's guidance, he launched a young man, Jackie Robinson, who rose to great heights, and has taken thousands of his brothers with him, earning the respect and adulation of all races.
>
> I hope Jackie will see his fellow man in a new light, knowing this story. May he ever remember Branch Rickey's soul-searching in the presence of the God of us all, on his own "Days of Decision."

Unfortunately Mrs. Fifield did not provide the date of this remarkable meeting, and now all the principals, including Mrs. Fifield, are dead.

When considering Rickey's motive in signing Robinson, the words of June H. Fifield are convincing. It was overwhelmingly a moral decision, indeed a modern revelation, as powerful, in its way, as the revelation on the road to Damascus that knocked St. Paul off his horse.

FOUR

THE BATTLE LINES OF THE REPUBLIC

INTEGRATION IN AMERICA SURGED FORWARD throughout the 10 major-league years of Jackie Robinson. During Robinson's turbulent and triumphant seasons, baseball was the unquestioned leader of American sport and Robinson was its most exciting player.

Briefly to summarize—later we will see him in more detail—I here cite a passage from *The Boys of Summer*:

> Robinson could hit and bunt and steal and run. He had intimidating skills, and he burned with a dark fire. He wanted passionately to win. He charged at ballgames. He calculated his rivals' weaknesses and measured his own strengths and knew—as only a few have ever known—the precise move to make at precisely the moment of maximum effect. His bunts, his steals, and his fake bunts and fake steals humiliated a legion of visiting players. He bore the burden of a pioneer and the weight made him more strong. If one can be certain of anything in baseball, it is that we shall not look upon his like again.

Once Tim McCarver tried, with reasonable amiability, to sandbag me during a television interview. "You said in one place that Jackie Robinson was the greatest player you ever saw. Somewhere else it was Willie Mays. Which is it?"

Mays had the greatest raw ability of anyone in my time. Speed, power, defense, throwing arm. Probably, although one can't be sure of this, even greater skills than Joe DiMaggio. But Robinson was the most *exciting* player. No episode in baseball was as rousing as Jackie Robinson caught in a rundown, sprinting, stopping, sprinting, dodging, sprinting and finally breaking free. Of course there was mighty symbolism in the play. Quoting from a Negro spiritual, "Free at last, free at last. Thank God Almighty, we are free at last." But symbolism (and music) aside, it was wonderful baseball.

During Robinson's playing years, spring training concluded with a cavalcade of exhibition games. Two teams traveled together for 10 days or so in private Pullman cars and shuttled from place to place in the southern states, moving northward and giving thousands their only chance to see major-league baseball firsthand. The Giants, who trained in Phoenix, moved out with the Indians, who trained in Tucson. I journeyed with them when they spent six days traversing Texas. Two Pullman berths became your apartment, the lower for sleeping, the upper for storage. Personally I prefer seven rooms, river view.

The Dodgers, based in Vero Beach, matched with the Braves, who started in Bradenton. The primary purpose of these little odysseys was not to condition the ballplayers. They had already grunted and strained their way into shape among orange groves or desert sands. The purpose, as with all road shows, was to harvest cash. Everywhere, Robinson was the prime gate attraction. As a late sportswriter, the talented Wendell Smith, wrote:

Jackie's nimble,
Jackie's quick.
Jackie's making the turnstiles click.

Apartheid ruled the American South well into the 1950s. The famous Supreme Court decision demanding integration of public schools did not come until 1954. Three years later Governor Orval Faubus of Arkansas defied the Court and ordered National Guard soldiers, armed with rifles, to stop African American students from attending Little Rock Central High. Apartheid was persistent, like a plague, and it still was raging when Robinson retired from baseball in 1956. But his career smoked out the bigots almost everywhere they lurked and then revealed America's homegrown racism in a blazing, inextinguishable light.

The Brooklyn where I grew up was hardly free from bigotry. Much of the hatred was channeled into sewer anti-Semitism promoted by pseudo-religious Roman Catholic groups such as the Christian Front. Some priests preached about Jewish plots to dominate the world. (Perhaps they should have been talking about Hitler.) Others maintained that communism was an international Jewish conspiracy.

A teammate on the Froebel football team, "Fats" Scott, once snapped at me, "You're a dirty Jew." I ignored Fats, but I did not ignore Donald Kennedy, the team captain, who started to laugh. "Then you're a dirty Presbyterian," I said. Kennedy stopped laughing and we grappled.

A passerby once snapped at me and a friend as we shot marbles on a sidewalk, "You're Jews, huh? Wanna own the world, huh!" At the time, we were nine years old.

Many Catholic clerics looked back in anger at the crucifixion. "All right, already," one exasperated Jew is said to have cried out to a threatening mob of Christian Fronters. "We did kill Christ. All right, already. But wouldn't he have been dead by now anyhow?"

Jews were visible, accounting for a significant portion of the total Brooklyn population of two million. Contending with the ambient anti-Semitism gave many Jewish people a feeling of identity with other victims of discrimination, including blacks. Brooklyn Jews rooted for

Jackie Robinson to succeed as passionately as Alabama Klansmen rooted for him to fail. In turn, Robinson became a ferocious foe of anti-Semitism. When I once sneered at a Dodger utility player as "the dumbest Jew I've ever met," Robinson laced into me for 10 minutes.

In long-ago Brooklyn you seldom saw blacks. A cleaning woman and a postman were the only blacks I encountered as a child. During my four years at Erasmus Hall I attended class with only one black student. That was second-year Latin and the black youngster, totally isolated, performed poorly. From the towers of the Ivy League down to street corners and gutters, the North exuded a bigotry of its own. But Southern racism was a thing apart.

Public water fountains throughout the South, gathering places for children on hot summer days, were marked "White" and "Colored." So were toilet facilities. No leading Southern hotel or restaurant accepted blacks. A black man couldn't even buy a beer at a working-class bar. In refined Southern social circles the term nigger was shunned, but neither did you hear the then acceptable word Negro. Southern ladies and gentlemen referred to blacks as "nigras," pronounced NEE-gras. Nowhere, except at a Klan meeting or a lynching, was Southern bigotry more evident than at the ballparks.

During Robinson's 10 major-league springs the Dodgers played in a wide variety of Southern ballparks. To cite a few, the spring cavalcade brought them to Hartwell Field in Mobile, Pelican Stadium in New Orleans, Ponce de Leon Park in Atlanta, Sulphur Dell in Nashville and LaGrave Field in Fort Worth. These parks varied in size and appearance. The one constant was segregation. Good seats were available only to whites. This rule was enforced not merely by ushers, but was also supported by state troopers carrying pistols.

When the Dodgers and Braves came to Pelican Stadium one April day in 1953, the sections reserved for whites did not sell out. The black stands were overflowing. Gathering notes, I was standing on the field with Robinson, who was playing catch with Reese when the Louisiana troopers made a decision. They opened up a few corridors of empty white seats to black fans. The blacks swarmed in, then burst into cheers for the white troopers.

Robinson stopped playing catch. "You stupid bastards," he shouted. "Don't cheer those fucking cops. They're only giving you what's rightly yours." He continued shouting until Reese said in his gentle way, "Jack. Did you come out here to warm up or make a speech?"

At Hartwell Field no seats were available for black fans. Attendants strung rope in center field and the blacks who wanted to see the Dodgers play the Braves had to see it standing behind rope. Of course this changed the dimensions of the playing field and distorted the game. Any ball hit into the outfield crowd, but not over the fence, became a ground-rule double.

The cynosure of neighboring eyes was Jackie Robinson. He fouled a pitch. Strike one. The white fans cheered. A curve bounced. Ball one. Now, from behind the ropes, came a cheer from the blacks. The high-decibel competitive cheering persisted and grew louder. I had found a seat in the press box, which was supported by slim poles and had walls of glass. I thought suddenly, *When the race riot starts and the poles get knocked down, how many reporters will be killed by shards of glass?* Nor was I alone in anxiety. George "Shotgun" Shuba, who was playing left field, said he began considering how, when the riot began, he could climb the wall behind him to escape.

There was no riot, just another uncomfortable afternoon of racism. Then we all boarded an (integrated) dining car to eat shrimp cocktail and steaks before moving to our berths or into the (integrated) club car for cards or reading or chatter. But the next day, when we debarked in Montgomery, the racism surrounded all of us again, as strong and virulent as ever. I think a good description of life with the Dodgers in the South back then is contained in the current psychological term "bipolar." We had a pleasant integrated existence in the train. Then as soon as we stepped off—raw apartheid.

But beyond our shuttling through what the crusading sports editor Stanley Woodward called "the Hookworm Belt," something beautiful was happening. Like it or not the racists saw—they had to see—that right there before their eyes on the ball fields blacks and whites were working together and usually, since the Dodgers won most of the time, working together in triumph.

"And even beyond that," Rickey said, proudly, "in the daily papers. A box score tells you who made hits and who scored runs. It does not tell you anything about a man's religion nor does it even suggest the color of his skin."

Anyway, each and every April I was glad to get the hell out of Dixie.

◆ ◆ ◆ ◆ ◆

AS I HAVE MENTIONED before, and may well mention again, Rickey traced his integration decision clear back to 1903, when the manager of the Oliver Hotel in South Bend tried to bar Charles Thomas from lodging for a night. To a devout Christian believer such as Rickey, the incident resonated with the Bible story of the first Christmas in Bethlehem. Once again, there was no room at the inn. The episode was fundamental to Rickey's emotional development and to his long-held determination to bring blacks into the major leagues. When finally he acted, when finally he was free to act, no fewer than 43 seasons later, he found himself ambushed at a secretive baseball meeting held in Cleveland on April 26, 1945. That is another story now clamoring to be told. But to understand the forces that were at play on that contentious afternoon, one first needs to remember that Rickey was a lawyer long before he established himself as a premium baseball man. He did not move to integrate the game until he determined that the law was on his side. Even so, if Rickey read T. S. Eliot—I am not certain that he did—he would have agreed that April is the cruelest month, although not simply because it mixes memory and desire. Rickey's April of '45 mixed ostracism, anger and bigotry.

Again, as with the fans at Ebbets Field, we encounter that special closeness between Jews and blacks, for baseball integration proceeded from the passion of a white Methodist Republican (Rickey), the foresight of a conservative Episcopalian governor (Thomas E. Dewey) and a Jewish counterstrike at anti-Semitism.

For a significant part of the 20th century organized medicine—the American Medical Association and the governing bodies at medical schools—sharply limited the number of Jews allowed into the lucrative business of doctoring. One reason was coldly economic. The WASPs at the top did not want to share the shekels—so to speak—with Jews. Another was irrationally emotional. Do we want to have leering Jews examining our naked Christian ladies?

The situation was particularly dramatic in New York City, where thousands of outstanding Jewish science students were routinely denied admission to medical schools, notably the ones affiliated with the Ivy bastions, Columbia and Cornell. As in Brooklyn, Jews made up a significant percentage of the voters in the city at large, and that was the wedge that various Jewish groups, led by the famous reform rabbi Stephen Wise, used to persuade the state legislature to hold hearings in 1944.

These proved to be a disaster for the Establishment bigots. One dean at Cornell Medical School said that of course a Jewish quota was in effect. No matter how many qualified Jews applied, no more than 5 percent of a freshman class "could be followers of the Hebrew religion." The dean defended the quota with such stubborn arrogance that some listening to his words heard echoes of Hitlerism. Out of that came the drafting of the so-called Ives-Quinn law, which made job discrimination on the basis of race or religion a crime in New York State. (No mention of age or sex discrimination appeared. Those would have to wait for another time.) Soon journalists and others were calling this new law, remarkable in its day, FEP, for Fair Employment Practices.

Governor Dewey signed the FEP bill on March 12, 1945, using 22 pens during a crowded ceremony at the Red Room of the state capitol in Albany. The right-wing columnist Westbrook Pegler furiously attacked the new law as "pernicious heresy against the ancient privilege of human beings to hate." But the Federal Council of [Protestant] Churches; the American Jewish Congress; the Roman Catholic archbishop of Boston, Richard J. Cushing; and Thurgood Marshall of the NAACP figuratively cheered.

A prominent black news photographer, the late Alfredo "Chick" Solomon, covered the 22-pen signing and drove 150 miles at high (and probably illegal) speed from the state capitol to the Hotel Theresa in Harlem, where quite coincidentally officials of the Negro National League were holding a routine meeting. Chick Solomon was exultant. He brought copies of the new law with him. "Listen everybody," he said, "the law is on our side now, doesn't mean we're gonna make Christians out of the bastards who run the major leagues. But at least there's nothing now that can stop a black ballplayer from going up and demanding a tryout."

Solomon's view of the power of the law proved optimistic. Change did not come in a rush. (It was not until 10 years later, for example, that the New York Yankees employed their first black major leaguer, the redoubtable catcher Elston Howard. (I have not known a finer gentleman in the game.)

◆ ◆ ◆ ◆ ◆

I FIRST HEARD ABOUT the 1945 baseball meeting at which Rickey was excoriated from his grandson, Branch B. Rickey, then president of the Pacific Coast League and himself a man of considerable eloquence. On the night of September 23, 1997, in the sedate college town of

Princeton, New Jersey, Arnold Rampersad, then Woodrow Wilson Professor of Literature and African-American Studies, organized a campus evening called "Remembering Branch Rickey." Rampersad, who was born in the island state of Trinidad and Tobago, had written a well-received biography of the poet Langston Hughes and then a life of Jackie Robinson, authorized and to some extent controlled by Rachel Robinson, Jack's strong-willed widow. As Jacqueline Kennedy earlier demonstrated, the influence of a willful widow on the posthumous biography of a hero husband exemplifies the term "mixed blessing."

"Did Rachel have editorial control?" I asked.

"No," Rampersad said, "but she brought to bear emotional pressure."

Thus the Robinson one encounters in Rampersad's book is considerably less charged with testosterone than the Robinson I remember. Rampersad, an interesting black academic, told me his forebears on his father's side had come to the Caribbean from India. "It's a little ironic that I hold the chair I do at Princeton," he said, "because Woodrow Wilson, whatever his virtues, was a bigot." Rampersad later moved on to Stanford. In 2010 he was awarded a medal by the National Endowment for the Humanities.

That September night in Princeton the panelists were Branch B. Rickey; Sharon Robinson, Jack's daughter; and myself. Our moderator was another high-powered academic, Sean Wilentz, history professor and director of American studies at Princeton. (Wilentz made later news in the 2008 presidential campaign with slash-and-burn attacks on Barack Obama and "the liberal intellectuals who abdicated their responsibility to provide unblinking and rigorous analysis of him." Wilentz himself grew up among liberal intellectuals in New York, where his father, Eli, founded the Eighth Street Bookshop, a gathering place in Greenwich Village for such notable writers as W. H. Auden, E. E. Cummings and Jack Kerouac.)

Most interesting at the start in Princeton, at least to me, was the fact that our audience of several hundred included the entire varsity baseball team. Coach Tom O'Connell believed that remembering Branch Rickey was, or anyway should be, as important to young ballplayers as learning how to hit behind a runner. The most passionate speaker turned out to be Branch B. After his grandfather moved to break the big-league color line, Branch B. said, the other owners gathered in a secret meeting and denounced him. According to young Branch, the rival magnates stormed about and shouted that integration could very well destroy baseball. Talk about slash and burn. "To a man," young Branch said, in ringing tones, "everyone in the room condemned my grandfather. No other owner, not a single one, stood up for him. Among men he thought were colleagues and friends, my grandfather found himself utterly and completely alone." In the shocked silence that followed Branch's speech, I remembered words that my own father said were uttered once by Abraham Lincoln. After a contentious debate during which every member of the cabinet opposed his decision to go public on a matter of consequence, Lincoln said calmly, "One man in the right constitutes a majority." The next day he issued the Emancipation Proclamation.

When the Princeton proceedings ended, Branch and I eased back with a few drinks at the Nassau Inn, a Princeton tavern that dates from 1756, when Princeton was a mostly Quaker town, a small colonial landmark between New Brunswick and Trenton. I asked where he had heard about the meeting that so roundly condemned his grandfather. "From my grandfather himself," Branch said. "He spoke about it more than once."

Criticism from the media bothered Rickey, but usually only to a mild degree. He recognized that he was more literate and more intelligent than the sportswriters who busied themselves slamming him. When such attack dogs as Dick Young and Jimmy Powers of the raucous tabloid New York *Daily News* referred to him as "El Cheapo," Rickey contained himself. "After all," he told me once, "Young didn't like Jackie Robinson, either, and I understand"—a malevolent chuckle burst forth—"he is not even enthusiastic about his wife." Young was renowned throughout press boxes as a philanderer. No cocktail waitress's private parts were safe after a night game when Dick Young, nicknamed Young Dick, came to town.

To Rickey the assault from other baseball men was far more wounding than press criticism. It was a shattering explosion detonated by people whom he had regarded as colleagues and friends. Rickey found their racism devastating. Their attack left him feeling threatened and humiliated. For all his days Rickey clung to a mystical sense of the goodness of baseball as a homegrown American institution. He never got over the bigoted attacks directed against him from within the game's fraternity and in time he even exaggerated their magnitude. People do that, of course. We all exaggerate the pain of episodes that hurt us badly, be it a divorce, a dislocated knee or a proposed expulsion.

Keeping blacks out of organized ball for more than six decades was the work of many people and proceeded with the tacit—and sometimes outspoken—approval of American society at large. As far as I can learn, there were no sustained calls from any groups, black or white, to boycott alabaster baseball, to hit the magnates where they were most sensitive. That place was not the heart, but the wallet.

One eloquent individual protest survives from 1939. It was issued by Wendell Smith in the prominent black newspaper the *Pittsburgh Courier.* Under the heading "A Strange Tribe," Smith wrote:

> Why we continue to flock to major league ballparks, spending our hard earned dough, screaming and hollering, stamping our feet and clapping our hands, begging and pleading for some white batter to knock some white pitcher's ears off, almost having fits if the home team loses and crying for joy when they win, is a question that probably never will be answered satisfactorily. What in the world are we thinking anyway?

> The fact that major league baseball refuses to admit Negro players within its folds makes the question that much more perplexing. Surely, it's sufficient reason for us to stop spending our money and time in their ballparks. Major league baseball does not want us. It never has. Still, we continue to help support the institution that places a bold "Not Welcome" sign over its thriving portal. . . . We black folks are a strange tribe! . . .
>
> We have been fighting for years in an effort to make owners of major league baseball teams admit Negro players. But they won't do it. Probably never will. We keep on crawling, begging and pleading for recognition just the same. We know that they don't want us, but we still keep giving them our money. Keep on going to their ballgames and shouting until we are blue in the face. Oh, we're optimistic, faithful, prideless—we pitiful black folk.
>
> Yes sir—we black folk are a strange tribe!

Presidents from William Howard Taft to Franklin Delano Roosevelt had appeared for cameras on Opening Day, dutifully throwing out a first ball and turning a blind eye toward segregation. The mainstream press accepted segregated baseball quite matter-of-factly. The Establishment press practiced segregation itself, informally but no less rigidly. Nor was this just the policy of the wealthy elitists who published, say, the *New York Times*. In 1939, when Wendell Smith applied for membership in the Baseball Writers' Association of America, a group consisting of and run by working sports reporters, he was turned down.

Major-league baseball was integrated for 15 years before mainstream newspapers generally began hiring black sportswriters. During that time, writers from such prominent black newspapers as New York's *Amsterdam News* were required to sit in the back rows of press boxes, as if they were riding buses on rural blacktops in Alabama.

A prominent newspaperman named Tom Swope, sports editor of the *Cincinnati Post,* filled the press box air with racist slurs. When

Jackie Robinson came to bat, Swope liked to crow, "The jig is up." When I told him to bridle his tongue, Swope said, "What's the matter? Can't I call a spade a spade?" Then Swope laughed. In 1956 Bob Teague became the first black sportswriter to work for a white-owned New York newspaper. He was employed by the *New York Times.* Some time after that, he engaged me in an intense discussion. Teague said he hoped that the *Times* had hired him because he was good, not just because he was black. We never found out how good a sportswriter Teague might have become, because a few years later he jumped to TV news.

The tide was running against the bigots, and it had been for some time.

◆ ◆ ◆ ◆ ◆

AS THE DECADE OF the 1930s arrived, and with it the Great Depression, calls for change (and cries for help) rumbled through America. As a third of the nation scrambled for food and shelter, as college graduates sold apples from street carts, people collectively began to realize that the dream of a "more perfect union" had not yet arrived. In 1933 the American unemployment rate reached 24.9 percent. Put differently, 11,385,000 Americans were out of work. Millions more were grossly underpaid or had to pursue pathetic make-work occupations. I remember walking with my father on St. Mark's Avenue in Brooklyn one pleasant May afternoon when a stranger approached us holding several boxes of yellow pencils. He had a thin, intelligent face, but his clothes were shabby.

"Pencils?" he said to my father. "Three for a dime."

My father fumbled a bit and found a dollar bill. "Good luck," he said. "I'll pick up the pencils another time."

After we moved on, I asked, "Why didn't you take the pencils, Dad?"

"Because now he can sell them to somebody else."

Beyond the cities, hundreds of thousands of farmers were losing their land, their herds, their homes. Foreclosures swept across the Great Plains. The nation had never experienced anything like this before and the American people and the American Establishment were shaken clear down to their ganglia.

Woody Guthrie, from Okfuskee County, Oklahoma, gave voice to the people—mostly people of the left—when he sang:

Oh, I don't want your millions, mister.
I don't want your diamond ring.
All I want is the right to live, mister.
Give me back my job again.

... ...

We worked to build this country, mister,
While you enjoyed a life of ease.
You've stolen all that we've built, mister,
Now our children starve and freeze.

... ...

Think me dumb if you wish, mister,
Call me green or blue or red.
There's just one thing that I know, mister,
Our hungry babies must be fed.

It is instructive to look at the results of the 1932 presidential election.

Franklin D. Roosevelt	Democrat	22,821,857	57.3%
Herbert Hoover	Republican	15,761,841	39.6%
Norman Thomas	Socialist	884,781	2.2%
William Z. Foster	Communist	102,991	0.3%

Although the actual bloc on the far left, 2.5 percent, may not seem large, almost a million Americans—987,772—voted either Socialist or

Communist. Not a mighty wind of change, perhaps, but certainly a noticeable breeze. Subsequently the Communist Party, USA, became a leading advocate for baseball integration.

In 1933, the year of Franklin Roosevelt's inaugural, none of the 16 major-league clubs drew as many as 750,000 fans at their 77 home games. One club, the St. Louis Browns—sportswriters customarily called them the *Hapless* Browns—drew fewer than 100,000—for an entire season. In the National League, the Philadelphia Phillies—in sportswriter jargon the *Phutile* Phillies—drew barely over 150,000. We are talking about gatherings of 1,200 to 2,000 fans on sunny afternoons in ballparks built to hold crowds of 35,000. When my father took me to Ebbets Field during the mid-1930s, we could arrive 15 minutes before game time and find good seats between home plate and first base priced at $1.10. Until I grew taller than the old-fashioned Brooklyn turnstiles, I was admitted free. That was the policy, kids shorter than the turnstile gained free admission, provided, of course, that they were accompanied by an adult who paid for his ticket. (The range went like this: bleachers 55 cents; general admission $1.10; reserved seats $1.65; boxes $2.20. Luxury boxes? There was no such animal.)

Inside, a nickel bought you a scorecard featuring the lineups and an advertisement for Between the Acts Little Cigars. These scorecards appeared in black and white. Glossy color scorecards had not yet been invented. All game long, vendors bellowed, "Hey, frank 'n' a roll here!" as they hawked Stahl-Meyer hot dogs. I remember those hot dogs as being just about the finest food on earth. They cost 10 cents. The Gulden's mustard was free.

In 1934 the Dodgers drew 434,188 for 70 home dates. Empty seats were the order of the day. The team wasn't much that year, finishing sixth under a novice major-league manager named Casey Stengel. Only one regular, third baseman "Jersey Joe" Stripp, hit .300. The pitching was mediocre except for the great fireballer Van Lingle

Mungo, who won 18. But losing games was not the greatest problem facing the Brooklyn National League Baseball Club, Inc. Unable to pay down their bank mortgage, the Depression Dodgers faced a continuing threat of bankruptcy.

Our family moved from Alsace, in eastern France, to Brooklyn in 1848, and came to develop great pride in their new native ground. But my father kept his civic pride well damped, except at the ballpark. Here, in casual conversations with other fans, he maintained, among the empty seats, that Brooklyn in truth was a great baseball town. The greatest. "If we had a decent team," he'd say, "we'd draw a million." (When the Dodgers won the pennant in 1941, after a wretched drought lasting 20 years, home attendance totaled 1,214,910, the highest in the major leagues by a margin of several hundred thousand. Branch Rickey came to agree with my father that Brooklyn was a great and special baseball town. It remained so until Walter O'Malley hijacked the franchise to Los Angeles.)

Like most other businesses in Depression days, baseball was dominated by frugality. Although Lou Gehrig finally drew $40,000 a year from the Yankees, the average major leaguer's salary in 1933 was $6,000. Ballplayers took winter jobs as factory watchmen, mill hands and clothing salesmen. (That persisted even into the 1950s when Gil Hodges, the Dodgers' slugging first baseman, sold Buicks in a Flatbush Avenue dealership during the winter.) The best Depression ballplayers—those with the most crowd appeal—turned to post-season barnstorming for extra revenue. Before television, just to see great big leaguers in uniform was an event to be remembered in a hundred American towns along a million miles of American railroad track. These rolling road shows were less tightly structured than regular-season baseball. Here, every October, in a country badly overdrawn, the common pursuit of cash wiped out the supposedly ineradicable cotton curtain.

Joe DiMaggio played in exhibition games against black teams in

1937 after his fine rookie season in New York, when he hit .323. He confessed later that doubts lingered about his own ability consistently to hit big-league pitching. But then he said, "When I was barnstorming I came up against [the Negro League right-hander] Satchel Paige, who was the best and fastest pitcher I ever faced. When I lined one of his fastballs for a single, I knew I'd be okay. If you could get a hit off Paige, you could hit anybody."

Jay Hanna "Dizzy" Dean, the most famous pitcher in the major leagues, lost an exhibition game to Paige by a single run. Afterward he announced cheerfully, "If Satch and I was pitching on the same team, we'd cinch the pennant by July fourth and go fishin' until World Series time."

After barnstorming with blacks, Johnny Vander Meer of Prospect Park, New Jersey, who would later throw consecutive no-hit shutouts for the Cincinnati Reds, said, "I don't see why the colored guys are barred." No fewer than four major-league managers, Burleigh Grimes of Brooklyn, Bill McKechnie of Cincinnati, Fred Haney of the St. Louis Browns and Jimmy Dykes of the Chicago White Sox, said that they had seen many Negro players with big-league potential, including Jackie Robinson, whom Dykes watched play ball for Pasadena City College. But when Herman Hill, a reporter for the *Pittsburgh Courier,* brought a very young Robinson to a White Sox spring camp in Pasadena for a tryout, Dykes turned him away. He said, "An actual tryout would have to be up to the club owners and Judge Landis." Neil Lanctot reports in his history, *Negro League Baseball,* that "several white players hovered around Robinson menacingly, with bats in their hands."

During the 1937 season, Satchel Paige made an astonishing proposal. He suggested that the World Series winner take on a team of all-stars from the Negro Leagues. Paige of course would pitch for the all-stars. Massive, genial Josh Gibson, "the black Babe Ruth," would catch. "Cool Papa" Bell, the fastest man in baseball, would play center field. Paige once observed, "If Cool Papa had known about colleges or if colleges had known about Cool Papa, Jesse Owens would have looked like he was walking." These black athletes would comprise a team of speed and sinew and spirit.

The 1937 World Series winner was (surprise) the New York Yankees, among the mightiest of ball clubs. Gehrig, at first base, batted .351 and hit 37 home runs. He drove in 159 runs. DiMaggio, in center field, hit .346 with 46 homers and 15 triples. Vernon "Lefty" Gomez won 21 games and led the league with a 2.39 earned run average. This Yankee squad collectively hit .278 and finished 13 games ahead of the second-place Detroit Tigers.

I believe that the match Paige proposed would have sold out Yankee Stadium, which then could hold 70,000 people. It might well have produced a ballgame for the ages. Paige, no slouch at business and a pretty fair gambling man, wanted all receipts after expenses to go to the ballplayers. He added an interesting proviso: Winner Take All.

What happened next? Nothing happened next. The white stars simply ignored Paige and this fabulous ballgame never took place. Some Yankees grumbled that they didn't want to play without a guaranteed check. But a larger consideration was at work. How would it look if the lordly Yankees, rulers of all they surveyed, unchallenged emperors of segregated baseball, were put to rout by nine itinerant black men? Not great for the forces of White Supremacy.

Organized baseball continued to ignore Satchel Paige until the season of 1948, when Bill Veeck signed him for the Cleveland Indians. During a tryout Veeck placed a book of matches on home plate and said to Paige, "I want to see you throw your fastball over that."

Paige asked, "Which match?"

As a 42-year-old major-league rookie, Paige started seven games for Cleveland. He won six.

◆ ◆ ◆ ◆ ◆

THE 1930S CONTINUED TO throb with pain and change. The Depression persisted. With Adolf Hitler unbound, the world, including isolationist America, lurched toward war. The alarming drumbeats of pain and change grew ever louder.

Ben Chapman, a Nashville native, played a strong right field for the Yankees, consistently batting .300 and stealing as many as 61 bases in a season. Chapman was an intelligent man and an accomplished bridge player. He was also a redneck with a trigger temper.

After he butchered a fly ball early in the 1936 season, fans began to jeer. Some chanted, "Chapman is a bum." He took the razzing for a while; it goes with the territory. But at length he turned and shouted into the grandstands, "Why don't you fucking Jew bastards shut up!"

Fans complained and the Yankee management responded quickly by trading Chapman to the Washington Senators for Alvin "Jake" Powell. Jewish New Yorkers were prominent purchasers of Yankee tickets. Two years later, on July 29, 1938, Bob Elson, a prominent sports broadcaster, was interviewing Powell for a radio program emanating from Comiskey Park in Chicago. "What do you do in the wintertime, Jake?" Elson asked.

"I'm a cop back home in Dayton, Ohio," Powell said. Actually, he was a private guard at a General Motors factory.

"I guess that keeps you in shape," Elson said.

"I stay in shape," Powell said, "by hitting niggers over the head with my nightstick."

The radio station cut off the program, but even in the raw racial climate of the time, Powell had crossed a line. Commissioner Landis suspended Powell for six games. "Judge Landis," wrote the black journalist Ed Harris in the *Philadelphia Tribune,* "is giving a lesson in decency and good sense."

Powell visited the Harlem offices of the *Amsterdam News,* where he read a statement prepared with the help of Yankee management. He had "high regard for the Negro people," Powell said. He employed black servants in his home. Should major-league integration ever come to pass, he would have no trouble accepting it.

Black fans and some whites booed Powell around the league and he never fully recovered. He was out of baseball a few years later. After being arrested in Washington, DC, on a bad-check charge in 1948, Jake Powell committed suicide.

A journalist named Jim Reisler has gathered the work of 10 black sportswriters into a collection called *Black Writers/Black Baseball.* In some areas of the integration story, Reisler is shaky. But we are not talking serious criticism, such as the prose of Alfred Kazin here, just basic research. Reisler has done very good work studying and transcribing the sports pages of defunct black newspapers. Less anger and fewer demands for integration appeared there than one might expect.

The two most renowned black sportswriters of my acquaintance were Sam Lacy of Baltimore, who wrote for a chain of *Afro-American* weekly newspapers, and Wendell Smith, a Detroit native who worked for the *Pittsburgh Courier,* then spent his halcyon years with white-owned newspapers and television stations in Chicago. Although each had to endure such humiliations as being barred from press boxes and press drinking rooms, neither was a firebrand. Sam was short and wiry, with sharp features inherited from his mother, a Shinnecock Indian. Wendell was bespectacled and mustached, mild mannered and with a ready smile.

Lacy said once, "Black players in general weren't bothered by the fact that they couldn't be in the majors. It's like Redd Foxx used to say, 'I never knew I was poor because everybody around me was poor, too.' Most of the black players [and perhaps Sam Lacy himself] were satisfied with what they were doing and thought the closed society was just something to be endured." In 1948 Lacy became the first black member of the Baseball Writers' Association of America. In 1997, on the day before his 94th birthday, he was admitted to the writers' wing of the Baseball Hall of Fame. Sam died on May 8, 2003, acclaimed as a pioneer, although the man I knew was soft-voiced, courteous and decidedly diffident.

Cancer killed Wendell Smith in 1972, when he was 58. The "strange tribe" story cited earlier was about as militant as Wendell got. I remember mostly a man of great geniality. Widely liked, he became part of the Establishment.

The one black journalist directly to confront the baseball color line was Joe Bostic, who was as much a promoter as a newspaperman. Bostic, who lived in Brooklyn and rooted for the Dodgers, spent three years as sports editor of the *People's Voice,* a short-lived Harlem weekly founded by the flamboyant preacher and congressman Adam Clayton Powell. The *People's Voice* carried a motto on its masthead: "A Militant Paper Serving All the People. The New Voice for the New Negro." Before settling in for a few years as sports editor of the *People's Voice,* Bostic had been a radio announcer and a theatrical publicity man.

During World War II, train transportation in the United States was hard to come by and baseball teams took spring training in the north. The Dodgers based at Bear Mountain, a resort renowned as a rugged playground and ski-jumping center about 50 miles north of New York City. Under the mountain, ample grassy meadows stretched on the west bank of the Hudson River. The Bear Mountain Inn, a rustic stone-and-timber structure with an upscale dining room, served as Dodger headquarters. Nearby stood the sprawling US Military Academy at West Point. When the days were mild, the ballplayers drilled on a meadow diamond called, pro tem, Durocher Field. When the weather turned cold and snowy the Dodgers worked out inside the vast Army field house. "The whole place surprised me," said young Duke Snider, a Southern California kid. "I'd never seen snow and I'd never owned an overcoat. Mr. Rickey gave me a very modest signing bonus, $500. My dad was away in the merchant marine and I gave almost all the money to my mom. Now at Bear Mountain I didn't have a coat and I couldn't afford to buy one. What did I do? What do you think I did? I was cold a lot."

With zero advance warning, Joe Bostic appeared at Bear Mountain on April 6, 1945, bringing along two athletes from the Negro National League. This was less than a month after Governor Dewey had signed the fair employment act, and Bostic now demanded tryouts. Terris McDuffie was a right-handed pitcher with the Newark Eagles. Dave "Showboat" Thomas was a big first baseman with the New York Cubans. According to their contemporaries, McDuffie and Thomas were journeymen rather than stars. The greatest Negro League players of the time were Paige, Bell and Josh Gibson, "the Black Bambino." Close behind came third baseman Ray Dandridge, pitcher–catcher Ted "Double-Duty" Radcliffe, and a rookie shortstop named Jackie Robinson.

Bostic later described his trip as "an epochal break in baseball's stone wall of Jim Crow." It was not exactly that. As Robinson later demonstrated, it would take nothing less than a super athlete to tear down that wall. (Make no mistake, Robinson was a super athlete. He won letters at UCLA in baseball, basketball, football and track. Some maintain that he was the greatest all-around athlete who ever lived. Jack and I competed once at a ping-pong table in Vero Beach, after I had defeated a string of Dodgers, mostly pitchers. Jack held the paddle facing downward, as some Chinese world-class players did, and no matter how hard or where I hit the little white ball, it came back harder and with a devilish spin. Robinson was totally concentrated, his face without expression. My ping-pong winning streak abruptly came to an end. "Now," Robinson said, finally smiling and meeting my gaze, "would you like to take me on in gin rummy? For dough?" I declined.)

On Durocher Field, Bostic approached peppery, toothy Harold Parrott, a former *Brooklyn Eagle* sports columnist, who was the Dodgers' traveling secretary and publicist. Bostic said he intended to see Branch Rickey. "I want him to give these fellows here a tryout."

Spring training tends to be informal, but asking to see the president of a ball club without first having made an appointment was and is a stretch. (Seeing some executives, such as George Steinbrenner in his later years, was a stretch—even *with* an appointment. Baseball organizations generally are about as transparent as carbon.) Parrott told Bostic that Rickey was watching an intrasquad game on another diamond and said, "I'll see if he'll talk to you later."

After 15 minutes Parrott returned with one of Rickey's assistants, an elderly front office aide named Bob Finch. "Mr. Rickey says to tell you that there is no bias in his organization," Finch said, "but we won't look at the players until we've set up workouts for them. That will take a little time. Now Mr. Rickey would like you and the ballplayers to be his guests for lunch."

In the dining room at the Bear Mountain Inn, Rickey told Bostic that personally he detested prejudice. Then, with great intensity, he repeated the story of Charles Thomas and the hotel in South Bend. Carried away by the memory, or by his own words, Rickey suddenly burst into tears. Embarrassed, Bostic focused on his roast beef. When Rickey recovered, he was not congenial.

"Look," he said. "You're pretty cute."

"No, I'm not cute," Bostic said. "I'm not concerned with being cute. I brought you two ballplayers."

"Yes," Rickey said, "but if I give these men a tryout, you've got the greatest sports story of the century. And if I don't give them a tryout, you've got the greatest sports story because it's an absolute showdown. I don't appreciate being backed into this kind of corner."

Rickey then agreed to look over McDuffie and Thomas a day later. He was true to his word, but apparently never forgave Bostic for publicly pressuring him. According to Bostic, subsequently he found himself cut off from Dodger press releases, not invited to Dodger press conferences and unable to reach Dodger people by telephone. In an angry outburst Bostic said, "Rickey treated me as though I was a 'fresh nigger.'"

The tryout took place early on a Saturday afternoon, April 7. McDuffie and Thomas reported to the Dodger dressing room in the West Point Field House, where uniforms had been laid out for them. Jackie Robinson was *not* the first black to wear a Brooklyn Dodger uniform. That man was either Terris McDuffie or Showboat Thomas. (I have been unable to determine which one first finished lacing up his spikes.)

It was a cold day and the tryout took place entirely in the field house. As he observed, Rickey was accompanied by two baseball men who had no racial prejudice: Dodgers manager Leo Durocher, later a surrogate father to Willie Mays, and Clyde Sukeforth, a onetime catcher from the village of Washington, Maine, who would later do extensive scouting work on Robinson.

At Rickey's direction the two athletes ran laps and then threw to one another. Sukeforth put on catching gear—the tools of ignorance, in the baseball phrase—and McDuffie began pitching. After a bit Rickey began calling pitches: curve, fastball, change. According to Bostic, Rickey "marveled at Mac's control."

Thomas got three turns at bat, 30 swings, against Claude Crocker, a fast 19-year-old left-hander. Bostic said Thomas sent several drives a long way. Then it was done. McDuffie and Thomas returned to the dressing room and donned street clothes. Neither ever heard from Rickey again. Bostic had a good sense of drama, but whether his Bear Mountain adventure advanced baseball integration is subject to question.

Rickey later said that McDuffie, then 32, "has a major flaw in his delivery. He does not follow through properly. That could take time to correct and McDuffie is not a young pitcher." Rickey had this to say about Thomas: "I have many better rookies than that fellow. I wouldn't be interested in Dave Thomas if he were 24 years old. And he's 34."

Writing in the black-owned *Chicago Defender,* Andrew "Doc" Young said, "If that was a fair tryout, I'm a billionaire. And I'm not." The leader of the mainstream white press, the *New York Times,* tried its best to ignore the episode. In later years I sat next to Roscoe McGowen, the *Times* Dodger beat man for several seasons, in press boxes. Roscoe was too genteel to indulge in the crude bigotry of a Tom Swope, but politically he stood, as the saying goes, to the right of Attila the Hun. He never championed Jackie Robinson's cause and he seldom missed an opportunity to underline any error Robinson made, even when the error had no bearing on the final score.

McGowen chose to ignore McDuffie and Thomas, and the *Times* elected to rely on an unsigned dispatch by the Associated Press that ran under a two-column headline:

TWO NEGROES ARE TRIED OUT
BY DODGERS BUT THEY FAIL
TO IMPRESS PRESIDENT RICKEY

Joe Bostic stayed in sports until his death in 1988 and during the 1970s, in a different racial climate, he worked as the ringside announcer at Madison Square Garden. But his greatest day, he always maintained, was the one in April 1945, when McDuffie and Showboat failed to make the Brooklyn Dodgers.

Just as well, perhaps. About four months later the FBI arrested Showboat Thomas. While playing for the New York Cubans he had been moonlighting as a security guard at the military facility called the Army Port of Embarkation, located on a number of piers in Brooklyn. Thomas, and several other guards, were charged with stealing 126,000 safety razor blades, which were to have been shipped to troops in Europe. The arrest brought to light another fact. Thomas was not 34 years old. He was 39. In time he avoided prison with a plea bargain. After that he sank into obscurity.

Where, then, can we find a hard-driving press arising and demanding, time after time, year after year, the integration of baseball here and now? Militant and unflinching protests appeared consistently in only one place, the sports pages of the *Daily Worker*, the newspaper of the Communist Party, USA. Who wrote most of those protest pieces and led the charge? A soft-spoken journalist from Brooklyn named Lester Rodney, who was born into a mercantile Jewish family. The Brooklyn Jewish–Negro connection never looked tighter.

Battle lines were being drawn even well before Bostic at Bear Mountain. On one side stood rednecks, racists and club owners, sometimes all embodied in a single person. *The game is white, the ball is white and both so shall remain.* Opposing this bunko-bunker thinking was Rickey, a man some called a full-scale religious nut. His steadfast ally: the principal sportswriter of the *Daily Worker*, published by the Communist Party of America, an organization that swore a solemn oath to atheism.

> *[Choir as a hymn]*
> *Integration is the path of righteousness.*
> *Hallelujah!*
> *May the Good Lord bless biracial second base.*

> *[Sing as a chant]*
> *Religion is the opiate of the masses.*
> *Most club owners are mini-minded jackasses,*
> *Ball Fans of the World—Unite!*
> *Better Red Than Wrong.*

FIVE

THE ORIGINAL BIG RED MACHINE

THE LESTER RODNEY I REMEMBER FROM THE long-ago press boxes of New York was slim, bespectacled and soft-voiced. Dick Young of the *Daily News* was caustic and loud. Benny Epstein of the *Daily Mirror* was funny and loud. Louis Effrat of the *New York Times* was opinionated and loud. Baseball writers were a swaggering lot back then, but Rodney was recessive. You might never have noticed him if you hadn't read his stuff.

In the middle of the 20th century I admired numerous warriors of the left: Henry Wallace, who ran for president as a Progressive in 1948 and spoke of "the century of the common man"; Paul Robeson, whose recordings of anti-fascist songs made even Bing Crosby's baritone sound thin; Howard Fast, who wrote *Citizen Tom Paine* and *Spartacus,* easy-reading novels—books for bright children, Ring Lardner Jr. said—that became political manuals for left-wing Americans. Myself, I was more left than right, but I was not comfortable having communists as close friends any more than I was comfortable with the extremist Roman Catholics who said Jews murdered Jesus, or the Protestant fundamentalists who said Darwin was a fraud. These folk, it seemed to me, followed inflexible directives and embraced a theopolitical mysticism that was a long way from the contemporary world of reason. (Ring, once Red as the flag of Soviet Russia, was the remarkable exception. His communism never interfered with his clear thinking.)

Lester Rodney and I exchanged greetings, little more, when I began covering baseball for the *Herald Tribune* in 1952. An episode that led to a humiliating Communist directive caused me really to notice him. The clubhouses at the old Polo Grounds were situated in a green blockhouse back of center field, about 500 feet from home plate. After games the ballplayers had to take a long walk or trot to the dressing room surrounded by clamoring fans. Following one game, a teenager ran up behind Leo Durocher, snatched the Giants cap from Durocher's bald scalp, and tried to disappear into the mob.

Rodney and Durocher got along. Lester told me once, with a flash of pride, that Durocher had said, "For a fucking Communist, you know your baseball." Observing the cap snatch, Rodney wrote a piece saying that ballplayers and even managers were working people and the fans, working people themselves, should treat baseball men with respect. Next day it developed that police had caught the cap thief. He was Puerto Rican. John Gates, editor in chief of the *Daily Worker,* issued a ukase along these lines: Puerto Ricans are a persecuted, exploited minority. The boy who stole Durocher's cap did what he did in response to white American capitalist prejudice. Therefore the theft was appropriate. That was the Communist Party line and a day later it rang out shrilly through the corrective column John Gates required Lester Rodney to write.

The *Daily Worker,* the official organ of the Communist Party, USA, began publication in 1924, the same year, coincidentally, that Fleetwood Walker died. The *Worker* attracted such gifted contributors as Richard Wright, the prominent black novelist, but for most of its span, the dominant aspect of the *Worker* was its adherence to the Communist Party line, as printed in red block letters by Josef Stalin in the Kremlin. The paper reached a circulation of 35,000 at its peak and I saw it on many newsstands around New York, proclaiming, "Communism Is Twentieth Century Americanism."

Many of the *Worker*'s editorial positions matched those of moderate liberals. For most of the 1930s it fiercely opposed Hitler and Mussolini. It supported the Spanish loyalists against the brutal fascist Francisco Franco. But some of its advocacy was bizarre. To deal with white American hostility toward Negroes, the *Worker* at one time proposed the creation of a self-contained all-black republic to be carved out of portions of Alabama, Mississippi and Louisiana.

"What will this new republic be called?" someone asked.

A non-communist answered, "The Ukraine."

Before Rodney, the *Worker* had taken a hard line on sports. "I don't believe that [New York Giant] Blondie Ryan is a conscious agent of the capitalist class seeking to dope the workers with his swell infielding," a *Worker* story began early in 1934. "But when a couple of dozen Blondie Ryans and [star first baseman] Bill Terrys, with the aid of hundreds of sportswriters, rivet the attention of millions of workers upon themselves rather than upon unemployment, wage cuts and wars, then we can draw the conclusion that Ryan, et al., consciously serve the purpose of the ruling class." The Giants won the National League pennant in 1933 when Terry, a sullen Southerner, batted .322. But Ryan, the "swell" infielder, made an appalling number of errors at shortstop: 42.

Aside from shaky reporting, you can hear in that *Worker* story an echo from antiquity. The Roman elite famously pacified the masses with bread and circuses. Alternately, you can regard the piece simply as ludicrous. When I covered baseball for the *Herald Tribune*, big-league play did indeed rivet my attention. But I recognized also that my salary, $72.50 a week, was outrageously low. It stayed low until I nailed an offer from *Sports Illustrated*. Then the *Trib* jumped me to $10,000 a year. Riveting on baseball in no way distracted me from trying to make a decent living. The big shift in the *Daily Worker*'s policies came in 1935. It was then that a Moscow conference, attended by

Communist Party leaders from 76 countries, the so-called Comintern, decided to campaign for a "popular front." Alarmed by the rise of fascism, the Reds would cease sniping at others on the left and now try to ally themselves with socialists and even liberals. Their newspapers would reach out beyond hard-line readers and court a broad audience. That Moscow decision, intended principally as a response to Adolf Hitler, is what brought Rodney, then 25, into the offices of the *Daily Worker* in New York and then into the struggle for integration. Hitler to Stalin to baseball: an unusual triple play.

Rodney's father, Max, was a Republican who lost both his business and his home in the 1929 stock market crash. Lester was 18. The family had been living comfortably in the section of Brooklyn called Bensonhurst and Lester, like so many other Brooklyn youngsters, worshiped at a shrine of baseball, Ebbets Field. "I'd rather watch the Dodgers and the Phillies battling for seventh place," he once said, "than see the best football game in the world." He played stickball and street hockey (no ice, no skates) and ran track for New Utrecht High School well enough to be offered a half scholarship to Syracuse University. But the market crash left the family unable to afford even half the Syracuse tuition. Rodney worked at an odd mix of jobs: summons server, chauffeur, lifeguard, and once in a while he wrangled an assignment from the *Brooklyn Eagle* to cover a local event—baseball teams from Consolidated Edison and the Brooklyn Union Gas Company meeting on Diamond One at the Parade Grounds.

The Depression drove Rodney away from his father's Republicanism, but he did not join the Communist Party until he landed the newly created job of sports editor with the *Daily Worker* in 1936. There was opposition from hard-liners. Rodney remembered an ideologue named Betty Gannett saying, "This is ridiculous. It's kid stuff. Does it make sense for a hard-pressed radical paper to give one-eighth of its space to games?" The Baseball Writers' Association, guardian of press credentials, refused Rodney membership for a year. He was given a pass to the grandstands, but was denied admission to clubhouses, playing fields and press boxes. Thus he had to write without interviewing. "But," he told me, "after they saw I was seriously covering the stuff they relented." He recalled run-ins with Jimmy Cannon and Milton Gross, both of the *New York Post,* then the most liberal mainstream daily in the city. McGowen and John Drebinger, the baseball reporters from the *New York Times,* and Dan M. Daniel, the grizzled veteran on the *World Telegram,* declined to speak to him. "But generally," Rodney said, "the other writers accepted me with just a little hazing."

"Such as?" I said.

"Such as 'Why do they have so many statues of Stalin in Russia?' At the time I said it was because the people loved Stalin for getting rid of the czar. Now"—this was 2009—"I know better."

No sensible person has ever accused the communist movement of subtlety. On August 13, 1936, Rodney prepared a boxed announcement that covered half a page.

OUTLAWED BY BASEBALL
THE CRIME OF THE BIG LEAGUES

> The newspapers have carefully hushed it up! One of the most sordid stories in American sports! Though they win laurels for America in the Oympics—though they have proven themselves outstanding baseball stars—Negroes have been placed beyond the pale of the American and National Leagues. Read the truth about this carefully laid conspiracy. Beginning next Sunday, the Sunday Worker will rip the veil from the "Crime of the Big Leagues"—mentioning names, giving facts, sparing none of the most sacred figures in baseball officialdom.

Three days later a front-page headline announced:

FANS ASK END OF JIM CROW BASEBALL

Not quite so. Not yet. An editorial followed, unsigned but written by Rodney. It read, "Fans, it's up to you. Tell the big league magnates that you're sick of the poor pitching in the American League. You want Satchel Paige out there on the mound. You're tired of a flop team in Boston, of the silly Brooklyn Dodgers, of the inept Phillies and semi-pro Athletics. Demand better ball. Demand Americanism in baseball, equal opportunities for Negro and white. Demand the end of Jim Crow baseball."

What happened to Rodney's opening blast? What became of it? Nothing happened. It did not become. Jim Crow baseball would live on for many years. But Rodney's impassioned prose drew mail, scores, hundreds of letters from fans. Lester's prose awakened thousands of people to baseball's prevailing bigotry and a groundswell began to rise. Coincidentally, the drive against alabaster baseball became a touchstone of the *Daily Worker.*

After my friend Ring Lardner Jr., the screenwriter and novelist, died in 2000, I wrote a memorial tribute for *The Nation.* A week later a letter arrived from Rodney, who was living in a retirement community located in Walnut Creek about 30 miles east of San Francisco. "Best piece," he wrote, "that I've read in quite some time." The letter served to renew our acquaintanceship and we met for a final time in the spring of 2009, when Lester was 97 years old. His wife, Clare, died in 2004. Now, while recovering from fractured ribs, he was living in the condo of his companion, Mary Reynolds Harvey. His voice was soft as ever, his gaze was steady and his memory was sharp.

He said I should be aware that when he began his *Daily Worker* campaign the times were growing right for integration. American Negroes, notably Jesse Owens, but also including Jackie Robinson's brother, Mack, dominated the Berlin Olympics of 1936. Joe Louis, whom sportswriters called "the Brown Bomber" and "the Dark

Destroyer," had become the most dynamic heavyweight champion since Jack Dempsey. With great enthusiasm Rodney recalled a conversation in 1937 with Burleigh Grimes, an old spitball pitcher who was managing a dreary Dodger team to a sixth-place finish.

At last credentialed, Rodney wandered out to right field where Grimes was working with Tom Winsett, a highly touted young outfielder whom the Dodgers had acquired for forty thousand Depression dollars. Winsett was fast becoming a Flatbush Flop. After some easy chatter Rodney said, "How are things going on the team?"

"Frankly I could use another pitcher," Grimes said, "and just one real good hitter. But we're doing the best we can."

"Burleigh," Rodney said, "how would you like to put a Dodger uniform on Satchel Paige and Josh Gibson?"

Grimes looked as though he had been clubbed by a Louisville Slugger. Sportswriters did not ask such questions in 1937. "Lester," he said, "you're just wasting your time. That'll never happen. Think about the hotels. Think about the restaurants. How could it happen? It'll never happen."

"Do you know about some of the good black players?"

"Of course I do," Grimes said. "So does everybody else. But let's talk about something different."

"Can I at least write that you know how good they are?"

"No. I'm not gonna stick my neck out."

"Not that you're in favor of signing them, Just that you know that Paige and Gibson are good."

"No, Lester. No, no, no."

◆ ◆ ◆ ◆ ◆

DURING THESE YEARS OF stirring racial currents, Rickey, the would-be second Great Emancipator, was out to lunch. With a masterfully constructed farm system he created championship teams in

St. Louis, the most segregated major-league city. Building on such homegrown stars as Enos "Country" Slaughter, Marty Marion and Terry Moore, the Cardinals in the late 1930s were on the rise again. But the team was all white, the farm system was all white and the home field, Sportsman's Park, was rigidly segregated. (Geographically, St. Louis was then the southernmost major-league city, except for Washington, DC.) In St. Louis black fans could sit only in distant right-field stands, the so-called pavilion. "As a point of fact," Rickey told me, "there was nothing I could do, I ran the team but it was owned by someone else, Sam Breadon. He had no interest in integrating baseball. And St. Louis itself was essentially a Southern city. Whites dominated. The whites made the rules. Negroes had to hide in the corners.

"You can only make a bold move when the time and place are right. When God ordains it, you might say. During my time in St. Louis, that was not the case."

Rickey, then, would not agree with me that he was out to lunch. He maintained that the absent party was God.

A blazing portrait of a Southern racist appears in Vachel Lindsay's mighty poem *Simon Legree, A Negro Sermon.* A few lines here can introduce us to Legree:

He beat poor Uncle Tom to death
Who prayed for Legree with his last breath.
Then Uncle Tom to Eva flew,
To the high sanctoriums bright and new;
And Simon Legree stared up beneath,
And cracked his heels, and ground his teeth:
AND WENT DOWN TO THE DEVIL.

... ...

And the Devil said to Simon Legree:
"I like your style, so wicked and free.

Come sit and share my throne with me,
And let us bark and revel."
And there they sit and gnash their teeth,
And each one wears a hop-vine wreath.
They are matching pennies and shooting craps,
They are playing poker and taking naps.
And old Legree is fat and fine:
He eats the fire, he drinks the wine—
Blood and burning turpentine—
DOWN, DOWN WITH THE DEVIL

Legree was fictive. The actual gatekeeper at baseball's racial barrier, its impenetrable cotton curtain, did not drink burning turpentine, but neither was he a pussyfooting slouch. "The Judge," wrote J. G. Taylor Spink, publisher of the *Sporting News* from 1914 to 1962, "was a tempestuous character who led a tempestuous life from the time he took his first breath in Millville, Ohio. There was never anything prosaic about him." A. L. Sloan, political editor of the *Chicago Herald-American,* wrote, "The Judge was always headline news. He was a great showman, theatrical in appearance, with his sharp jaw and shock of white hair, and people always crowded into his courtroom, knowing there would be something going on. There were few dull moments."

This tempestuous, theatrical showman-judge was, of course, Kenesaw Mountain Landis. He was the first commissioner and the most absolute commissioner ever. Landis did not want black players appearing in organized ball. Stories persist that in 1940, when the Phillies constantly were losing games and money, someone proposed dumping the whole bumbling squad and replacing them with gifted players from the Negro Leagues. Landis is said to have killed the plan. He had the power to throw anyone—player, owner, umpire—clear out of organized baseball if he felt the expulsion was "in the best interests of the game." Talk about an elastic clause. Landis was prosecutor, judge and jury all in one. After Oliver Wendell Holmes Jr. exempted baseball from the antitrust laws governing business in 1922, there was no appeal from a Landis decision—no appeal, no protest, no escape except perhaps to slit one's throat.

I am not sure about the black-ballplayers-for-Philadelphia story. Supposedly the would-be buyer was Bill Veeck, a friend of mine for more than 25 years. I visited him often at his home near Easton, Maryland, and we stayed up late many evenings talking baseball. Bill never mentioned Philadelphia. But he did tell me that in 1939, when he was running the Milwaukee Brewers in the Triple A American Association, he decided to sign a few black players to strengthen his club. Veeck dispatched scouts to Negro League games and Landis, who had more sources than J. Edgar Hoover, found out about the plan. He had long known Veeck's late father, once president of the Chicago Cubs. "Our families go back a ways," Landis told Veeck on a long-distance telephone line. "It would pain me greatly, Bill, to have to throw you out of baseball. But if you even try to sign a colored ballplayer, that's what I will do. Out of baseball, Bill. For life!"

I asked Veeck, "What did you say?"

"Not much. Just thank you for your time."

Landis was a complex and quintessential Midwesterner, the sixth child born to Mary and Abraham Landis in Millville, a small community in a southwestern corner of Ohio, centered around, predictably, a grist mill. It was less than 100 miles from Branch Rickey's birthplace, Stockdale.

Abraham Landis, a German immigrant, was a surgeon in the Union Army grievously injured during Sherman's March to the Sea. At the Battle of Kennesaw Mountain in northwestern Georgia, Landis was dressing the wounds of someone he recalled as "a beardless, blue-clad infantryman" when a nearly spent Confederate cannonball ricocheted off a tree and struck him full on one leg. The iron ball crushed flesh and shattered bone; another Army doctor had to amputate the leg. Curiously, Landis chose to memorialize this agonizing event by naming his fifth son after the battle that crippled him, Kenesaw Mountain. (Somewhere between Georgia and Ohio, Dr. Landis dropped a letter out of "Kennesaw.")

The injury made it impossible for Dr. Landis to make the rounds of a rural medical practice and he moved to Logansport, Indiana, and bought a farm. Ken Landis remembered a happy boyhood on the farm performing chores and, at every opportunity, playing baseball. In time he played for and managed the Logansport High team. After a smattering of courses at the University of Cincinnati, Landis studied law in Chicago at Union College of Law (now the Northwestern University School of Law).

Sometime after graduation Ken Landis found a position as assistant to Grover Cleveland's secretary of state, Walter Gresham. The young lawyer was hard-driving, patriotic and bright. When Gresham became ill, he designated Landis to sit in for him at meetings of the presidential cabinet. The future judge was on his way.

Following Gresham's death, Landis moved back to Chicago, where he developed a flourishing law practice. Then, in 1905, Theodore Roosevelt rewarded the bright young man—Landis was not yet 40 years old—by appointing him a federal judge. Landis became famous two years later when he found against Standard Oil in an antitrust trial and fined the mammoth company an unprecedented sum: $29 million. (On appeal the verdict was set aside.) He later presided over the trial of Jack Johnson, the black heavyweight champion, who was accused of transporting a white woman across a state line "for immoral purposes." An all-white jury convicted Johnson. Landis sentenced him to prison at Fort Leavenworth, Kansas.

He had always been a baseball fan and claimed to have played semi-pro ball as a teenager. But his first formal connection with organized baseball came in the courtroom. The Federal League was founded in 1912 and in 1914 began playing a full schedule of major-league baseball in direct competition with the National and American Leagues. Eight teams, from the Brooklyn Tip-Tops to the Kansas City Packers, competed and at least five Hall of Famers appeared in Federal League uniforms: Charles Albert "Chief" Bender with the Baltimore Terrapins; Mordecai "Three Finger" Brown, St. Louis Terriers; Bill McKechnie, Indianapolis Hoosiers; Eddie Plank, Terriers; Edd Roush, Newark Peppers; and Joe Tinker, Chicago Whales. This was and is the most serious challenge in the annals to the monopoly of the National and American Leagues.

It was expensive starting the league—think building new ballparks—and after beginning, the Feds hoped for some mergers with the established ball clubs. Getting nowhere, the Feds filed an antitrust suit, which led to the court of the old trustbuster, Judge K. M. Landis. In this instance, Landis did no trust busting, but let the case languish. The Federal League folded. Landis had shown himself to be a friend of Establishment baseball.

When later it came to light that seven or eight Chicago White Sox had taken bribes and dumped the 1919 World Series to the Cincinnati Reds, the country reacted with profound shock. This comes across in a passage from Scott Fitzgerald's signature novel, *The Great Gatsby*:

> "Who is he, anyhow, an actor?"
>
> "No."
>
> "A dentist?"
>
> "Meyer Wolfsheim? [In reality, Arnold Rothstein.] No, he's a gambler." Gatsby hesitated, then added coolly: "He's the man who fixed the World's Series back in 1919."
>
> "Fixed the World's Series?" I repeated.
>
> The idea staggered me. I remembered, of course, that the World's Series had been fixed in 1919, but if I had thought of it at all I would have thought of it as a thing that merely happened, the end of some inevitable chain. It never occurred to me that one man could start to play with the faith of fifty million people—with the single-mindedness of a burglar blowing a safe.

> "How did he happen to do that?" I asked after a minute.
> "He just saw the opportunity."
> "Why isn't he in jail?"
> "They can't get him, old sport. He's a smart man."

Nothing excluding earthquakes or tsunamis at ballparks near the sea can be worse for baseball than gamblers tinkering with final scores. Staged, which is to say fixed, professional wrestling matches could be advertised in many states only as exhibitions. By contrast, big-league ballgames were contests. Take away that element, the contest, the struggle to and fro grinding down to the final out, the final pitch, and you kill an essential part of baseball's appeal. Suspicions of the White Sox's effort surfaced even as the World Series was being played. Christy Mathewson sat next to Ring Lardner in the Chicago press box on October 1 as the Reds won the first game, 9 to 1. On Lardner's scorecard Mathewson silently circled White Sox plays that he thought looked suspicious. Then Lardner wrote a scathing song that he sang two days later after a few drinks of Prohibition whiskey in a Pullman car headed for Cincinnati: Based on the popular tune "Blowing Bubbles," Lardner's lyrics went like this:

> *I'm forever blowing ballgames,*
> *Pretty ballgames in the air.*
> *I come from Chi—*
> *I never try.*
> *But the gamblers treat us fair.*

Contemporaries said Lardner had a strong and on-key baritone voice. That day his voice and lyric carried far beyond the rattling Pullman car in which he was traveling.

Word of the fix spread and eight White Sox players were indicted, including the iconic Shoeless Joe Jackson, who somehow managed to bat .375 in a Series he was dumping. Thoroughly alarmed, the 16 club owners hastily agreed to form a commission of non-baseball men to supervise the game and, to be sure, restore public faith in the integrity of baseball. Asked to join the commission, Landis declined. But, he said, he would accept an appointment as the sole commissioner. Frightened, the owners readily agreed.

Further, Landis said, he would have to have unlimited authority to act "in the best interests of baseball." He would be a one-man arbitration panel.

In virtually a single voice, the owners said, "Yes, Judge."

And finally, Landis said, the decisions he made could not be appealed.

The owners, actually an arrogant lot, were in trouble and they knew they were in trouble. They submitted to Landis's autocratic terms without a whimper. This was just about the greatest handoff of power ever until 10 years later when Adolf Hitler took over the German Reichstag.

On August 2, 1921, a hometown jury acquitted the Chicago Eight. The ballplayers and the jurors then joined in a roaring alcoholic celebration. Next day, a cold-sober Landis banned the eight for life. He said that banning them was essential if baseball's favorable image was to be restored.

Soon sportswriters began calling Landis "Czar" and his reign lasted 24 years, until his death in 1944 at the age of 78. He wanted no funeral, no memorial, no flowers. "He was, I think, an atheist," wrote J. G. Taylor Spink. Whatever, Landis wanted to be remembered only for his life. It was in many ways an exceptional life, but it was marred and it is marred by racism.

"Certainly in many instances Landis made important decisions that favored baseball's working men, the ballplayers," Lester Rodney said at our final meeting. "Certainly with the New Deal and World War II the times were changing. At the *Worker* we prepared petitions to open the game to blacks. More than a million people signed them. Figuratively those petitions were dumped on Landis's desk. He was unmoved. The only end to his opposition to blacks in baseball was death. His own death. Within one year of Landis dying, our long campaign bore fruit. Rickey signed Jackie Robinson."

These intersections of viewpoints are no less than remarkable. The Psalm Singer (Rickey). The Rigid Self-Righteous Judge (Landis). The Brooklyn Communist (Lester Rodney). Jackie Robinson summarized the situation when he testified before Congress on July 18, 1949.

"The fact that it is a Communist who denounced injustice in the courts, police brutality and a lynching when it happens doesn't change the truth of his charges. Negroes were stirred up before there was a Communist Party, and they'll stay stirred up long after the Party has disappeared—unless Jim Crow has disappeared as well."

"A profound statement," I said to him years later.

"For a second baseman," said Jackie Robinson.

SIX

A MEETING FOR THE AGES

HY TURKIN, A SHORT, SLIGHT, BESPECTACLED tabloid sportswriter, was what we used to call a "Figure Filbert." He was a numbers man, forever considering and reconsidering the statistics and measurements that to some (mostly other numbers men) define baseball. Hy Turkin and Allan Roth, a supremely gifted Canadian statistician whom Branch Rickey brought to Brooklyn, were the founders of modern baseball numerology, subsequently practiced by Leonard Koppett, Bill James and such other numbers folk as John Thorn and Alan Schwarz. But the numbers folk are not universally popular. One day when Koppett arrived in a press box carrying a satchel, the columnist Jimmy Cannon snarled and said, "What you got in that bag, Koppett? Decimal points?"

The numbers were and are such stuff as on-base percentage, at bats per home run, fielding percentage; the arithmetic of baseball fills many volumes. One numeric rule, of particular interest in New York, stated that no outfield fence in a major-league ballpark could be closer to home plate than 250 feet. The thought obviously was to eliminate pop-fly home runs. Officials of the New York Giants maintained that the right-field foul pole in the old Polo Grounds was 257 feet distant.

But so many lazy fly balls reached the seats that numbers of us became suspicious. Hy Turkin was the man who took action. One morning in 1950 he showed up at the Polo Grounds with a yardstick. Turkin crouched at home plate and began measuring as he slouched his way out toward right field. He had just reached first base when three husky ballpark cops appeared and blocked his way. Under orders from the Giant management, they confiscated Turkin's yardstick and escorted him off the field. There were no laser range finders back in 1950s, so the actual distance to the right-field foul pole at the Polo Grounds remains a mystery, like the identity of Jack the Ripper or the true founder of the city of Rome.

During the 1940s, Turkin crossed paths with a cornet player named S. (for Shirley) C. Thompson who had played in John Sousa's famous marching band. Thompson was a professional musician, but almost all his spare time was devoted to baseball, its people and its history. In 1951 a sports book publisher, A. S. Barnes, issued the groundbreaking first *Baseball Encyclopedia.* It had been assembled by Thompson and Turkin. The book purported to contain the name of every man who had ever played major-league baseball, the teams for which he played, his positions, his birthplace and birth date and his vital statistics, good (home runs) and bad (errors). Lowell Pratt, the president of Barnes, said the work was so complete that he would personally pay $50 to anyone who came up with the name of a big-league player, living or dead, who was missing from the encyclopedia. (As I remember it, Pratt had to pay off only eight times.)

Rickey made no secret of his aversion to the tabloid press—this would cost him dearly—but the bespectacled little numbers man from the New York *Daily News* interested him and they developed a relationship. Rickey discussed with Turkin, as he did with very few, a bit of the selection process that led to Jackie Robinson.

According to Turkin, Rickey's first choice was a Cuban infielder named Silvio Garcia. "He hits for power and average," one of Rickey's scouts reported in 1945. "He runs well and his arm is unbelievable. When he's playing third and throws to first, it's as if an invisible hand at the pitchers' mound threw the ball again. That's how hard this Garcia flings it."

Walter O'Malley picked up the story from there. "I was the Dodger lawyer," O'Malley told me years afterward at a luncheon in Los Angeles. "I knew in legal confidentiality about Rickey's plan to integrate, and of course I approved. He said the scouts had found a superb player named Garcia. He told me to fly to Havana and do a background check. We understood that the first black would have to be a great ballplayer but also a man of character. I'd had some dealings with one of the leading Cuban Jewish families, the Maduros. They were active in a whole lot of areas, from cane sugar to baseball.

"I flew to Havana on a lumbering old DC-3. All the windows were painted black. This was just after the war and the windows were blackened to conceal the plane from anti-aircraft fire from German ships and submarines.

"Roberto Maduro, a good ballplayer in his own right, helped me out. He had a file on Silvio Garcia and it wasn't pretty. First, Garcia was in trouble with Cuban selective service. It looked as though he might be accused of draft dodging. Second, his personal health records showed that he had been treated for venereal disease.

"I thanked my friend Bobby Maduro, and flew home to New York in another plane with blackened windows. After I reported my findings to Rickey, our search for the right player moved elsewhere."

Subsequently, in 1949, Garcia signed with the Sherbrooke Athlétiques of the Provincial League in Quebec. This league was "independent," not affiliated with so-called organized baseball. There, Garcia tore up the turf of Canada. He led the league in homers, doubles and runs batted in. He hit .365. Finally, in 1952, Garcia broke a color barrier in organized ball playing infield for the Miami Beach Flamingos of the Class B Florida International League. But by then time was eroding his great skills.

One thinks of a memorable line Budd Schulberg wrote in another context. Except for bigotry, the now forgotten Silvio Garcia "coulda been a contender."

Rickey told me he spent "about $30,000" scouting ballplayers around the Caribbean. "That also cost me time and effort," he said. "In the end it only demonstrated that the best Negro ballplayers for my purpose were playing in the United States."

My recorded conversation with Rickey that the *Herald Tribune* published in 1954 drew considerable attention. Among those pleased with the story was Rickey himself. "My door is always open for you," he said afterward, "any time you want to visit for a talk." Early the next season, in Pittsburgh, I took him up on the offer. I wanted to discuss scouting; I wanted to learn as much as I could about the methodology that led him to Jackie Robinson. He would oblige, but first the man Red Smith called a checkers shark tried an amiable hustle. We were sitting in a private compartment in the low-ceilinged press box at Forbes Field watching a shaky Pirate team play the Dodgers. With Roberto Clemente in right field and Dick Groat at shortstop, these Pirates had potential, but that year there wasn't a single .300 hitter on the club.

"Wouldn't it be a fine thing to bring Sid Gordon home," Rickey began. Gordon was an experienced outfielder with good power, a fine arm and not much running speed. "You know he was born in Brooklyn." He knew that. I also knew Gordon was Jewish. A Jewish slugger from Brooklyn hitting home runs in Ebbets Field had great box office potential. But I also knew that Gordon was 38 years old.

"I imagine he could have some good days with that short wall out in left field."

"And right center," Rickey said. "He still has plenty of power to all fields." Rickey was hard at work planting a story, which he hoped I would write under a headline about like this:

SID GORDON AVAILABLE FOR RIGHT OFFER, RICKEY SAYS; VETERAN SLUGGER WOULD HELP DODGERS WIN PENNANT

That could generate pressure from fans on the Dodger front office and help along a sale that would put a fresh deposit into Rickey's bankbook. I said I would use a Gordon item in the notes that followed my regular Dodger story. Rickey seemed satisfied. He had made his pitch and if I wasn't buying all of it, at least I was paying attention. A few weeks later Rickey sold Gordon's contract to the New York Giants for $40,000. Gordon hit only .243 for the 1955 Giants in what was his final season in the major leagues. (Ten years later he died of a heart attack at the age of 57, stricken while chasing a long fly in a softball game in Central Park. His career total of 202 home runs places Sid Gordon fourth, after Hank Greenberg, Shawn Green and Ryan Braun, among all Jewish-born major-league sluggers, past and present.)

Rickey had profound ideas on the art and science of scouting. Buzzie Bavasi, the Dodger general manager for 17 seasons, told me shortly before his death in 2008, "Without question Mr. Rickey was the greatest scout who ever lived. He is really the father, or grandfather, of modern scouting."

That day in Pittsburgh, Rickey talked scouting at length. His thought processes were vivid. His phrasing was extraordinary. Almost everything he said was new to me, at least in the way he said it. I didn't know then that he had made many of the same points many times in closed meetings when he was running the Brooklyn Dodgers. Perhaps that's why the phrasing was so smooth.

Al Campanis, who succeeded Bavasi as general manager of the Dodgers, tape-recorded Rickey's dissertations and preserved the cassettes in an old shoe box, which he kept locked in his desk at Dodger Stadium. "The spirit of Branch Rickey still stirs in these offices,"

Campanis said when I was visiting in 1985 with my late son, Roger Laurence Kahn. Campanis peered into his shoe box and considered the labels. Then he read aloud:

> *"Luck Is the Residue of Design.*
> *"Is What We Are Doing Worthwhile?*
> *"Intestinal Fortitude.*
> *"The Cure Is Sweat.*
> *"Thou Shalt Not Steal (Defensively).*
> *"Thou Shalt Steal (Offensively).*
> *"Does He Like to Play?"*

Lecture titles for a postdoctoral course in the game of baseball.

"Do you have your managers, coaches and scouts listen to these tapes?" I asked.

"Damn right," Campanis said. "Every year. And I listen to them myself, too, about every six months. Mr. Rickey was the master. He's still teaching all of us, 35 years after these talks were recorded"—and more than 60 years later as I write these lines.

When we talked scouting Rickey asserted that there were three fundamentals, the arm, the legs and power. "You look at a boy and say, 'Can he throw?' Sometimes, particularly with outfielders, you have to watch many games to get an answer. Outfielders can go for a week without having to make an important throw. But this is primarily can he or can't he. If a boy can't throw at 18 he won't throw much at 28. You may tinker a little with grip and mechanics, such as arm angle, but not significantly. Either a prospect has a strong arm, or he doesn't. Look at the Brooklyn man in right field now [Carl Furillo]. He's about 30 years old, am I right, and famous throughout baseball for his arm. The base runners take no liberties with him. Well, I'll guarantee he had the great arm he has today when he was just a prospect, 10 years ago. I'll guarantee a good scout looking at him then would report, 'This man is armed.' Am I going too fast for you?"

"Not at all."

"With hitting I look for power."

"Batting average?" I said.

"No, no, no," Rickey said. "So many things affect a .300 hitter. The ballpark. The skill of the defenders. The strike zone of individual umpires. Now that boy out in center [Duke Snider] came to me at Bear Mountain with a magnificent, natural swing. That translated into tremendous power. But there was a problem. He had not learned the strike zone. He was a headstrong youngster, very willful and self-involved. I told him repeatedly and sternly that if he ever wanted to make the major leagues he would have to stop swinging at bad pitches. High and outside. He swung at everything high and outside the strike zone, swung at everything, swung and missed. So I ordered him to stand in the batter's box with a bat while I had a succession of pitchers throw. I told the young man, 'You may not swing. You are simply to call each pitch, ball or strike.' He pouted but obeyed. That went on for days, weeks. The Yankees scouted him carefully and in the 1949 World Series fed him bad pitches and made him look dreadful. He batted less than .200. But learning is an ongoing process and the last time he was in the World Series [1952] he batted about .350 and hit four home runs. The power was always there. That's why we invested so much teaching time in a headstrong young man. Today, as you know, he's a star."

"And still headstrong," I said.

"Perhaps," Rickey said. "But he seems to have learned that the strike zone is not high and outside.

"My third fundamental is a pair of fast legs. Foot speed. If I were to write four units on a blackboard, I would give two to the legs and one to arm and one to power. The arm is used only defensively, no matter what the position. Power is used only on offense. But the legs are much in evidence offensively and defensively.

"Do you know that speed forces errors? When a slow man hits the ball to deep shortstop the fielder takes his time and throws him out. When a fast man hits a similar ball the shortstop has to hurry, and in hurrying may throw the ball away.

"My ideal team is fast and young. My ideal pitching staff is intelligent and seasoned.

"What I look for first in a pitcher is size. Christy Mathewson—he and I served together in France during the First World War—is my favorite among all pitchers and he is remembered today for poise, the fade-away [the modern screwball] and for his remarkable control. But don't forget that Matty was a big, strong man, well over six feet tall. So was Walter Johnson. So was Dizzy Dean. Every one over six feet.

"If I have to name a favorite pitch it would be the overhand curve. Thrown properly—watch Carl Erskine—it breaks straight down, making it equally effective against right- and left-handed batters. A flat curve breaks along the plane of the bat so the hitter has a significant stretch of wood with which to make contact. But against the overhand curve he has only the diameter of the bat and inside that diameter only an inch or so that will produce a solid drive.

"But picking a favorite pitch is an incomplete approach, since pitches come in sequences. Each pitch relates to what has gone before. If you are going to throw three curveballs in a row, the second one has to be better than the first and the third one has to be better than the second. One of my favorite pitchers, now a coach, Whitlow Wyatt, says simply, 'The best pitch in baseball is a strike.'" A laugh rumbled up from Rickey's chest. "'Simply.' I used that word didn't I? But a strike is seldom a simple pitch."

The Rickey papers are stored in 131 boxes in a warehouse at the Library of Congress, and it was there that I found a brief and succinct example of Rickey's pitching acumen. Subject: The highly neurotic but just about incomparable Sandy Koufax. As Rickey viewed him in a memo written in 1960:

> This boy comes nearest to perfection in pitching as anyone in either of the major leagues at the present time. He has more speed than [Warren] Spahn and almost perfect control of a slow curve that really curves. A daunting combination for even the finest hitter. He has an exceptional fastball and occasionally throws a change-up off that fastball. He has four different pitches that he can throw for strikes on any occasion. Perhaps the best thing about Koufax is that he is a good thinker and uses all four, three of them [not the straight change] constantly.
>
> This fellow has so much stuff and has such perfect control that I am compelled to think the hitter's best hope is swinging at the "cripple," the 3 and 0 pitch. But Koufax does not go to 3 and 0 often. Like Mathewson long before him, he is not likely to walk anybody.

A catcher from the Bronx, the late Bob Berman, once told an interviewer that Rickey was going to sign him for the St. Louis Cardinals in the spring of 1917 but changed his mind. "He was interested," Berman said, "until he found out I was Jewish. That killed the deal." Berman then signed with the Washington Senators.

Ezra Pound ultimately called this sort of generic response "stupid suburban anti-Semitism." For decades it was endemic in baseball and American society at large. A touch of it colors some of Christy Mathewson's memoir, *Pitching in a Pinch,* and invades passages of T. S. Eliot's poetry and even the famous Hemingway novel *The Sun Also Rises.* I can testify personally that Rickey bested any suburban anti-Semitism within him during his later years, and indeed reached out to Jewish people after the revelation of the Holocaust. "How," he asked in a moving speech, "among Christian nations could such a thing be?" But a curious question remains. After the young pitcher's dazzling tryout with the Pirates at Forbes Field in 1954, why didn't Rickey sign Sandy Koufax on the spot?

Koufax was born in Brooklyn to Evelyn and Jack Braun, but his parents divorced when he was three. Six years later Evelyn married an accountant named Irving Koufax, whose name young Sandy assumed. Divorce was infrequent and considered somewhat immoral in Bensonhurst, the staid Jewish community where the family lived. (For some years Koufax concealed his family history.)

Sandy starred in basketball at Lafayette High and for an amateur baseball team in the Coney Island Sports League, run by a man named Milton Secol, nicknamed "Pop." Informally the organization was called the Ice Cream League. Later Koufax enrolled at the University of Cincinnati, hoping to become an architect, but sports continued to hold him in its thrall. He made the baseball varsity as a freshman. Mostly with his fastball, he struck out 51 batters in 31 innings.

Now word spread through baseball about the Brooklyn kid with the blazer. Koufax tried out for the Giants at the Polo Grounds but later said he was so nervous he forgot to bring his glove. He was wild and the Giants took a pass. Then he traveled to Forbes Field, where Rickey watched with his favorite scout, Clyde Sukeforth. Another Rickey favorite, a former Cardinal catcher named Sam Narron, crouched behind the plate. Koufax threw harder and harder until a fastball broke Sam Narron's thumb—a thumb that was protected by a catcher's mitt. Rickey said quietly to Sukeforth, "This is the finest arm I've ever seen." After a bit Sukeforth told Koufax, "Mr. Rickey is thinking of a generous signing package. Something like $15,000."

The Ice Cream League star said he would have to think about it. He went back to Brooklyn and tried out for the Dodgers at Ebbets Field. Al Campanis, then the Dodgers' chief scout, took a stance in the batter's box when Koufax was ready to pitch. He memorably described what happened next. "Only twice in my life," Campanis told me, "has the hair on the back of my neck literally stood up straight. The first time was when I saw Michelangelo's Sistine Chapel. The second time was when I saw Sandy Koufax's fastball."

Today a legion of agents would come marching up to the door of a young pitcher with an electric arm and set up a bidding war at once. But this was happening during the mid-1950s, when baseball executives refused to talk to agents. The Dodgers quickly cobbled an offer together: a $6,000 signing bonus and a salary of $14,000. In short, a $20,000 package. Under the rules of the time any bonus over $5,000 meant that the player was guaranteed a spot on the major-league team for at least two seasons. Like Bob Feller before him, Koufax would skip the endless bus rides of the minor leagues. Besides, as Koufax and his stepfather saw matters, the $20,000 would cover tuition through architectural college if the baseball career fizzled. And wouldn't it be a fine thing to play big-league ball not far from the Flatbush fields of the old Ice Cream League?

As far as I know Sandy Koufax, apprentice architect, never did design a building. And two years after Sandy joined the Dodgers, Walter O'Malley hustled the franchise, including Koufax, out of Brooklyn to California, where superstardom awaited the intense left-hander. "In all the years I was working in Brooklyn," O'Malley subsequently told me during an amiable lunch at Perino's Restaurant on Wilshire Boulevard, "I would have given my right arm for a star Jewish ballplayer. What that would have done for our gate.

"I come out here where I could fill the ballpark with nine fucking Chinamen, and what do I get? Koufax." O'Malley laughed genially. Then he said, "Remember, you promised to pick up the lunch check."

As for Branch Rickey, in this instance he struck out. For the man who signed Jackie Robinson is also the man who failed to sign Sandy Koufax.

◆ ◆ ◆ ◆ ◆

WITH LANDIS'S DEATH LATE in 1944, a primary obstacle to integrating baseball was interred. As New York State's fair employment bill began moving through the legislative process, the path to integration was being secured. The men who directed the major leagues—Red Smith described them as "the fatheads who run baseball"—began to realize that the times were changing and possibly, just possibly, they might have to change as well.

Imperious to the end, Commissioner Landis directed St. Luke's, the Chicago hospital where he lay dying, to issue only upbeat bulletins. "The judge is doing fine." Sam Breadon visited in early November and reported, "The judge's mind is as sharp as ever." A few days later a committee including Breadon, Rickey and Ford Frick, president of the National League, recommended offering Landis a new seven-year term as commissioner. What that would have done to Rickey's developing integration plans is a good question. It became moot in the early hours of Saturday, November 25, 1944, though, when Landis died peacefully within an oxygen tent.

Uncertainty followed, along with a wild scramble for Landis's job. Candidates lobbied hard to become the second baseball commissioner, a job that paid $50,000 a year, five times the salary of a United States senator at the time. The suitors formed a cavalcade of sporting-life celebrities: hard-nosed J. Edgar Hoover of the FBI; liberal Supreme Court justice William O. Douglas; the essentially conservative New York governor, Thomas E. Dewey; Franklin Roosevelt's pragmatic aide James A. Farley (a one-time semi-pro first baseman); and Ford Frick, who eventually would become commissioner but not just yet. Most media people were surprised in April 1945 when the owners plucked from the ranks of the United States Senate one Albert Benjamin "Happy" Chandler, an ambitious, cornpone politician from rural Kentucky. After meeting him, Dan Parker of the New York *Daily Mirror* wrote, "There is an astonishing contrast between straight-laced, stern Judge Landis and his ebullient, sophomoric successor, Senator Chandler."

Chandler opened an office in a Cincinnati skyscraper and, when receiving visitors, liked to point across the Ohio River. "Kaintucky," he would say. "God's country." The contrived down-home country boy manner so irritated Red Smith that Smith began referring in his columns to the new commissioner as "A. Benny Chandler." Not easily squelched, Chandler took to calling the newspaperman "Whiskey-head Smith." (Smith liked to drink but almost always handled the hard stuff well.)

In his later years Chandler portrayed himself as a champion of integration and in truth he did nothing to block Rickey's plan. But during the presidential election of 1948, Chandler supported a fiery racist candidate, the Dixiecrat Strom Thurmond.

During the interregnum between Landis and Chandler the owners created a so-called Major League Committee on Baseball Integration. Its members were Rickey, Sam Lacy, a black Philadelphia magistrate named Joseph Rainey, and Larry MacPhail, who had just bought the Yankees (with two multimillionaire partners: copper heir Dan Topping, a former husband of the lusty movie actress Arline Judge, and Del Webb, whose construction company built the rickety camps in which Japanese Americans were confined during World War II). Perhaps the most remarkable thing about the integration committee is this: It never met.

Rickey had no intention of sharing his grand design, but many have faulted MacPhail's "stalling tactics" and depict him as an unyielding foe of integration. We talked for a few days at Larry's Maryland farm in 1952 and he presented quite a different picture. "Some things have to move fast," he told me. "In this instance I thought they had to move slowly.

"The Negro Leagues were just chaotic. Uncertain schedules. Rough conditions for the players. Few if any contracts and some owners who were just one step ahead of the law. Numbers racket hoodlums ran teams. If I know anything about baseball, it is that you can't have gambling people running ball clubs.

"My approach was that the majors should pitch in and stabilize the Negro Leagues. That would take a few years, but when it happened organized baseball could systematically begin buying the contracts of the better Negro League players and assigning them to the high minors or even, in a few cases, to the majors."

"But in Brooklyn, Larry," I said, "you were an opponent of gradualism. You defied the ban on radio broadcasts and summarily brought in Red Barber. You installed lights at Ebbets Field and suddenly we had night games. When you moved, you moved fast."

"Integration is totally different," MacPhail said. "You also have to consider your fans. When you hire Negro players you'll attract Negro fans and you know as well as I that there are bad elements in Harlem. Drug dealers. Tough guys carrying booze and packing knives or even guns. How are you going to police them in your ballparks?"

"With cops," I said.

"It isn't that simple," MacPhail said. "You have two cultures here that clash, and those clashes could lead to riots in the ballparks. Figure it out. The white fans get scared and stay home. Attendance collapses. That way lays financial ruin."

Whatever, the Major League Committee on Baseball Integration disappeared.

◆ ◆ ◆ ◆ ◆

RICKEY SAID THAT SCOUTING black ballplayers cost the Dodgers $30,000. Since the leading Dodger scouts, Sukeforth, George Sisler and Tom Greenwade, began appearing regularly at Negro League games, Rickey needed a cover story to explain their presence. All three were well known in the two worlds of baseball, white and black. With Rickey's customary craft he spread the word that he wanted to organize a new Negro league, more reputable than the ones already existing, and he was organizing his linchpin team, the Brooklyn

Brown Dodgers. My *Herald Tribune* colleague, the gifted Al Laney, who had been covering the Brooklyn White Dodgers, said Rickey's story made sense. "We knew the Yankees were making money, perhaps as much as $100,000 a season, renting the stadium for Negro League games. But the Dodgers were getting nothing, because there was a rickety old field called Dexter Park, out near the border of Brooklyn and Queens, which was home to a semi-pro outfit called the Bushwicks. When the Negro teams wanted a Brooklyn crowd, they usually played the Bushwicks in Dexter Park, which could hold about 20,000 fans. Rickey's third Negro league would move the Negro games to Ebbets Field and bring him a nice rental income. Or so we thought. We knew Rickey liked income of any sort."

Sam Lacy said Jackie Robinson was not the best Negro League player in 1945. "Not the best," Lacy repeated, "but the most suitable." Buzzie Bavasi told me, "The Negro League player with the most talent was Don Newcombe. But Mr. Rickey wouldn't sign him to be the first because Newcombe was 19 years old. He felt that Newk was too young to face the pressure we knew was coming." Such comments created a general underestimation of Robinson's pure athletic ability.

As a senior at UCLA Robinson led the football team in rushing, total offense and scoring. He was fast and strong and shifty. California sportswriters called him Lightning Jack. Playing basketball—he was a power forward and a strong rebounder—Robinson led the southern division of the Pacific Coast Conference in scoring during his junior and senior years. Basketball cut into the track season, but without much practice Robinson made a running broad jump of 25 feet and became the 1940 NCAA champion. Longer leaps are not uncommon today, but training and equipment, such as track shoes, are much improved. In 1940 the four-minute mile was still regarded as an impossible dream.

Playing shortstop for the Bruins in the spring of 1940, Robinson batted only .097. That is a puzzler, and I brought it up directly with

Robinson in his North Stamford home one social evening in 1970. His late son, Jack Jr., had joined us. "Yeah, Dad," young Jack said, as a bit of familial rivalry flared. "How come you couldn't even hit a hundred?" Robinson bristled, but only briefly. "I was dog tired," he said. "Playing and practicing all the sports I did without a break just wore me out."

Rickey reviewed Robinson's records at UCLA. He had assistants discreetly investigate the family. Robinson's father, Jerry, sired five children and disappeared during the Spanish flu epidemic shortly after Jackie was born in Cairo, Georgia, on January 31, 1919. "Disappeared" is a gentle word. Jerry Robinson abandoned his wife and children in Georgia and moved to Florida with another man's wife. He never saw his family again. "My mother was not the most sophisticated woman," Robinson said, "but now that she was on her own she had the sense to get out of Georgia as quickly as she could." In Georgia the Robinsons were sharecroppers, farming acres on a plantation owned by a white racist named Jim Sasser. "My mother said we ate what we grew," Robinson said, "and we never got much meat. When Sasser had hogs slaughtered the ham and bacon went to the white people. Negroes only got entrails, like the liver or the intestines that people called 'chitterlings.'"

When Jerry Robinson fled, Sasser turned on Mallie. As Jackie told me the story, Sasser said Mallie should have warned him that Jerry was planning to leave "so I could get the sheriff to stop him." Sasser didn't like losing a farmhand.

"The sheriff?" Mallie said. "Slavery's over, Mr. Sasser. A man can go where he pleases."

Sasser said, "You're too damn uppity for your own good." (In a later time some said the same about Mallie's most famous son.)

Mallie Robinson scratched together fare and moved with her brood to Pasadena, where she heard she could find work as a domestic. "We went by train," Mallie said years afterward. "We were riding out of Georgia to a new life so I called it the Freedom Train." From

Pasadena she wrote in wonder and happiness to one of her former teachers back in Georgia, "Tell my girl friends that to get here I crossed a river so wide you couldn't see from one side to the other, climbed mountains so tall the tops were hidden in the clouds—and the Freedom Train was so long that on the sharpest curves you could lean out of the last car and light a cigarette by the fire of the engine."

Athletics ran in the family. Jackie's older brother Matthew, called Mack, won a silver medal in the 1936 Olympic Games held, as I've mentioned, in the Nazi capital, Berlin. Competing in the finals of the 200-meter dash, Mack finished four-tenths of a second behind Jesse Owens. Both broke the prior Olympic record. The genial German host, Adolf Hitler, refused to shake the hand of either black man, and his propaganda lackey, Josef Goebbels, issued a statement condemning America's use of "black auxiliaries."

Mack graduated from the University of Oregon in 1941, but he had a hard time finding an appropriate job. For many years this college graduate with an Olympic silver medal worked as a garbage collector in Pasadena, stabbing litter and filth with a spiked stick and pushing a stinking garbage barrel on wheels.

Although Jackie's boyhood was fatherless and hard, he remembered only two episodes of California bigotry that upset him. When he was small, a white girl living across the street greeted him with a nasty chant:

Soda cracker's good to eat.
Nigger's only good to beat.

On his mother's orders, Jack did not respond.

Blacks were forbidden to use the Pasadena municipal pool, so one very hot day Robinson and some of his black friends went wading in the city reservoir. Someone called the police. Soon a sheriff and some deputies appeared, guns drawn. "Looka there," the sheriff shouted. "Niggers in my drinking water."

The boys, 16 in all, were hauled off to a police station and crammed into one sweltering room. Just before sunset the sheriff, again with his pistol drawn, opened the door and dismissed them with a single word, "Git!"

For a time Robinson ran with a group called the Pepper Street Gang, but, he went to pains to tell me, it was not violent like gangs of later years. "Some of us stole fruit off street wagons," he said, "or we hid in bushes at a golf club and stole balls after long drives landed on the green. Nothing to brag about, but that was about as bad as it got. I ran with the gang for a time, but more and more sports were taking over my life."

Others say the Pepper Street Gang was rougher than Robinson admitted. "Jack got himself arrested lots of times," said Ray Bartlett, a high school classmate and friend. "The sheriff even got to know him by his first name." But no one disputes that sports were drawing Robinson away from the uncertain life of a street kid.

Leo Durocher said of himself when the Chicago Cubs hired him to manage in 1965, "I'll tell you one thing. They ain't getting no maiden." After a sometimes-contentious youth, Robinson left college during World War II to accept a commission as a cavalry lieutenant. A few months later he was court-martialed for refusing a captain's order to move to the rear of an Army bus. He was acquitted. Still, with the Pepper Street Gang and an Army court-martial in his background, the Robinson Rickey signed was—in Durocher English—"no maiden neither."

To Robinson the most remarkable aspect of the signing was not his own background, but Rickey's age. "When he offered me a contract," Jack said, "he was 65 years old. Isn't that when most people are retiring?"

Records from the old Negro Leagues tend to be uncertain. You can read that Robinson, as shortstop for the Kansas City Monarchs in 1945, hit .433. Or he hit .382. Or whatever. But by all accounts he was a punishing batter, a sure-handed infielder and a superb base runner.

There was some question about his arm. Could he move to his right at shortstop, pluck a grounder, then fire a long throw to first the way all the great big-league shortstops do? That question was bothering Clyde Sukeforth when he traveled to Chicago to watch a brace of Negro League games.

In 1953, after Jackie and I started the magazine called *Our Sports,* he asked me to help him with a column he was preparing, "The Branch Rickey They Don't Write About." With the column in front of me now, I can repeat, for the first time since their initial publication, Robinson's exact words of 60 years ago.

> In Chicago, summer of 1945, someone said, "There's a man outside the clubhouse who wants to see you."
>
> I went over to see "the man."
>
> "My name's Clyde Sukeforth," he said. "I'm with the Brooklyn Dodgers. How are you feeling?"
>
> "Pretty well, thanks. My arm's a little sore from a fall on the base paths, but I'm okay."
>
> "I've been watching you for a while. Would you mind going out to the infield and throwing a few from short to first?"
>
> "I don't think I can. My arm is so sore I can't play."
>
> "Never mind then," Sukeforth said.
>
> Then he asked me something I'll never forget. "Can you come to New York with me to see Branch Rickey, the Dodger president?"
>
> "Sure," I said. "Sure."
>
> I was thinking much more than that one word. I was thinking that this might be a gag, a cruel gag. I didn't dare think of becoming a Dodger. Hundreds of other things entered my mind, and I was still thinking when we got off the train in New York.

"How did you travel?" I said.

"Pullman. Not bad. But Clyde took the lower berth and made me take the upper."

The first meeting between Robinson and Rickey, on August 28, has become the stuff of both legend and fairy tales. In 1953 Robinson lay back on a bed in his room at the Hotel Schenley in Pittsburgh and while he talked I took notes, using my Smith-Corona portable typewriter. What follows is verbatim.

> The first time I saw Branch Rickey he was setting up a smokescreen with his cigar. Behind the smoke was a face revealing sincerity.
>
> "Do you think you are capable enough to play baseball in the major leagues?" Mr. Rickey began.
>
> "I don't know. I've only played professional baseball for one year. I don't know how the Negro Leagues stack up against the minors, let alone the majors."
>
> Mr. Rickey did not wait to deliver his punch line. "I am willing to offer you a contract in organized baseball. Are you willing to sign it?"
>
> Now I was the one who did not hesitate.
>
> "Certainly," I said.
>
> Then Mr. Rickey began to speak. He spoke of barriers to be broken and how to break them. He spoke of bigotry and hate and how to fight them. He spoke of great things to be done and how to do them.
>
> He spoke of himself and how his own family had advised him against signing a Negro because at his age the bitterness he'd have to face might make him sick, or even kill him.
>
> He spoke of my future in baseball and of the taunts and insults that would be hurled in my face and the dusters that would be hurled at my head.
>
> He spoke of others who would wait for me to slip so they could say that Branch Rickey had been wrong and that baseball was no place for Negroes.
>
> All this he hurled at me like thunder. And then he asked me if I still wanted to sign.
>
> "Certainly," I said again.

The small hotel room near Forbes Field in Pittsburgh had become electric with emotion. "What a story, Jack," I said.

That was as far as Robinson would go or could go on that particular day. With time came embellishments from Jack, from Sukeforth and from Rickey himself, never one to shy from center stage in a dramatic situation. Supposedly in that first meeting Rickey went to great lengths to impersonate bigots. He took off his jacket and swung his arms and pretended to be a rival base runner assaulting Robinson. "Take that, you nigger bastard," Rickey claims he shouted.

Robinson was shocked but kept his poise. Now Rickey became a hotel clerk refusing Jackie a room, a white waiter declining to serve him a meal, a white railroad conductor barring his way to his assigned berth in a Pullman car. "We don't allow no nigger boys in there!"

Robinson said that though the outbursts did indeed shock him, he also felt stirred. "As I kept listening, I knew I had to do this thing for myself and for my race and then I began to feel I had to do it for this spellbinder I had just met, Branch Rickey."

Suddenly Rickey produced a book. He was always a great one for books. This was a 1923 bestseller called *The Life of Christ,* a novelization of parts of the New Testament, written by an erratic Florentine named Giovanni Papini. (Other bestsellers that year were H. G. Wells's *The Outline of History* and Sinclair Lewis's *Babbitt.*) Rickey indicated a passage from Papini and directed Robinson to read.

> Ye have heard that it hath been said, An eye for an eye, and a tooth for a tooth. But I say unto you, that ye resist not evil. But whosoever shall smite thee on the right cheek, turn to him the other also. And if any man will sue thee at the law, and take away thy coat, let him have thy cloak also. And whosoever shall compel thee to go a mile, go with him twain.

These words are, of course, a cornerstone of Christian belief.

Robinson reading Papini on nonviolence is a story that has been told several times, always with deference and approval, even reverence, and often with cross-references to the nonviolence of that other Mahatma, Mohandas Gandhi. But every source I have found neglects a profoundly disturbing fact. Giovanni Papini, the author Rickey chose to cite at this extraordinary moment, was a bigoted Fascist.

To quote from one biography: "In 1937, Papini published his *History of Italian Literature,* which he dedicated to Benito Mussolini: 'Il Duce, friend of poetry and of the poets.' Subsequently the Fascist government awarded him top positions in academia. Papini supported Mussolini's racial discrimination laws of 1938, which among other things prohibited marriage between Jews and Christians."

Mussolini's views on blacks were yet more vicious. He sent his modern armies into Ethiopia, an independent black African nation, in October 1935, and completed a colonialist conquest the following May. In the course of the war Mussolini violated international law by using mustard gas against the Ethiopian forces. Mussolini's invaders killed roughly 275,000 black Africans. Having seen the face of fascism up close, the Ethiopian emperor, Haile Selassie, spoke before the League of Nations in Geneva. "If it is us today, tomorrow it will be you." Haunting words, but the leaders of the League, hurtling toward World War II, did not respond.

When the Fascist regime crumbled in 1943, Papini retreated behind the walls of a Franciscan convent. Although never prosecuted as a war criminal, he was thoroughly discredited by the subsequent non-Fascist Italian regime.

Did Rickey's small-town Christian zealotry blind him to Papini's fascism? Was Rickey unaware of Mussolini's war crimes against blacks? Or did he simply not care, believing in his zealotry that Jesus's message trumped all other considerations? I never got a chance to bring up these questions with him. My belief is that his zealotry was blinding.

As for Robinson, in later years he attended university seminars on dictatorships and racism, but in 1945 he had never heard of Papini. When Alan Paton, author of the great antiapartheid novel *Cry, the Beloved Country,* visited Ebbets Field in 1953, Robinson had never heard of him, either. The old four-letter varsity star was still developing intellectually. How would he have reacted if he knew Rickey was feeding him words composed by a man who believed that it was acceptable for a mechanized white European army to bomb and shoot and gas black Africans? The Jackie Robinson I remember would have walked out. But he did not know and he did not walk out. Instead, the meeting lasted three hours, Rickey constantly emphasizing the need to turn the other cheek. At one point Robinson said, "Are you looking for someone who doesn't have the courage to fight back?"

"No," Rickey said. "I'm looking for someone who has the courage *not* to fight back." The old spellbinder went on, "We've got no army. There's virtually nobody on our side. No owners, no umpires, very few newspapermen. And I'm afraid that many fans will be hostile. We'll be in a tough position. We can win only if we convince the world that I'm doing this because you're a great ballplayer, a fine gentleman.

"Jackie, I just want to beg two things of you: that as a baseball player you give it your utmost and as a man you give continuing fidelity to your race and to this crucial cause you symbolize.

"Above all, do not fight. No matter how vile the abuse, ignore it. You are carrying the reputation of a race on your shoulders. Bear it well and a day will come when every team in baseball will open its doors to Negroes."

Rickey lowered his voice. "The alternative is not pleasant."

Robinson agreed to accept a bonus of $3,500 and a salary of $600 a month to play baseball in 1946 for the Montreal Royals, the Dodgers' top farm team, in the Triple A International League. There he would establish himself as an outstanding second baseman, steal

40 bases and lead the league in hitting at .349. He was also a significant gate attraction. More than one million people went to games involving Robinson in 1946, an amazing figure by the standards of any minor league.

But off the field many communities coldly rejected him. Summing up that memorable season the witty, acerbic (and corrupt) Dick Young wrote, "Jackie Robinson led the league in everything except hotel reservations."

SEVEN

SHOW THE BUMS THE DOOR

THE INTEGRATION OF BASEBALL, HEROically engineered by Branch Rickey, heroically executed by Jackie Robinson, would be called the Noble Experiment and become the stuff of books, essays, seminars, doctoral theses and, within the world of baseball, unending self-congratulation. Put briefly, Robinson's debut season in Montreal, summer of 1946, was a sheer, if stressful, triumph. He hit, he ran, he fielded and he led the Royals to victory in the ultimate minor-league playoff, the Little World Series. But for Branch Rickey, who shared that triumph as Robinson himself invariably pointed out, the times brought not only triumph but also trappings of disaster. His Brooklyn Dodgers, of Pee Wee Reese, Dixie Walker and Carl Furillo, lost a tight pennant race to the St. Louis Cardinals, of Stan Musial, Terry Moore and Enos Slaughter. (Rickey, the architect, designed both teams.)

But the New York press did not gush with praise. As exemplified by the tabloid *Daily News,* then selling two million copies a day, the press generally declined to applaud Rickey's merits. In fact, Dick Young, the *News*'s most prominent and virulent baseball writer, turned on Rickey with a vengeance worthy of Macbeth. To Young,

Rickey was first of all a skinflint and a hypocrite. "But a great baseball man, Dick," I said, after we had become contentious acquaintances. "Surely you'll give the old boy that."

"Maybe it's something in me," Young said, "but I just can't seem to appreciate a pompous tightwad son of a bitch who is always quoting the Psalms . . . even if he does know the game."

RICKEY CLAIMS THAT 15 CLUBS VOTED TO BAR NEGROES FROM THE MAJORS

Declares He Used Robinson Despite Action Taken at Meeting in 1945—Officials Deny Dodger Head's Charges

Despite this headline, which appeared in the *New York Times* of February 18, 1948, this remarkable story—Baseball Bigotry's Last Stand—has lain fallow for many years. No written records of the meeting survive, although I know from various sources that a high-level baseball meeting occurred at the Blackstone Hotel in Chicago on August 29, 1946. But no one present at the meeting seemed to recall the overwhelming anti-Negro vote. The source, the only source, on baseball bigotry's last stand was Branch Rickey himself. In our discussions of the anti-Negro vote—and we had several—Rickey always insisted that I keep his words off the record for all the rest of his life. "It ill becomes one," he said, "publicly to turn and curse the leaders of a game that has nurtured him for almost all his days."

William Wilberforce was an early-19th-century English abolitionist and a convert to the Methodist religion. He led the parliamentary campaign against Britain's lucrative slave trade, which persisted until 1807. Previously, British ships legally transported captured black Africans to lives of slavery in America's racist South. The practice of slavery was profitable for more than one country. Both the town of Wilberforce, Ohio, and Wilberforce University, which is located there, were named in his honor. The African Methodist Episcopal Church founded Wilberforce University in 1856 and today it stands as one of the three oldest private predominantly black colleges in the country.

The devoutly Methodist Rickey accepted an invitation to speak to his coreligionists at the Wilberforce annual football banquet on February 17, 1948. His audience was small, no more than 250 people. As far as I can learn, the only reporter there was someone from the Associated Press. He took careful notes and filed a story that would shake the rulers of baseball to their ganglia.

The AP man—anonymous to this day—quoted Rickey at length from a speech he called "candid and impassioned."

"After I had signed Robinson, but before he had played a game," Rickey began, "a joint major league meeting adopted unanimously a secret report prepared by a joint committee [representing both the National and American Leagues] which stated that however well intentioned, the use of Negro players would hazard all the physical properties of baseball.

"You can't find a copy of that report anywhere, but I was at the meeting where it was adopted.

"I sat silent while the other 15 clubs approved it.

"I've tried to get a copy of the report, but league officials tell me all were destroyed.

"But let them deny they adopted such a report, if they dare.

"I'd like to see the color of the man's eyes who would deny it."

According to the AP reporter, Rickey grew increasingly impassioned at the Wilberforce banquet. "I believe," Rickey said, "that racial extractions and color hues and forms of worship become secondary to what a man can do.

"The American public is not as concerned with a ballplayer's pigmentation as it is with the power of his swing, the dexterity of his slide, the gracefulness of his fielding or the speed of his legs.

"Who thinks of the inconsequential when great matters of common challenge and national interest confront us? It is not strange that Robinson should be given a chance in America to feed and clothe and shelter his wife and child and mother in a job he can do better than most.

"It is not strange that a drop of water seeks the ocean."

Rickey expected his comments to attract praise. Instead his eloquence drew a firestorm of rage from his old deputy, Larry MacPhail, and barefaced contempt from his once and future enemy, the populist New York *Daily News*. Two days after the Wilberforce speech, the *News* published a prominent headline:

RICKEY 'LYING'; M'PHAIL REFUTES NEGRO CHARGE

In a written statement MacPhail said no secret report existed. A report was indeed filed. MacPhail himself retained a copy. It recommended certain "changes in the structure of the major leagues." "Other copies," MacPhail maintained, "were collected because they contained a criticism of the commissioner [Chandler], written by me, which the commission felt was unfair and unproductive.

"If and when Branch Rickey said that my committee recommended that Negroes be banned from major-league baseball, Branch Rickey was lying."

The usually voluble MacPhail would take no questions. He would let no one see his copy of the disputed report. After that Rickey never again spoke to MacPhail.

Is it plausible to believe that Rickey, in an orgy of self-praise, fantasized the anti-Negro meeting? It certainly does not appear that way here. Rather it seems likely that MacPhail, in a fit of passion, went on a rant against his old boss for accomplishing something in Brooklyn that MacPhail, for all his innovations and promotions, schemes and dreams, had failed to realize. I don't think Larry was innately a bigot.

But, particularly when drinking, he was one of the notorious hotheads of his time. "Part genius," said Leo Durocher, "and part madman." On the issue of integrating baseball, and indeed America, starting in Brooklyn, in an Ebbets Field that MacPhail had repainted and restored, it seems the madman in MacPhail knocked the genius in MacPhail clear over Canarsie and out of sight, somewhere above the waters of the stormy North Atlantic.

That was not the editorial opinion at the *News*. The sports columnist there, the ambitious Jimmy Powers, had this to say. "Branch Rickey gets up at Wilberforce U and showers rose petals on himself. . . . We are wondering just what purpose this blast at other baseball executives serves at this time. As an admirer of Negro Jackie Robinson we realize that some owners were, for good and sufficient reasons of their own, against the breaking down of the color line. We also happen to know that many of these people are now in favor of Robinson and accept him as a gentleman of culture and irreproachable conduct. Others are still opposed to the whole setup, as is their privilege. Why stir up these prejudices today just to pose as a superior human being?

"It is significant that all of Rickey's moves save him money. He is paying Robinson only $5,000 a year, not even a hundred dollars a week. We will be the first to toss our hat into the air and pelt rare Brazilian orchids at El Cheapo when we see that a single one of his magnanimous acts COSTS him money out of pocket."

Dick Young followed up with sarcasm. "No longer do baseball personalities squirm on the spot if their own backfired remarks claim that they've been 'misquoted,'" Young wrote. "But rather that they've been 'misinterpreted.' That was the position taken yesterday as the Dodger prexy attempted to square himself with his fellow owners. . . . "

Some years later I asked Rickey specifically how he had reacted to the Powers piece. "Neither my wife, Jane, nor I was accustomed to being subjected to such vitriol," he said. "To put it succinctly, we were stunned."

"Did you realize that this column was in a sense a declaration of war?"

"Not at the time," Rickey said. "With hindsight, however, I accept your characterization."

As for Powers, he appeared conveniently to be forgetting the lines he wrote in the *News* when Rickey broke the color line. With absolute certitude, Powers declared: "Jackie Robinson will not make the grade in the big leagues this year or next. He is a 1,000-1 shot." It is not superfluous to point out that good journalism begins with reporting and Powers had never seen Robinson play.

The meeting officially was organized to contend with issues other than integration. The lords of baseball felt threatened by a new independent Mexican League, which was signing big leaguers in defiance of the American reserve clause. A second matter was the rising demand voiced by outstanding major leaguers, including Allie Reynolds and Ralph Kiner, for recognition of a players' union.

A Latin entrepreneur named Jorge Pasqual had organized the so-called "outlaw" Mexican League, backed by $50 million, and he was staffing it in part with well-known big leaguers. Among these were Mickey Owen, the former Dodger catcher; Max Lanier, an accomplished Cardinal left-hander; and (almost) Stan Musial, to whom Pasqual offered a bonus of $50,000 in cold cash. Musial, then earning $11,500 annually from the Cardinals, told me, "He laid out the money in big bills right on the double bed in a hotel suite. He said sign and then I could put all that money in my pocket. Not later. Right then. I thought long and hard. I finally decided that I just didn't want to move my family to Mexico."

At the Chicago meeting the Establishment owners elected to impose a lifetime ban on any ballplayer who signed a contract with Jorge Pasqual. This feudal decision led to lawsuits and in time to both cash settlements and reinstatements. The most notable star coming back from a Mexican fiesta was the rugged right-hander Sal "the Barber" Maglie, later famous for fastballs clipping whiskers from Dodger batters' chins.

Within a decade the Mexican League ceased to be a problem. Blowing through $50 million, it went bankrupt. Some 30 years would pass before the players' union became strong enough to overturn the reserve clause. But at the Blackstone Hotel that August, Rickey's integration was here and now.

"I remember," Rickey told me, "that Larry MacPhail was very angry. He had just bought the Yankees and he claimed that Pasqual had hired one of your colleagues on the *Herald Tribune* to recruit Yankee ballplayers for the Mexican League. Recruit them right there in the Yankee Stadium clubhouse. He was insisting that the *Tribune* fire the reporter, a man named Rud Rennie, who always seemed to me a decent sort. [Rennie denied the charge and Wilbur Forrest, the executive editor of the *Tribune,* hotly refused MacPhail's demand.]

"Ford Frick presided at the meeting. Where was Happy Chandler, our new commissioner? I'm not really sure. Frick passed out a report on integration prepared under the direction of MacPhail and Phil Wrigley, the chewing gum manufacturer who owned the Cubs. As I said, MacPhail was angry. He stood up and glared at me. Robinson was then playing for Montreal. Did I realize, MacPhail said, that when Montreal played in Baltimore and Newark more than half the fans in attendance were Negroes? And did I further realize that all those Negroes were going to drive away our white fans?

"He was raging. I made no answer. We read a report that essentially said the time was not right for bringing Negroes into the major leagues. I hoped someone would challenge the report. No one did. Then Frick asked all of us to return our copies to him. After that was done the MacPhail–Wrigley report against Negroes simply vanished from the face of the earth.

"I cannot tell you how dismayed I was. These were my colleagues and, I had thought, my friends. I had only the good sense to hold my tongue. Then over the next few days I sent letters to the baseball people I considered most important, calling their attention to the Ives-Quinn law.

"Discrimination had always been wrong.

"Now, I pointed out, it was also illegal."

Rickey believed that the strongest human emotion was sympathy. "The word derives from the classical Greek *sumpatheia,* which suggests mutual understanding which blossoms into affection," he said. "I believed that when my ballplayers saw what Jackie Robinson was going through, sympathy would make them reach out to him. Eventually most of them did, but it took more time than I had anticipated.

"Ballplayers love money. They love World Series checks. I thought when they saw how good the colored boy was, when they realized that he could get them into the World Series, they'd pretty much force me to promote him from Montreal and make him a Dodger. After that, one problem—Robinson's acceptance by his fellows—would solve itself."

During spring training 1947, Rickey arranged for the Dodgers and the Montreal Royals to play a seven-game series, touring the Canal Zone. Robinson, still on the minor-league roster, rose majestically. In the seven games, he stole seven bases. He batted .625. When he won one game for Montreal with a squeeze bunt, Hugh Casey, the Dodgers' best relief pitcher, picked up the baseball, cursed and threw the ball over the grandstands.

In considering the Holocaust, Jean-Paul Sartre defined bigotry as a passion and passion is, of course, irrational. You cannot talk someone away from avarice; you can't reason a person away from lust; you could not argue Nazis out of their murderous anti-Semitism. The core of veteran Dodger players was not roused by Jackie Robinson's success. They felt no sympathy, none at all, for a brave, solitary black man. Instead, the veteran core felt passionate outrage. Bigoted ballplayers would hate Robinson if he batted 1.000, which he damn near did. "How dare a colored fella be that good?"

In Panama the Dodgers were billeted briefly in an Army barracks at Fort Gulick on Gatun Lake. There, one night in March, Clyde Sukeforth, working as a bench coach, told Leo Durocher that some veteran players had drawn up a petition that said simply, brazenly: "We the undersigned will not play on the same team as Jackie Robinson." Dixie Walker, a literate and intelligent man and a native of Georgia, had done the phrasing. (In 1976 Walker, then 66, told me, "Starting that petition was the dumbest thing I did in all my life.")

But back in 1947 the petition began to catch on. Bobby Bragan, a backup catcher but a clubhouse leader, signed. So did Hugh Casey. Both men were Southerners. Carl Furillo signed. He grew up in Pennsylvania. Next came Cookie Lavagetto, a native of the San Francisco Bay Area. But a youthful Gil Hodges flatly refused. Pete Reiser, the gifted center fielder, said that when one of his children was gravely ill, the only person who would help out was a Negro doctor. "So I got nothing against the colored people, nothing at all." Now the petitioners turned to Pee Wee Reese, from whom they expected strong support. Reese was raised amid segregation in Louisville, Kentucky.

"It was a terrible moment," Reese told me years afterward when we had become close friends. "I knew what these fellers were doing was wrong, just plain wrong, but they were my buddies." In a quiet, nonevangelical way, Reese was a practicing Christian. "As a Christian," Reese said, "how could I deny another human being the right to inherit a small portion of the earth? That was what was in my heart. Jackie Robinson had that right." But at the time Reese was not comfortable speaking so intensely to his teammates. "It could have sounded too churchy or too uppity." Instead he told them, "This thing might rebound, fellers. If we sign, we all might get the boot. I can't take that chance. I just got out of the Navy. I got no money and I have a wife and baby to support. So, fellers, just skip me." The petition lost momentum but did not die.

"Who told you about this fucking petition?" Durocher asked Sukeforth.

"Kirby Higbe, after he had some beers."

"Must be another Kirby Higbe," Durocher said. "Our guy comes from South Carolina. They don't care for colored people down there."

"It is our Hig," Sukeforth said. "He told me when his pitching was going badly, the Dodger organization took a chance on his arm and let him restart his career. Hig says he owes the Dodgers. He's afraid the petition will tear the team apart."

"This is big, Sukey," Durocher said. "Let me sleep on it a while."

But Durocher could not fall asleep on his army cot in the faraway Panama Canal Zone. At one o'clock in the morning Durocher decided that there was no reason why he should sleep. No reason at all. *Get the hell up!*

Durocher roused his coaches and told them to bring all the players into a big empty kitchen behind an army mess. The team assembled in night clothing and underwear. "Boys," Durocher began in a loud bray that rattled spinal disks. "I hear some of you don't want to play with Robinson. Some of you have drawn up a petition."

The players sat on chopping blocks and leaned against cold stoves. Durocher, possessed of a phenomenal, if selective, memory, told me he could recall his exact words.

"Well, boys, you know what you can use that petition for?

"Yeah, you know.

"You're not that fucking dumb.

"Take the petition and, you know, wipe your ass.

"I'm the manager and paid to win and I'd play an elephant if he could win for me and this fellow Robinson is no elephant. You can't throw him out on the bases and you can't get him out at the plate. This fellow is a great player. He's gonna win pennants. He's gonna put money in your pockets and mine.

"And here's something else. He's only the first, boys, only the first.

There's many more colored ballplayers coming right behind him and they're hungry, boys. They're scratching and diving.

"Unless you wake up, these colored ballplayers are gonna run you right out of the park.

"I don't want to see your petition. I don't want to hear anything about it.

"The meeting is over. Go back to bed."

Did any manager ever have a finer moment?

Early the next day Durocher placed a phone call to Rickey, who was briefly back in his Brooklyn office. "I was appalled by what I heard but I entirely endorsed Durocher's statements, if not his vocabulary," Rickey told me. "I believe, I have always believed, that a little show of force at the right time is necessary when there is a deliberate violation of the law and the law here was the fair employment act. I knew that a reasonable show of force was now the best way to control this thing. When a man is involved in an overt act of violence or a destruction of someone else's rights, then that is no time to conduct an experiment in education or persuasion."

After the Panama tour, Rickey summoned a number of players into his office, one by one. "I talked to them singly," he told me. "I wanted to rob them of safety in numbers. I read each of them the riot act. Bobby Bragan argued with me hardest. I reminded him that we had other catchers and that he was not indispensable. An intelligent man, but he remained obdurate. I thought that his bigotry might be changed by proximity to Robinson, as given time it was. I did not then cut him from the squad.

"Hugh Casey, our best relief pitcher, was indispensable but curiously insecure for a great competitor. When I told him he might end up relieving in the minor leagues, he simply wilted. I told Cookie Lavagetto, a popular veteran, that frankly I was ashamed of him. Lavagetto hung his head."

"What did you tell Furillo?" I asked.

"Nothing. I did not bother to speak to him at all. I regarded Furillo as a man in whom talk could arise no moral dilemma because he had no basic moral compass of his own. I would almost have wagered that later Furillo would argue as rabidly in Robinson's behalf as he was arguing against Robinson in those days."

During the early 1950s, when I started covering the Dodgers on a daily basis, Furillo warmed up before each game by playing catch with a teammate of his choice, the great receiver from the Negro Leagues, Roy Campanella. And of course he had a moral compass. "I was fucking wrong five years ago," he told me. "That's why right now I play catch with Campy every day."

Whether Bobby Bragan actually did change remains questionable. In 1983, when I bought the Class A Utica Blue Sox, Bragan, then president of the Texas League, telephoned to wish me well. "Most people lose money in the minors," he said, "but you don't have to worry about that." Then, referring to my partially Jewish heritage, he went on, "Your kind always makes money!"

Bragan remained a Dodger into the season of 1948. Neither Rickey's persuasive power nor playing alongside Jackie Robinson weaned this smart and essentially likeable man away from his entrenched stereotyping of others.

Utica won the 1983 pennant in the New York–Penn League. Keeping the team in business for a single season cost me $17,000. Despite being whatever "kind" I may be, that was a net loss. The local utility, a voracious company called Niagara Mohawk Power, refused to supply electricity for the ballpark lights until I had written a personal check for $7,500 as a deposit. Clubhouse lights? That would be an upfront $1,000 more. "We ought to socialize you bastards," I said genially to a bloodless clerk, who did not answer.

In retrospect destroying the racist petition was an unalloyed triumph for that decidedly odd couple, Branch Rickey, the eloquent teetotaler, and Leo Durocher, baseball's Loud Lip. But as Scott Fitzgerald famously reminded Ring Lardner, life is larger than a diamond. Off the field Durocher, a long-term Rickey reclamation project, was running with a dangerous crowd, on Broadway and in Hollywood. The hallmarks of Leo's bicoastal friends were a passion for gambling and rampant lust, both of which would have a significant impact on Durocher's managerial career and Rickey's noble experiment. Here are some leading characters in *Le Gang Durocher*:

George Raft, movie tough guy, and offscreen friend of the notorious gangster Owney Madden. Raft was a heavy baseball bettor and a card shark. He sometimes organized crooked dice games. He always brought the dice. Married at the age of 22 in a Roman Catholic ceremony, Raft never was able to obtain a divorce from Grace Mulrooney. Offscreen the movie tough could be warm and attentive and he was a ballroom dancer almost in a class with Fred Astaire. Estranged from Grace for more than 45 years, Raft plunged into affairs with Betty Grable, Marlene Dietrich, Mae West and Norma Shearer. "I just don't like to sleep alone," he said. During the 1940s, Raft let Durocher share his Hollywood mansion in the winter months and join his crap games and frolics along with his friends, his women and his fellow desperados.

Max "Memphis" Engleberg, a big-time bookmaker, who set the odds and point spreads that his colleagues used to run their gambling businesses. As detectives later established, the point spreads Engleberg created were a key to prodigious betting on the college basketball doubleheaders that regularly sold out Madison Square Garden. For at least 10 years, games involving City College, St. John's, NYU, Kentucky and Bradley Tech, among others, routinely were fixed. Hard-eyed gamblers ordered the fixes. Fresh-faced college athletes carried them out.

Conrad "Connie" Immerman. During Havana's swinging pre-Castro days he ran the casino at the elegant Hotel Nacional. Gambling was legal then, prostitution flourished and on almost every corner in Havana you found all-night shops selling coffee and condoms.

"Bugsy" Siegel, born Benjamin Siegelbaum, gently played by Warren Beatty in a popular 1991 movie but in reality a savage hoodlum. Following a mob dispute Siegel was shot to death in June 1947.

Joe Adonis, born Giuseppe Antonio Doto, a Mafia thug. Adonis was deported to his native Italy in 1956. During an interrogation by Italian police he suffered a fatal heart attack.

The list of additional hoods ran very long. "Of course Leo ran with a rat pack," someone has said. "Only this one had real rats."

As commissioner, Landis kept files on Durocher, but he was most active in 1943 considering the now forgotten case of a lumber millionaire named William D. Cox, principal owner of the Phillies, who stood accused of betting on ballgames. He bet *on* the Phillies, not against them, but any baseball gambling by an owner violated the game's prime directive: *Do not bet!* Landis found the charges valid and ruled sternly on Cox: "You are hereby declared ineligible to hold any office or employment with the Philadelphia National League Club, or any club or league party to the Major-Minor Agreement." (This was decidedly more draconian than commissioner Allan "Bud" Selig's 2011 action deposing Fastbuck Frank McCourt as CEO of the Dodgers. The charge against Frankie Fastbuck was not gambling, but overall fiscal irresponsibility, spelled greed, which contributed to his mismanagement of what had been a gorgeous ballpark at the center of what was once a golden franchise. Unlike McCourt, Cox, a Yale graduate, went quietly. After no more than token resistance, he broadcast a farewell on a popular New York radio station, WOR. Cox concluded, "Good luck and goodbye to everyone in baseball.")

Durocher, who sprang from a pool-hall boyhood in Springfield, Massachusetts, became a gambling man in the rousing world beyond the old neighborhood pool halls. He loved cards, dice and betting at the racetrack. He publicly praised Memphis Engleberg as "the best horse race handicapper I've ever met." As we've seen, Landis's office was created in the wake of the Black Sox scandal, and the judge was hypersensitive on issues of gambling, legal or otherwise. He maintained that he would allow no one with racetrack connections to buy a major-league team. "My constant battle," he said, "is to keep baseball clean and away from the gamblers."

But Landis did make exceptions. Rogers Hornsby, perhaps the greatest right-handed hitter in the annals, was never far from a copy of the *Daily Racing Form.* Landis looked away. He regarded Durocher as a talented, truant schoolboy who could well be reformed. Landis summoned Durocher to his Chicago office more than once and cautioned him, but in a fatherly way. According to Durocher, Landis said, "Son, I don't want you hurting yourself by running with the wrong crowd and getting into trouble."

Durocher was bald-headed, brash and loud, and his vocabulary often exploded with obscenity. But Leo the Lip also could exude cloud banks of charm. Living with George Raft opened his way to the boudoirs of movie actresses, and Durocher energetically put his charm to work.

Someone has described Laraine Day as a B-plus movie star. She was better than those cute anonymous female leads in B movie westerns, but she was never on a par with such major performers as Joan Crawford or Bette Davis. Day starred in the Hitchcock thriller *Foreign Correspondent* and played Cary Grant's love interest in *Mr. Lucky,* but her signature role was as prim, pretty nurse Mary Lamont, whom she played in seven Dr. Kildare films.

She was born La Raine Johnson into a prosperous, devoutly Mormon family. Her great-grandfather, three of his six wives and a few dozen of his 52 children were early California settlers in the town of San Bernardino. (The family history of indiscriminate polygamy never broke into Laraine's MGM press releases.)

She was an established actress in 1942 when she married one Ray Hendricks, a former Air Force flight instructor who became manager of the Montebello Airport, eight miles east of downtown Los Angeles.

In a few years of marriage, Laraine claimed, Hendricks evolved from a social drinker into a confirmed alcoholic. This rendered him virtually impotent just as Laraine was blossoming.

On a slow train through Texas during spring training 1954, Durocher recounted an ensuing event. He and Laraine began to hold secret meetings after the 1946 season, while Durocher also struck up a seeming friendship with Laraine's husband, Ray. One night the three began to watch one of Laraine's movies in the screening room of the large home she had purchased in the West Hollywood hills. Hendricks soon drank himself to sleep. Leo and Laraine embraced and proceeded to have at it full blast on a piano bench. Suddenly the reel of film snapped in the projector and began flapping loudly. The noise woke Hendricks. He turned on the lights. On the piano bench Laraine and Leo were heaving in each other's arms.

Durocher recovered first and pulled up his pants. "I had to be ready," he told me. "The guy might have charged." Laraine stood up and began to speak in breathless tones. "I love Leo," she said. "He loves me. We want to be married."

At the subsequent divorce trial Hendricks testified, "The rapidity and shock of these events completely humiliated and overwhelmed me. In my opinion Leo Durocher is not a fit person for Laraine to associate with. She's only a young girl, 26 years old. Durocher is more than twice her age. [Actually Leo was 41.] He is guilty of dishonorable and ungentlemanly conduct. He clandestinely pursued the love of my wife under my very roof, while pretending to be a family friend." The Los Angeles *Herald Examiner* summed up that day in court with a catchy headline: "Durocher Branded Love Thief."

A California judge named George A. Dockweiler granted Laraine the divorce she wanted on January 20, 1947, with the stipulation that she could not marry again in California for a full year. A day later in Ciudad Juarez, Mexico, Laraine and Leo married. Some said the residency requirement for marriage in Juarez was three minutes.

Furious, Dockweiler ordered Laraine to show cause why her divorce should not be set aside. Durocher, never shy, telephoned Dockweiler to ask if Laraine could return to California without being hauled into court. She could, the judge ruled, as long as she and Leo did not live together. Laraine said through tears, "Doesn't the judge care about my happiness?" Then she moved into her mother's home in Santa Monica. Leo then leased a suite in the Miramar Hotel, which was located in, of all places, Santa Monica.

As Durocher had pounced on Laraine, *Life* magazine pounced on the story. The publication ran a lively text and photo essay under the headline: THE CASE OF LEO AND LARAINE; BASEBALL'S LOUDMOUTH AND HOLLYWOOD'S NICE GIRL MAY BE PUT OUT AT HOME.

Life, primarily a picture magazine, ran strong shots of Durocher arguing with umpires. Another section, called "Leo and the Ladies," featured three photographs of Durocher. In one he was sunning himself with a leggy Copacabana chorus girl named Edna Ryan. In another he was hugging the blonde movie star Betty Hutton. In the third he was being kissed by the dark-haired beauty Linda Darnell. That week a downtown Brooklyn movie theater showing *Mr. Lucky* posted an arresting message on its marquee: *Starring Cary Grant and Mrs. Leo Durocher.*

Branch Rickey, the epitome of monogamy, told the newspapermen that he would have no comment.

Baseball people had behaved scandalously before. Babe Ruth often asked his teammate Joe Dugan to go through his fan mail. "Keep the stuff with checks and from broads," Ruth would say in his customary bellow. "Dump the rest." Joe DiMaggio was well known as a serial seducer of chorus girls. But in the days of Ruth and later DiMaggio, journalists did not write such stuff. What was unique about the Follies Durocher was not the sex but the press coverage of the sex. It never stopped.

A popular promotion throughout the major leagues brought

thousands of youngsters into the ballpark without charge on slow weekday afternoons. The idea was to build a future fan base. The Dodger version was a heavily promoted venture called the Knothole Gang, from distant days when children watched ballgames free through the knotholes of wooden outfield fences. The leading participant in the Dodger Knothole Gang was the Brooklyn Catholic Youth Organization, 50,000 boys strong and directed by a zealous priest named Vincent J. Powell.

Powell gained an audience with Rickey and said that Durocher was a bad example for Catholic youth and indeed for youngsters of all faiths.

"Doesn't your church," Rickey said, "still dispense mercy and forgiveness?"

Whoops. Wrong response. Powell had not traveled to the Dodger offices to discuss comparative religion with a Methodist. In those days the Catholic Church in New York City had so much general influence that it was colloquially known as the Powerhouse. Father Powell was about to turn on the power, which came with a mighty surge. If the Dodgers did not replace Durocher as manager, Powell said, he would have no choice but to withdraw the CYO from the Dodger Knothole Gang. He then suggested that an overall Catholic boycott of Dodger games could be in the works. More than 750,000 Roman Catholics lived in the borough of Brooklyn.

All this was happening within two months of Rickey's planned promotion of Jackie Robinson to the Dodgers. Rickey had long since decided that Durocher, who was completely devoid of racial prejudice, would be the ideal manager for modern baseball's first integrated team. Under pressure in his office, he made a quick choice between the integrator and the priest. But controlling himself, Rickey quietly told Powell that he took the priest's remarks seriously and would discuss them as soon as possible with the team's board of directors. Shortly after Powell departed, Rickey summoned the club lawyer,

Walter O'Malley, an Irish Catholic who had major connections within the Brooklyn diocese.

Two versions describe what followed. William Shea, the real estate lawyer for whom the Mets' former stadium was named, told me over dinner at Gage and Tollner, a gaslit restaurant on Fulton Street in Brooklyn, that the problem came down to this: "Walter O'Malley was one lousy lawyer."

"How can that be, Bill?" I said. "O'Malley has made more money out of baseball than anyone in history."

"That's right," Shea said, "but he was one lousy lawyer. O'Malley was the most brilliant businessman I've ever met, but we're talking law here, aren't we?

"Of course he lost when he tried to plead Durocher's case with that priest. He wasn't trying to embarrass Rickey. He just lost.

"I wouldn't have let O'Malley plead a parking ticket for me."

By far the best of recent Dodger books is Bob McGee's affectionate biography of Ebbets Field, *The Greatest Ballpark Ever.* McGee writes, "It was inconceivable that Walter O'Malley's influence within the Church could not defuse the [Durocher] situation. But the fact was O'Malley didn't much care for Rickey or Durocher and enjoyed their difficulty." McGee then cites a voluble Dodger executive named Harold Parrott. "One word from O'Malley and the anti-Leo priests would have piped down.

"But the Big Oom never gave the word.

"Rickey had reason to wonder who had put the churchmen up to this. The Catholics never boycotted Hitler or Mussolini the way they went after Leo Durocher."

I am a little regretful that in all of my conversations with Walter O'Malley, stretching across 35 years, I never asked him about Durocher and the Roman Catholic Church. As I say, a little regretful, but no more than that. Walter was an outstanding fabulist. Had I asked, there is no reason to think he would have responded with the truth.

The continuing Catholic threats so alarmed Rickey that he dispatched his personal assistant, Arthur Mann, to the offices of the new commissioner, Happy Chandler, in Cincinnati. Mann was to "air out" the Durocher situation. Chandler insisted that he was already on top of the matter because had been reading Judge Landis's Durocher file. "There are certain people," Chandler said, "that Leo simply has to stop seeing." He named Raft and Bugsy Siegel and Joe Adonis. Mann was surprised Chandler had so much information, but he agreed and said he spoke for Rickey, whose opposition to gambling was resolute.

A few weeks later Chandler ordered Durocher to meet him at the Claremont Country Club in Oakland, California. Leo later said, "Happy had always been a good friend. I used to see him with fast company at the Stork Club in New York. Always gave me a big hello and that hamfat drawl. 'Ah loves baseball!'" At the Claremont, Chandler bought lunch and then produced a sheet of paper with a list of now familiar names. Durocher was surprised. He had thought, he told me, Chandler wanted to talk about the Laraine Day affair. But as always Durocher responded quickly to an unexpected situation.

Bugsy Siegel? "I was introduced to him once in a barber shop."

Joe Adonis? "Never even met him, but he would say hello to me at the ballpark. I would nod. I told Chandler, Okay, I'll stop nodding."

Memphis Engleberg? "Sure, he was a friend. Whenever we went to the racetrack, he'd mark my card. But I sure as hell can't tell you whether he ever bet on baseball. I know I never did."

Connie Immerman? "If the casino he runs in Havana is controlled by criminals, hell, that's news to me. I thought it was controlled by Cubans."

George Raft? "We've hung around together, but if you tell me I can't stay at his house anymore, and I gotta turn down his invitations, well, you're the commissioner. I'll feel like a louse, but I'll do it."

The claims of innocence sound a touch belligerent. Durocher was endlessly a belligerent character. But the Durocher gambling issue of the mid-1940s ran deeper than questionable associations. Bill Veeck, the brilliant and inventive executive who variously owned the Cleveland Indians, the St. Louis Browns and the Chicago White Sox, always had a fondness for gangsters. He explained this to me one day: "When my daddy was on his death bed he said all he wanted on earth was a final glass of Napoleon brandy. This was during Prohibition time. You couldn't just go out and buy the stuff. So I went down to Al Capone's headquarters at the old Lexington Hotel and explained the situation. Capone knew about my daddy. My daddy was president of the Cubs. Al said, sure kid, and gave me a bottle of the best Napoleon brandy in his stock. That made my daddy's final wish come true. Ever since I've been a little soft on hoodlums."

When Veeck took over the Cleveland Indians in 1946, the *Plain Dealer* was calling a swaggering local named Alex "Shondor" Birns "the city's No. 1 racketeer." Birns supposedly ran Cleveland's numbers game and was also operating a restaurant, the Alhambra Lounge on Euclid Avenue, "that was considered the in place to go. Famous persons [including Bill Veeck] were frequent customers.

"The secret charges against Leo Durocher," Veeck told me, "were that he dumped the 1946 pennant race to the St. Louis Cardinals. At least that's what Shondor Birns told me. He said he and some other gamblers paid off Leo to mishandle the Dodger pitching rotation. Shondor said that's what Leo did. Shondor said he personally made a killing."

Mob reports of a Durocher fix also reached the offices of Ford Frick, president of the National League. Frick asked New York district attorney Frank Hogan to investigate. Nothing materialized.

The 1946 pennant race ended in a tie with both the Dodgers and the Cardinals finishing at 96 victories and 58 losses. Frick then ordered a best-of-three playoff series, the first in the long history of the National League.

For the opening game at Sportsman's Park, St. Louis, Eddie Dyer, the Cardinals manager, went with his 20-game-winning ace, the slim, elegant left-hander Howie Pollet. Durocher responded with a young right-hander, who in time would become famous as the worst pitcher in all the history of post-season playoffs, Ralph Branca. Only 20 years old back then, Branca spent much of the season with the Dodgers' St. Paul farm team. Brooklyn's big winner had been the hard-drinking, hard-throwing veteran, Kirby Higbe.

The Cards scored once in the first and two innings later knocked out Branca. Then, with the game slipping away, Durocher called on Higbe. Too late. Pollet stayed in command and the Cardinals won, 4 to 2.

Back at Ebbets Field, Durocher started a durable left-hander, Joe Hatten, in Game 2. The Cards knocked him out in the fifth inning and went and won handily, 8 to 4. (The Cards then defeated the Boston Red Sox in the World Series, four games to three.)

By themselves box scores will not always reveal crooked play. Shoeless Joe Jackson admitted that he was paid $5,000 to help lose the 1919 World Series when he was playing for the Chicago White Sox. Dumping that Series, Jackson batted .375. So you cannot say for certain that Durocher's unusual decision to start a rookie in the playoffs is proof of any criminal intent.

While working on my book *The Era* in 1990, I had several conversations with Durocher. In one I brought up the 1946 rumors. He gave me a very hard look. "Outrageous," he said. "Fucking outrageous. You writers either say I tried to win too hard or that I didn't try to win at all. Double fucking outrageous, and you can print that anywhere you want."

Earlier, in 1973, I had no more success in developing a dialogue with Frick, who retired as baseball commissioner in 1965. We were seated side by side at a winter baseball banquet and I said, "Ford, what can you tell me about the Durocher gambling rumors of 1946?"

"Have you ever seen the Ardsley Curling Club? " Frick said.

"I've been trying to get a line on that pennant race."

"Curling is truly an underappreciated sport," Frick said. "If you come by the club I'll give you some pointers."

"About Durocher . . ."

"It is critical to use your curling broom vigorously."

This remains one of the more interesting no-comments of my experience.

What about word from Bill Veeck's underworld acquaintance, Shondor Birns? I was late getting to him. According to the Cleveland *Plain Dealer* of March 29, 1975:

> Alex (Shondor) Birns, Cleveland numbers racketeer, was blown to bits at 8 last night, seconds after he entered his car parked behind a West Side bar.
>
> Police, who made the identification, said Birns was hurled through the roof of a 1975 light blue Lincoln Continental Mark IV. The upper torso was found beside the opened front passenger door. . . .
>
> Police speculated that the car's ignition may have been wired to several sticks of dynamite. . . .

On April 9, 1947, four days before opening day, Happy Chandler suspended Durocher for one year. He cited "conduct detrimental to baseball." He would have no further comment on the matter then or ever.

Few, if any, anticipated the ruling. By a stroke of a novice commissioner's pen, Branch Rickey had lost his reckless, fiery manager and, on the very brink of the integration of major-league baseball, Jackie Robinson had lost the man who would have been his champion.

When Chandler's contract as commissioner expired in 1951, it was not renewed.

EIGHT

THE POWER OF THE PROSE

DAVE ANDERSON, THE VETERAN SPORTS COLUMNIST for the *New York Times* who won a Pulitzer Prize in 1981, has called Dick Young the best newspaper baseball writer of his experience. Anderson, who has a well-deserved reputation for fair-mindedness, covered the Dodgers during the team's final five years in Brooklyn. Rickey was gone by then, exiled to Pittsburgh, where his masterly touch was not yet clearly evident. (A season later, 1958, the Pirates finished second and the Dodgers, disoriented in their new Los Angeles surroundings, finished seventh.)

Why didn't Rickey remain in Brooklyn, where his signing of Jackie Robinson and his creation of the team I called the Boys of Summer became a triumph, glorious to behold? There had never before been such sociological drama and baseball success anywhere from Canarsie to Brooklyn Heights. Surely one huge factor in the exile was the maneuvering of Walter O'Malley, whom Rickey called "the most devious man that I have ever met." O'Malley's lust for power and money was extraordinary. But another consideration was Rickey's own avarice. It left him vulnerable to O'Malley's ambushes. But finally a major additional element was the relentlessly anti-Rickey prose, much of it written by

Young, published in the lurid popular tabloid, the New York *Daily News*. "New York's Picture Newspaper," as the tabloid billed itself, was selling two million copies a day and twice that many on Sunday. If you wondered about Errol Flynn's rapaciousness, Franklin Roosevelt's perfidy or the multitudinous flaws in the character of Branch Rickey, the *News* was an indispensable source. At one point the paper's right-wing politics got so extreme that President Roosevelt interrupted a press conference to present John O'Donnell, a crypto-Nazi *Daily News* columnist, with Hitler's highest military honor, an Iron Cross.

I agree with Anderson on Young's remarkable reporting skill, but other considerations temper my evaluation of this short, loud baseball writer. Young's ego grew without restraint until, as happens with some journalists, the ego interfered with telling a straight story. Beyond that he was—as Walter O'Malley and Buzzie Bavasi repeatedly demonstrated—readily subject to corruption. Then there was Young's vulgarity. Not even Leo Durocher was quite so militantly obscene.

As I wrote earlier, I had a close but contentious acquaintanceship with Young, formed during my years of covering the Dodgers for the *New York Herald Tribune*. We sat side by side in press boxes for hundreds of summer days and afterward, in bars, on planes, on trains. I heard him out on his money problems, his extramarital affairs and his simplistic view of life. "You got to remember this," he said after three or four bourbons, "there are only two kinds of people in the world. The good guysh and the bad guysh." Sometimes, for no apparent reason, he turned on me. Once when I joined him for breakfast at a hotel coffee shop, he stared up through a hangover and said, "If I fucking looked like you do in the morning, I'd fucking kill myself." I moved to another table.

When Young discovered that the fine Dodger pitcher Clem Labine designed men's sportswear during the winter months, he decided that Labine must be gay. Young disapproved of gays and he began in print to question the manliness and courage of Labine, who was a former paratrooper. At length Labine marched through the clubhouse stripped to the waist and presented himself to the Dodger trainer, a soft-spoken osteopath named Harold Wendler. "Doc," Labine said. "I want you to tape my right arm behind my back."

"Why?"

"Just do it, Doc." When Wendler finished, Labine sought out Young. "Some of the stuff you've been writing about me," Labine said, "is so out of line, the only way we can settle this is with our fists. But I'm bigger than you. I want the fight to be fair. That's why my right arm is taped behind my back.

"Are you ready, Dick?

"Let's go."

Young fled.

After I left the *Tribune* and began writing books and magazine articles, I encountered Young from time to time. He usually said something like "You had enough sense to get out of the fucking newspaper business. If I were younger, I would, too." I never truly caught Young at full foul blast for many years. That came about in April 1972, as *The Boys of Summer* rose to the top of bestseller lists from Brooklyn to San Francisco. The NYU Varsity Club honored me with a banquet and an award—a modest pewter platter—and asked Young to introduce me from the dais at the NYU Club, then located a few blocks from Times Square. A fine crowd arrived, including Dean John Knoedler, who had taught a lively Shakespeare course with a stress on Shakespeare's sexual humor, and Sid Tanenbaum, an All-American basketball guard whose smooth, sure-handed performances influenced and inspired many lesser players, including me. Kudos and smiles. The great Tanenbaum shook my hand. The dean asked if I remembered why the character Enobarbus died in *Anthony and Cleopatra*. "He took thought and died," I said, echoing one of Knoedler's finest lectures. "Full credit," the dean said. "Let me buy you a drink." Then Young was called on for the formal introduction. He had been drinking bourbon whiskey at great speed.

"Lotta you maybe think I never went to college," Young began. "Well, fuck that. I took a writing course at NYU. Teacher was damn pretty. I couldn't write much back then but I fucked the teacher. She gimme an A. Couldn't a' been for my writing. That was lousy. So I figure she gimme an A in fucking."

You could feel discomfort in the room. Young was oblivious. "Now I gotta introduce this fucking guy," he said. "Only covered the Dodgers for around three, four years and he writes a book and it's a fucking bestseller. Go fucking figure. Here he is."

When I got my hands on the microphone I looked at Young and said, "Why did you agree to introduce me if you didn't want to introduce me?" After that evening we seldom spoke. (Young died in 1987.)

It may seem curious that such an ineffable boor could write, but Young wrote very good, hard-edged tabloid stuff. When he wanted to point out that the Dodger pitching staff, specifically Ralph Branca, was choking under pressure, he began a story, "The tree that grows in Brooklyn is an apple tree and the apples are in the throats of the Dodgers." When the columnist Jimmy Breslin started a feud—the subject was Mets' pitcher Tom Seaver—Young lashed back, repeatedly referring to Breslin as "Fatty the Writer." Seaver moved on to Cincinnati, Breslin retired from the field.

Joseph Medill Patterson founded the *Daily News* in 1919, and it is generally regarded as America's first tabloid newspaper. The *News* was easier to read than a full-sized newspaper while one traveled New York's crowded subways, and this surely contributed to the paper's success. But so did its extensive and groundbreaking use of pictures, its intense coverage of celebrity scandal and, almost from the start, a much livelier sports section than you could find in, say, the *New York Times*. Paul Gallico, the hard-driving sports editor of the *News* during the 1920s, scored heavily with what is now called participatory journalism. Gallico sparred with Jack Dempsey in 1923, when Dempsey was training for his dramatic bout with Luis Ángel Firpo. At six foot three and 192 pounds, Gallico was bigger than Dempsey. No matter. Dempsey knocked him out in 1 minute and 37 seconds. Gallico wrote that after the fall he heard the referee counting, "Thirty-eight, thirty-nine, forty." Gallico followed up by swinging at Herb Pennock's curveballs, golfing against Bobby Jones and racing laps against the swimming champion Johnny Weissmuller, famous for playing a bare-chested Tarzan in a series of movies. Gallico himself became a national celebrity. Then, in 1936, after covering the Berlin Olympics, he quit newspaper work with a memorable essay called "Mine Eyes Have Seen the Glory."

"That was a marvelous era that is past," Gallico wrote.

> And yet in all those long days of endless excitement, I found myself usually too busy reporting to do much evaluating. Why did we love Dempsey? What makes us go to ballgames to the number of ten million spectators a year? Why do we stand for dirty football? What makes women athletes such wretched sports? Why are Negroes athletic? What makes Gene Tunney tick?
>
> Sportswriting has been an old and good friend and companion to me. One does not, it seems, barge ruthlessly out of such a friendship. Rather one lingers a little over the good-by, sometimes even a little reluctant to leave, and uncertain, turning back as some old, well-loved incident is remembered, calling up again the picture of vanished friends, having one's last say, lingering as long as one dares before that final, irrevocable shutting of the door.

He then began writing books and finished no fewer than 41, many quite popular.

"I'm a rotten novelist," Paul Gallico said near the end of his days. "I just like to tell stories. If I had lived 2,000 years ago I'd be going around to caves, and I'd say, 'Can I come in? I'm hungry. I'd like some supper. In exchange, I'll tell you a story.

"'Once upon a time there were two apes. . . .'"

Joseph Patterson had served under Douglas MacArthur during World War I, attaining the rank of captain. That was how he liked to be addressed in the years that followed. But neither Captain Patterson, nor anyone else, could find another tabloid sports editor with all the gifts of Gallico. Instead he promoted a loud, hustling Midwesterner named James Powers, who immediately began writing a daily column called, reasonably enough, the Powerhouse. A decade before Rickey took over the Dodgers, battle lines were being drawn for a small, savage war that in time drove Rickey to fury. As Buzzie Bavasi has said, Rickey was the greatest baseball scout who ever lived. But he had no idea, not a suggestion of a clue, of how to contend with an aggressive and belligerent tabloid press. Many things, including his innate contempt for tabloids, stood in the way. (Curiously, or perhaps not so curiously, Bavasi himself better understood the media. In fact, handling the tabloid press, specifically Dick Young, was his forte.)

I have seen, but have not been permitted either to photocopy or keep, old Dodger financial records, circa 1930, that show weekly payments of as much as $150 from the team to the sportswriters who were covering the ball club. In many instances this exceeded the salary the writers were drawing from their newspapers. This money went not to the journalistic stars: Gallico, Ring Lardner, Heywood Broun, all of whom, I believe, would have turned down such payments. Rather it was paid to the so-called "beat" reporters, the men who wrote game stories about the Dodgers more than 150 times a year. Today youthful journalists sometime ask why old-line sportswriters did not punch out tougher stuff. Why didn't they swarm into clubhouses and write controversial inside stories, covering such matter as the feuds and jealousies that often arose? The answer seems clear. The newspapermen were taking Dodger money not to embarrass or criticize the home team, but to root for it. They came to praise Caesar, not to bury him. The practice of under-the-table payoffs to sportswriters was widespread throughout the major leagues. The term for the supposedly quiet money was "ice."

In addition, when I began covering the team, the Dodgers paid travel expenses, meal money, hotel rooms and first-class Pullman berths for reporters from six of the nine metropolitan New York dailies that assigned writers to the team. (The three newspapers that paid their own way were the *Herald Tribune,* the *Times* and the *Daily News.*) The Dodgers maintained a comfortable and free press restaurant and bar tucked near the roof of Ebbets Field behind home plate. As standard policy the Dodgers invited the sportswriters' wives and children to be their guests in Florida during the six or seven weeks of spring training. No one talked about corrupting the press. Instead the idea was to create a sense that the Dodgers—the players and the management—and the sportswriters were all part of one happy extended family. Only rarely did disharmony appear. Mike Gavin, a portly character from Hearst's *Journal-American,* liked to sip Napoleon brandy after dinner. He ordered a pony from the Dodgers' spring-training barkeep, a genial character named Babe Hamberger, then took a Havana cigar, also provided by the Dodgers, and before lighting it dipped the cigar tip into the brandy. "Brings out the flavor of the tobacco," Gavin said. Then he tossed out the first pony of brandy and ordered a second one to drink. Buzzie Bavasi watched the practice with increasing annoyance. One night he said to me angrily, "Do you think Gavin does that at home?"

Not until 1978 was I able to modify what I perceived as an incestuous culture between ball clubs and the working press. Writing a series of sports columns for the *New York Times,* I mentioned in one the free dining room and saloon that the Yankees maintained for sportswriters amid the catacombs underneath the old stadium. Arthur Gelb, a tall, solemn character who was managing editor, knew a great deal about the life and dramas of Eugene O'Neill, but when it came to sports Gelb was a naïf. He said to me that surely *Times* sportswriters did not accept free food and drink from the team that they were being paid to cover. I said they surely did. Two things resulted. First, the *Times* henceforth insisted on paying for meals and drinks served to its reporters at the stadium and other ballparks. Second, the *Times*'s lead baseball writer stopped speaking to me.

Despite its pervasive right-wing politics, the *Daily News* took a few populist positions, one of which placed it squarely against the equally pervasive right-wing ways of the baseball Establishment. As far back as February 1933, with Gallico still in charge of the sports section, Jimmy Powers wrote an article headlined: "Colored B. B. Players—O. K."

This was a full 14 years before Jackie Robinson's debut at Ebbets Field. Main-lining a resolute stance in favor of integrating the major leagues is the only instance known to mankind where the right-wing *Daily News* and the Communist *Daily Worker* stood shoulder to shoulder and side by side.

Powers's piece was carefully reasoned. Golf and tennis, he wrote, were country club sports. Bigotry at the clubs came as naturally as snobbishness. But two sports, boxing and baseball, were "born out of the lower class." Joe Gans, who was black, won the lightweight championship early in the 20th century. The defiant and ultimately tragic Negro Jack "L'il Arthur" Johnson was heavyweight champion from 1908 to 1915. Powers mentioned a baseball gathering in 1932 called to honor John J. McGraw, the iconic longtime manager of the New York Giants, whose years were winding down. Powers brought up integration at the function, and the audience of baseball people, which included Branch Rickey, "displayed a refreshing open-mindedness." Everyone except John McGraw. The aging sage, a native of an all-white central New York village called Truxton, said in a growling tone that Negroes should be content to play in their own leagues.

"But," Powers wrote, "I believe it is only a question of time before the colored player is admitted into the big leagues. I base this upon the fact that the ballplayer of today is more intelligent—and liberal—than yesterday's leather-necked, tobacco-chewing sharpshooter from the crossroads. White college men who have hung up their football cleats or track spikes in the same locker rooms with their colored teammates are not suddenly going to assume the old bias when they enter the runways of the Stadium or Polo Grounds."

◆ ◆ ◆ ◆ ◆

AT THE URGING OF George V. McLaughlin, president of the Brooklyn Trust Company, the bank that had held an $800,000 mortgage on Ebbets Field, the Dodgers trustees signed Rickey as club president and general manager in October 1942. Stepping away from baseball to join the struggle against Hitler, the previous president, Larry MacPhail, had enlisted in the Army and drawn the rank of colonel. Under MacPhail the Dodgers had just finished a remarkable but frustrating season. Peopled with such stars as Dolph Camilli, Billy Herman and Dixie Walker, the Dodgers won 104 games, an all-time record for the borough of Kings. But Rickey's Cardinals, with strong pitching from Mort Cooper and Johnny Beazley and solid performances by Terry Moore, Stan Musial and Enos Slaughter, won 106 and won the pennant. They then defeated the Yankees in the World Series, four games to one. After victories in eight earlier World Series, this was the first time the Yankees had lost one since 1926.

MacPhail was a big winner, a big drinker and a big spender. New York State bank examiners were pressing George McLaughlin on the unproductive Ebbets Field mortgage. In urging Dodger trustees to hire Rickey, McLaughlin, a banker but also a hard-core Brooklyn ball fan, knew he would be getting a great baseball man who, all reports indicated, was as far from being a big spender as anyone in all the front offices in all the cities in the game.

The Dodgers needed Rickey. The Brooklyn Trust Company needed Rickey. The Brooklyn citizenry wanted Rickey. Well aware of such needs and wants, Rickey negotiated for himself one fabulous contract. The term was five years. The base salary was $90,000, with various bonus arrangements including 15 percent of the proceeds of all player sales to other big-league clubs. He could and did gross over $100,000 a year. (The average annual income for US workers in 1942 was $1,290.)

The magnitude of Rickey's compensation glitters like gold when matched against the salaries of the stars on his first Brooklyn championship team. Jackie Robinson came up in 1947 and signed for $5,000. Ralph Branca, briefly a pitching ace, was paid $7,000. Center fielder Carl Furillo drew $7,500. Shortstop Pee Wee Reese earned $12,500. While Rickey was banking his $90,000 plus, the collective salary for the entire Dodgers' starting nine in 1947—the team that would win the National League pennant—came to $87,500. All by himself, Rickey outearned his entire ball club.

Jimmy Powers's *Daily News* comments were not kind. "When El Cheapo [his new term for Rickey] moved into the gold mine franchise of Brooklyn, a heavily populated boro that is almost the size of Chicago, his payroll was and is disgracefully low."

Powers presently spoke at a baseball banquet and surprised his listeners by announcing, "I've just found out that Skinflint Rickey dislikes money."

The audience murmured and waited for elaboration.

"The skinflint," Powers said, "dislikes money in the pockets of other people."

What a distraction. Under Rickey, Jackie Robinson was integrating baseball and the country. Under Rickey, the greatest of all Brooklyn teams was coming together with Hall of Fame players at shortstop, second base, home plate and in center field. The Boys of Summer had arrived! Yet the most popular paper in New York blew no triumphal trumpets. Blind to both panoramic happenings, the *News* kept its focus tightly on the ledger, even as a dismal bank clerk in a drab setting drawn by Dickens.

I am aware that ballplayers at the time had their struggles. When I was working with Robinson on the magazine *Our Sports,* he told me of a special problem he faced as a $5,000 Dodger rookie: where to live. It was difficult for a middle-class black couple with a baby to find what they considered suitable housing within their means. At the start the Robinsons had to settle for a hotel room in the McAlpin, situated in a commercial district on Thirty-Fourth Street in Manhattan. "It was particularly rough on Rachel," Jackie said. "In that one room she had to deal with diapers and formula and bathe the baby. Whenever we got a breather there always seemed to be some newspaperman knocking on the door." Though Robinson was becoming a national figure, he spent much of the 1947 season living with his family in a single room. Playing major-league baseball back then generally provided a decent living, but rarely wealth.

The *News*'s sharp but superficial baseball coverage reminded me of its notorious reporting of a Hollywood trial in 1942, when the swashbuckling actor Errol Flynn was accused of rape for having had consensual sex with a pretty 17-year-old named Peggy Satterlee. The trial was appropriately lurid for the tabloid's passions, particularly when prosecutors asked Satterlee to recount specifics. She testified that while she was in a bedroom on Flynn's yacht, he took off all her clothes.

"So you were naked?"

"Yes."

"Then what happened?"

"Mr. Flynn took off his clothes."

"All of them?"

"He was in a hurry. He didn't take off his shoes."

A generation of *News* readers soon was speaking variations on the comic line "Errol Flynn does it with his shoes on."

Amusing at the time, but the *News* missed a more important, underlying story. Later investigators discovered that people in the office of the Los Angeles district attorney were accepting payoffs from the big studios to look the other way when stars were caught bedding underage women, driving while drunk and committing other such breaches. After a while the district attorney and his aides demanded a heavy increase in their payoffs. The studio heads refused and as a response the DA elected to go after Errol Flynn. In time a jury, wowed by Flynn's earthy, masculine glamour, returned a verdict of not guilty.

The *News* never asked *why* Flynn was being prosecuted for casual sex in a Hollywood community where casual sex was the norm. Similarly the *News* didn't ask *why* Rickey was keeping baseball salaries in Brooklyn so low. When I brought up that question with Rickey one afternoon in his private box at Forbes Field, he told me an intriguing story.

"I recognized that Brooklyn was a great baseball town, but the Dodger franchise seldom achieved its potential," he began. It was a warm day, but he wore a jacket and tie. Except when he was teaching on a diamond, I don't recall seeing Rickey moving about in shirtsleeves. "History is a great instructor and the Dodger history was heavy with disappointment. There had been some fine individual ballplayers in Brooklyn. Nap Rucker was as good as any left-hander in his time. Zack Wheat was a first-class hitter. Then there was Babe Herman and Dazzy Vance. Are you familiar with those names?"

"My father started following the Dodgers before 1910," I said.

"Then those I mentioned were probably gods in your household," Rickey said. "But baseball is a team game and Dodger teams were too often mediocre. They won pennants in 1916, 1920 and more recently in 1941, but winning three pennants in a half a century is no great accomplishment. It forks no lightning. Worse yet, the Dodger pennant winners were patchwork teams. They were built with good trades or intelligent purchases, but they were not the stuff of dynasty. Under John McGraw the New York Giants were consistent winners. So were the Yankees after they acquired Babe Ruth. Although in a sense

Brooklyn is a world unto itself, it should also be regarded as part of the greater New York area. And in the area, home to three major-league teams, the Dodgers were team number three.

"As I said, they'd had some splendid players. The team had hired able managers, among them Wilbert Robinson and Casey Stengel. What then was the problem? I am a great believer in what I call addition by subtraction. Take away players and managers as problems and what does that leave? The executive branch, what sportswriters call the front office."

Rickey had done his homework. For many years two families shared control of the Dodgers. The first prominent owner, Charles Ebbets, was an architect who designed Ebbets Field. (He is also said to have been the inventor of the rain check.) When Ebbets needed money to pay construction costs, he sold 50 percent of the team to Ed and Steve McKeever, brothers and partners in a contracting business. The ballpark, considered a wonder when it opened in 1913, occupied an outsized city block, bounded by Bedford Avenue, Montgomery Street, Sullivan Place and McKeever Place. It originally seated about 18,000 people. (Yankee Stadium, opening in the next decade, seated 58,000.)

A heart attack killed Charles Ebbets at the age of 65 in April 1925. He was interred on a cold, wet day in Brooklyn's imposing Green-Wood Cemetery. Standing at the gravesite during services, Ed McKeever caught a cold, which turned into pneumonia. He died that May. Steve McKeever then assumed the presidency, but subsequently the Ebbets and McKeever families fell to squabbling and litigating. As a result, for many years the Dodgers were essentially leaderless. One glaring consequence came clear in 1937.

The Dodgers were paying a grizzled ex-spitball pitcher with the English manor house name of Burleigh Grimes to manage. (Grimes, a surly sort, once punched a Brooklyn child who had the audacity to ask him for an autograph after a loss.) The Dodgers were also paying off

Casey Stengel, who had been fired as manager at the end of the 1936 season. Stengel's Dodgers had finished seventh. On top of that they were still paying off Max Carey, born Maximilian Carnarius, a star center fielder in his day and a man who led the National League in stolen bases 10 times. Carey had been fired as Dodger manager after the season of 1933. Carey's Dodgers had finished sixth. Thus the 1937 Dodgers simultaneously were paying a Brooklyn troika, one man to manage the team and two men not to manage the team. The 1937 Dodgers finished seventh. It is a wonder that they finished at all. During this period, the Dodgers' years in the wilderness, Eddie Murphy of the New York *Sun* wrote an amusing comment one spring. "Overconfidence may cost the Dodgers fifth place."

Late in the booming decade of the 1920s Steve McKeever decided to enlarge Ebbets Field by extending the upper deck all the way down the right-field foul line and above the border of right from the center-field side. He could not completely enclose the playing area because Bedford Avenue, which ran beyond the right-field wall, was a major Brooklyn thoroughfare, four lanes of heavily traveled cobblestone. Neither the city fathers nor borough sachems were inclined to build an underpass, in retrospect a significant error in urban planning. The right-field wall, topped by a stiff screen, interrupted by a scoreboard, stood as long as the Dodgers played in Brooklyn. Caroms shot off that wall in difficult and unpredictable ways. Dixie Walker and later Carl Furillo played those caroms brilliantly, and the wall became a wonder of the game. When Duke Snider saw film of a wrecker's iron ball smashing the right-field wall to rubble, he reacted in an understandable way. The Duke of Flatbush wept.

The remodeled Ebbets Field would seat 28,000. Steve McKeever's expansion plans required money and here is where George V. McLaughlin and the Brooklyn Trust Company entered the world of baseball. The bank lent the Dodgers $800,000, with Ebbets Field posted as security.

Very soon the loan ran smack into the Great Depression. The Dodgers of 1930 had a good but not outstanding team in an exceptional baseball season. Hack Wilson, who stood five foot six but had an 18-inch neck, walloped 58 home runs for the Chicago Cubs. Bill Terry, a truculent character who played first base for the Giants, batted .401. This prompted Ogden Nash later to write in *Sport* magazine:

> *T is for Terry*
> *The Giant from Memphis*
> *Whose .400 average*
> *You can't overemphis.*

The Dodgers, who had in Dazzy Vance arguably the best pitcher in the National League, finished fourth. Hack Wilson's Cubs finished third. Bill Terry's Giants came in second. The pennant winner? None but Branch Rickey's St. Louis Cardinals, who went on to win an exciting World Series over Detroit, despite the hard hitting of the Tigers' G-men, Charley Gehringer and Hank Greenberg.

The general baseball excitement of that season fueled an attendance record in Brooklyn, 1,097,329, or better than 15,000 paying customers for each home date. But as the team slumped and the Depression struck, the seventh-place Dodgers of 1934 drew only 434,188, a disastrous drop to about 6,000 fans per home date. That season the Dodgers regularly played to 22,000 empty seats, most of which were in hock to a bank.

I well remember my father taking me to games in '34. I was six years old but already in love with baseball. Games started at 3:15 and even when we got to Ebbets Field as late as 3:00, a good assortment of seats remained vacant in the grandstands, near first base and third. Good news for my dad and myself, but a financial horror story for the Mac boys, Keever and Laughlin.

The team's poor play and, more than that, the new huge debt frightened Steve McKeever, now in his 80s, and alarmed the various heirs of Charlie Ebbets. McLaughlin was a haughty character, but he had a good feel for baseball. He knew something had to be done, beyond firing a manager every few seasons.

Backed by the promissory notes, McLaughlin asked the trustees to let him hire a new chief executive. "With all respect," he told McKeever, "you're not a youngster anymore." The creditor's request had the force of a loaded pistol.

McLaughlin talked to Ford Frick, the president of the National League. Frick said he was enjoying his current job. McLaughlin telephoned Branch Rickey in St. Louis. If Rickey's messianic mission to integrate baseball was stirring, he kept it concealed. You could not reasonably start the integration of baseball in St. Louis, the most overtly racist city in the major leagues. But Rickey said he was content with the Cardinals. He recommended that McLaughlin contact Larry MacPhail, who was doing interesting things in Cincinnati, including, on May 24, 1935, staging the first night game in major-league history. (The Reds defeated the Phillies, 2 to 1.)

The modern Dodgers can fairly be said to date from January 18, 1938, when Larry MacPhail met with George McLaughlin and laid down his terms for taking over management of the team. He said the old leadership would have to step aside. He and he alone would run the Dodgers. McLaughlin agreed. MacPhail needed continuing support from the bank. Ebbets Field had fallen into disrepair. Some seats were broken. All needed paint. Cement was crumbling in the dugouts. All told, he had to have $200,000 for ballpark improvements. He got it. He had to bring in more baseball talent quickly and that would cost more money. McLaughlin lent him $50,000 to buy the premier first baseman, Dolph Camilli, from the Phillies. A day later Steve McKeever died at the age of 83, supposedly of pneumonia. But the author Bob McGee suggests that what really happened was this: When Old Man McKeever found out that the Dodgers were paying $50,000 for the contract of just one player, he died of shock.

In June of 1938, MacPhail hired Babe Ruth as first-base coach for a salary of $15,000. At the age of 43, the big man still had power and crowds came to see him drive batting practice fastballs over the screen in right. Brooklyn fans were excited at the prospect of Ruth managing the Dodgers a year later. So was Ruth. When the job went instead to Leo Durocher, Babe Ruth burst into tears. (MacPhail felt Ruth lacked the essential inside baseball shrewdness he felt that managers should have.)

Later MacPhail cobbled together a $75,000 package to buy Pee Wee Reese from the Boston Red Sox farm team in Louisville. The manager of the Red Sox, aging shortstop Joe Cronin, was happy to see Reese go to another league. And in 1941, putting together a pennant-winning ball club, MacPhail gave $65,000 to the Chicago Cubs for the great second baseman William Jennings Bryan Herman, who answered to Billy.

As the bank had big bucks, MacPhail had a fine eye. He brought in two seeming journeymen from the American League. Dixie Walker became a National League batting champion. Whitlow Wyatt won 22 games for the Dodgers in 1941. That season Brooklyn won its first pennant in 21 seasons. In 1937, the year before MacPhail arrived, the Dodgers drew 482,481 fans, or about 6,200 for each date at Ebbets Field. In 1941 the Dodgers drew 1,214,910 fans, the highest total in baseball. The team was now averaging more than 15,000 customers for each home date. You could no longer find empty seats close to first base or third near game time at Ebbets Field. When I went now with my father he bought reserved seat tickets in advance. They were priced at $1.65.

MacPhail brought night baseball and Red Barber to Brooklyn. He experimented with baseballs colored yellow, like today's tennis balls, and, courting the Brooklyn Irish, he ordered new uniforms of Kelly green. Neither idea worked out but MacPhail was always experimenting, always hustling, and as we learned in Brooklyn, always restless. Some say he was the first to hold a Ladies Day. On some such occasions the women were presented with silk stockings in addition to admission for 10 cents. (Many ladies to be sure brought dates, who had to pay full price, ranging up to $2.20 for a box seat.) "The shrill cries of the female rooters," wrote Frank Graham in the New York *Sun,* "pierced the ears of passers-by blocks away."

Hokum, grumbled the old-line conservatives who had followed the drab Dodgers of Steve McKeever. But MacPhail and his team so roused the borough that after the Dodgers clinched the 1941 pennant, the *Brooklyn Eagle* reported that a million fans watched the victory parade along Flatbush Avenue. That would be every second resident of the borough, including shut-ins, newborns and hospital patients. The *Eagle* was a rooting paper and its number seems absurdly high, but photographic evidence shows that many Brooklynites on the parade route held signs that read: "Pee Wee Reese for President."

The year 1942 was a mixed bag. As I've noted, the Dodgers won 104 games, but the team lost its best player on July 1, when Harold "Pete" Reiser ran headfirst into the center-field wall in St. Louis and fractured his skull. He was chasing an Enos Slaughter drive. Reiser was never again the same luminous star; Leo Durocher told me that without that injury Pistol Pete "would have been every bit as good as Willie Mays." At the very least the point is open for debate.

Given another close pennant race, the fans kept coming to Ebbets Field. For the second straight year, the team drew over a million fans and led the major leagues in attendance. The Yankees, with more than twice as many seats in their stadium, won another pennant, but failed to reach a million and would not until the postwar boom. Small ballpark or no, the Dodgers were the hottest and most profitable franchise in baseball. That Brooklyn was a great baseball town is, quite simply, a matter of public record.

McLaughlin the fan was delighted to have a winning team in Brooklyn, but McLaughlin the banker was not satisfied with the ledger. It is axiomatic in baseball that the concessions people will generally cheat a little, under-reporting sales of beer and even Cracker Jack. They then quietly pocket some of the proceeds. But McLaughlin detected a great diversion of the cash flow. He brought in a tough collection lawyer, who had offices in the Lincoln Building near Grand Central Terminal, to look into profit and loss. That was how Walter Francis O'Malley came into baseball, sniffing down dollar bills and dimes.

Each day's proceeds have to go promptly into a bank. Leaving them at the ballpark is an open invitation to larceny, thieves at midnight quietly ransacking the empty offices until they strike gold. The Dodgers transferred their receipts from Ebbets Field to the Brooklyn Trust Company downtown, a 20-minute van ride, in large gray duffel bags that were unsealed. Who was stealing and how much was stolen never has been precisely defined, but a Dodger official named Jack Collins, who had been drawing a salary of $7,500, abruptly retired during O'Malley's investigation. He then bought himself a large motel situated on a prime Florida beach with, I suppose, some of my father's hot dog money.

"It was so bad," O'Malley said, "that I couldn't rectify everything as an outsider. I told McLaughlin that I needed to get inside and become a trustee." O'Malley was a sure hand with money. He was a season boxholder in Brooklyn, but his interest in baseball seemed no more than casual. McLaughlin lent him $250,000, with which the lawyer bought a 25 percent interest in the Dodgers. The duffel bag pilfering soon stopped. A bit later so did Brooklyn Dodger baseball.

Before McLaughlin died, in 1967, he had stopped speaking to O'Malley. But the banker certainly experienced what sportswriters would call a "torrid" streak. In a stretch of five years he gave audience to three of the most commanding executives in baseball history,

MacPhail, Rickey and O'Malley. All today have plaques in their honor nailed to a wall at the Baseball Hall of Fame.

Apparently it was patriotism alone that moved Larry MacPhail to resign as Dodger president, a week before the end of the 1942 season. Suddenly the hottest franchise in baseball faced problems. MacPhail may or may not have paid off the long-standing mortgage. He insisted that he had, but the banker, George McLaughlin, remained a power in the Dodger offices, partly because the heirs of Charlie Ebbets had appointed him trustee for their 50 percent share of Dodger stock.

◆ ◆ ◆ ◆ ◆

BACK IN PITTSBURGH YEARS afterward, Rickey was describing his first meeting with McLaughlin. "Did Larry MacPhail tell you that he paid off the Dodger debt?"

"He said so on the farm he had in Maryland," I said.

"That is not my recollection," Rickey said. "MacPhail always was better at spending new money than repaying old obligations. His creditors grew whiskers whilst they waited.

"At any rate I had determined that McLaughlin was critical to the success of my Brooklyn venture and a part of that, surely not all, was proceeding with integration. I believed that the Negro in America was legally but not morally free. I had begun to think that if the right individual, one who possessed great athletic gifts *and* great self-control, could be located, we could make a difference that should be celebrated."

He paused. The Pittsburgh players, who were underperforming before us at Forbes Field, are mostly forgotten now. Gair Allie at shortstop. Curt Roberts at second. Toby Atwell catching. No Cooperstown plaques for these people. These Pirates of 1954 would finish last, 44 games out of first place.

"I remember that it was a bitter cold January day," Rickey said. "I can still envision the gray and somewhat forbidding bank building. It was located at the corner of Montague and Clinton streets, not two blocks from my office at 215 Montague, and constructed of gray stone in a style modeled after buildings of the Italian Renaissance.

"McLaughlin knew baseball as a fan, which is by no means a criticism. He was the financier and a leader of the Brooklyn Roman Catholic Establishment. I was a Midwestern Methodist, a grown-up farm boy, from out of town. But I was learning about the remarkable borough called Brooklyn and I tell you with no false modesty that I knew the game of baseball.

"I told the banker that for all the Dodgers' recent success under MacPhail, the team was in a precarious position. The stars MacPhail acquired were not young men. Dolph Camilli, Billy Herman and Whitlow Wyatt were moving toward the downward side of their careers. My ideal team, as I may have told you, consists of youth at the eight positions, youth with speed that is a factor offensively and defensively. But I retain a preference for older pitchers. They know the craft and are possessed of poise. 'Have I ever put together an ideal team?' you may ask. The answer is 'Not up to this time.'

"But the Cardinals of '42 came reasonably close. We had outstanding position players in Slaughter, Musial, Marion and Walker Cooper. We had experienced pitchers like Mort Cooper and Max Lanier. Not only did that team win 106 games, they simply blew away the mighty Yankees in a five-game World Series. Simply blew 'em away." To emphasize his point Rickey blew a thundercloud of cigar smoke into the already polluted Pittsburgh summer air.

"All well and good for St. Louis and myself, but now I was in Brooklyn. I told George McLaughlin that I would have to work very hard with a reasonable budget or else when peace returned the Cardinals would dominate the National League for many years."

"I am going to have to expand the Dodger farm system," Rickey told McLaughlin. "I want to hire the best scouts in the country."

McLaughlin absorbed Rickey's brilliant analysis with some surprise. Jeopardy? Not really, although Rickey would be spending a lot of the bank's money. The Brooklyn team had just won 104 games. But as the banker considered them with some thought, Rickey's points made sense. "But one thing I'm going to urge," he said after a pause, "is economy. MacPhail was terrible at thrift. That's why we are still having to carry Dodger debt on our books. We want you to win. We also want the ball club to be solvent. That's why I brought in a tough lawyer, Walter O'Malley, to keep an eye on spending."

"I'm glad you brought in this fellow O'Malley," Rickey said, probably for the only time in his long lifetime.

During the seven years in which the *Daily News* attacked Rickey as a tightwad, no one at the tabloid appeared to know or care that he was operating under directions from a bank.

He dropped his real bombshell almost casually. "In order to be ready for the end of the war, we are going to have to beat the bushes, and that might include a Negro player or two."

According to papers filed by one of Rickey's aides at the Library of Congress, McLaughlin's eyebrows shot up. The Brooklyn Irish Catholic Establishment was just emerging from a decade in which one of its hallmarks was raw bigotry, specifically street-corner anti-Semitism. Everywhere people quoted the high priest of prejudice, Father Charles Coughlin, who insisted that all rich Jews were dangerous international bankers and that all poor Jews were dangerous Communists. But by this point, to paraphrase Bob Dylan from another period, the times were a-changing. (Walter O'Malley's special affection for me hardly characterized the behavior of an anti-Semite.)

McLaughlin was a businessman, not an ideologue. More blacks were moving into Brooklyn. They could swell attendance figures at Ebbets Field. The borough was heavily New Deal Democrat. This was not Atlanta or Birmingham. Rickey's revolutionary plan could work and open a large new market. Finally McLaughlin spoke. "If you are doing this to improve the ball club," he said, "go ahead. But if you're doing it for the emancipation of the Negro, then forget it."

Rickey could not remember his response. The proper, but probably dangerous answer would have been "Both." Instead he pressed forward. Could McLaughlin quickly arrange a meeting for him with the board of directors? He would like their approval on his overall approach and particularly for his idea of bringing in a Negro.

A week later the directors and possibly Walter O'Malley met for lunch in a spectacularly inappropriate setting on Central Park South, the fervidly racist New York Athletic Club. The New York AC categorically barred Jews from membership. Admitting a Negro was unthinkable. I brushed up against the club on several early assignments from the *Herald Tribune,* where a press card temporarily trumped bigotry. At one point I asked a club official, John F. X. Condon, what the club policy was on Jews and blacks. "We don't accept either Jews or black as members," he said in a genial tone, "any more than we would accept dogs."

According to papers in the Library of Congress, the luncheon gathering with Rickey included McLaughlin and his banking associate, George Barnewell; Joseph Gilleaudeau, representing the interests of the Ebbets family; and James Mulvey, a forceful executive at MGM, representing the McKeevers. (Eight years later McKeever's daughter Ann would marry Ralph Branca.) No record exists of an O'Malley presence, although he later claimed that he was there. It became important to him in later years to maintain that he was prominent in the decision to integrate, which he was, but it is reasonable to doubt that he was present at the creation. I almost always could catch Buzzie Bavasi's misstatements. Walter was a more difficult case. Whenever I pressed him harder than he wanted to be pressed, he turned jovial and announced, "You have to remember that only half the lies the Irish tell are true." Although he personally disliked Jackie Robinson—"an inveterate seeker of personal publicity," O'Malley once called him—he was proud that the Dodgers had integrated the game and deeply envious of the credit that eventually fell like manna onto the shoulders of Branch Rickey.

That summer day in Pittsburgh, 1954, Rickey told me that he was aware of wintry chill between Gilleaudeau and Mulvey. The Ebbets and McKeever families never reconciled. "I wanted to avoid a situation at that luncheon where if one man said yes, the other would automatically say no," Rickey said. "Barnewell was most helpful in steering away from that. 'We,' Barnewell said, referring to all of the various people in Dodger management, 'probably haven't tapped the Negro market enough.' I followed up along those lines being very careful not to sound either too zealous or too ideological. Courting the Negro market would simply be good business. After a while and without any real debate everyone agreed that I could go ahead with my grand plan."

"Were you aware that the New York Athletic Club barred Jews and Negroes from its ranks?"

"Not at that time. But over the next few years, I gave myself an intense course in racism and bigotry in America. I would not attend a meeting at the New York Athletic Club today."

Now Rickey began to resemble the legendary horseman who rode off in all four directions at once. He read Gunnar Myrdal, a Swedish socialist who wrote on the discrepancy between America's stated ideals and its actual treatment of blacks. He learned that in the first draft of the Declaration of Independence Thomas Jefferson had written, "all men are created free and equal." Benjamin Franklin crossed out the word "free." Rickey thought that was ironic. Jefferson was a slaveholder. Franklin was not.

Rickey wanted the process of baseball integration to proceed without violence, and he began studying the passive resistance methods of Mohandas Gandhi. More than once he cited one of Gandhi's observations:

> *"I object to violence because when it appears to do good, the good is only temporary; the evil it does is permanent."*

Overhearing that, Tom Meany, a very sharp baseball writer for the remarkable and forgotten newspaper *PM,* nicknamed Rickey himself "the Mahatma." Except in the *Daily News,* that wonderfully apt nickname stuck.

Now the directors were on board, but what was to be done about Negro players during spring training in the South? Where would they eat; where would they live? Despite its winter influx of tourists from the north, derisively known as snowbirds, Florida was as racist as Alabama, particularly small-town Florida, where so many exhibition games were played. How should he prepare the other Dodgers for playing alongside a Negro? He might have to do some evangelical preaching in the clubhouse. The gifted Dodger sportscaster Walter Lanier "Red" Barber was a proud Southerner, raised among fierce racist traditions. Faced with black Dodgers, would Barber quit? Other teams were eager to bid for his services, which, as I've mentioned, included such homespun Southern phrases as "tearin' up the ol' pea patch." That meant that the Dodgers were rallying.

How would the rival owners react not to a theory but to a reality, a black man wearing a Brooklyn Dodger uniform? What about the press? Aside from Lester Rodney, the Communist columnist, only a few, Dan Parker in the New York *Daily Mirror,* Shirley Povich in the *Washington Post,* had announced themselves as pro-integration. "I was busy with the day-to-day details of running the Brooklyn club," Rickey said, "but my mind was constantly racing ahead, trying to envision the future." To the *Daily News* and Jimmy Powers's Powerhouse, however, the future was now. And now was sordid.

Although I never seriously considered Rickey's suggestion that I go to work for him in Pittsburgh, when he wanted someone urgently his sales pitch would put the gabbiest used car salesmen to shame. His persuasive power and his great baseball gifts brought a wide variety of talented people into the once atrophied Dodger organization. These included his son Branch Jr., nicknamed Twig, a baseball-wise hard-drinking diabetic; Allan Roth, the founding father of modern baseball statistics; E. J. "Buzzie" Bavasi, smart and charming and as devious as a counterspy; and Arthur Mann, a former newspaper reporter who gained renown by playing the role of Branch Sr. in skits staged by the New York baseball writers at their annual dinner in the Hotel Waldorf Astoria. Mann looked a bit like Rickey, sounded a lot like Rickey and was Rickey's choice to collaborate on Rickey's memoir. (A heart attack killed Mann at the age of 65, before the memoir was even begun.)

Mann monitored the *News* and specifically studied the Powerhouse on a daily basis. He counted a total of 154 columns that blasted Rickey with varying degrees of severity. Powers wrote that Rickey secretly disliked Brooklyn and was trying to quit and take over the Yankees. He wrote repeatedly that "El Cheapo Rickey pays his players coolie salaries." He demanded that the Dodger stockholders fire Rickey. He then asked readers to vote upon two choices: "Shall we send Rickey over Niagara Falls in a barrel? Shall we maroon him on a Bikini atoll?"

The *News* ran these angry pieces even as Rickey was assembling the greatest baseball team in Brooklyn history. Among the white stars-to-be that he signed were Gil Hodges, Carl Erskine, Clem Labine and Duke Snider. The black stars, Robinson, Campanella and Newcombe, followed close behind.

Within just a few years, Rickey had established ownership or working agreements with no fewer than 27 minor-league teams. That meant contracts for about 500 players. Newport News of the Class D Piedmont League, equivalent to a Single-A league today, numbered 15 athletes 17 years old or younger on its roster. Jake Pitler, one of the few Jewish minor-league managers, ran the club and commented, "Our kids were so young that our team bus was loaded with comic books and candy bars, but practicably no shaving cream." Two of the youngsters were Clem Labine and Duke Snider. Rickey showed me Pitler's scouting report on Snider, dated September 2, 1944.

"Well built and moves good," Pitler noted. "Good fielding. Good power. Very good arm. Must improve on hitting curveball. Has a lot of ability. Might go all the way." Snider, of course, went all the way to Cooperstown. But Jimmy Powers did not look into what was really going on in Brooklyn, much less on the vital but faraway farms. In something like four seasons of covering the Dodgers pretty much every day, I never once saw Powers at Ebbets Field. Why not? He never went to Ebbets Field. He was committed to rage rather than reporting, and he even managed to attack Rickey on the issue of integration.

"We question Branch Rickey's statement that he is another Abraham Lincoln," Powers wrote. (I never heard nor can I find a record of any such statement. Rickey did hang a picture of Lincoln above his desk, but that evidenced admiration, not ego. For the same reason a replica of Leo Cherne's bust of Lincoln, presented to me by the Union League Club, sits prominently on a bookshelf in my own office.) Jimmy Powers continued, "We resent pontificating sports promoters who talk a lot. What we wish to see is how much money these 'liberals' are personally willing to sacrifice to back up their fancy speeches. You will usually find they are framing their pretty press releases primarily to make money out of the colored people and the colored athletes."

Sometimes, when Powers was occupied with other matters, he ordered Dick Young to ghostwrite the Powerhouse, directing the thrust of what Young was to type. On one occasion Young approached my *Herald Tribune* colleague Harold Rosenthal and said, "I got a date. I need you to write tomorrow's Powerhouse for me." Rosenthal agreed, then told me merrily, "I'm ghosting a column for Dick Young ghosting a column for Jimmy Powers."

"A ghostly trio," I said, but Harold didn't hear me. He had already started typing.

When Powers found time to write his own column, he continued his barrage. The Cardinals' success, pennants in 1942, '43, '44 and '46, was largely the work of good field managers, Billy Southworth and Eddie Dyer, not the efforts of "Old Man Rickey" upstairs. Ebbets Field needed refurbishing. That would never happen with "El Cheapo" Rickey running things, Powers announced. He wouldn't even pay to modernize the restrooms. Brooklyn fans, Powers wrote, were proving to be the best and most loyal anywhere in baseball. Despite their small home ballpark, the Dodgers led the major leagues in attendance five times in an eight-year stretch during the 1940s. What was happening to all those gate receipts? Powers asked. The fans of Brooklyn had a right to know. (Among other persons, places and things, the money went to fund the best farm system in baseball, pay a superb scouting staff and outstanding coaches and to build Dodgertown, the matchless spring-training facility where black and white players would live comfortably side by side, even though they were situated within the borders of Vero Beach, a small, all-white, racist Southern town.)

A curious tempest broke in February 1948, when Ralph Branca, coming off the best season of his career, was negotiating a new contract with Rickey. Branca grew up in suburban Mount Vernon, New York, and one February day the local paper there, the *Daily Argus,* broke a story that Branca had signed a new Dodger contract calling for about $13,000 a year. Dick Young immediately grew furious. He and the mighty *Daily News* had been scooped by the *Daily Argus.* Rickey became just as angry. His policy dictated that signings were to be announced by the ball club office, not by individual players.

Young telephoned Rickey about the *Argus* story. "Not accurate," Rickey said.

"But I happen to know," Young said, "that you've held private meetings with the kid."

"Indeed," Rickey said, "covering a range of issues, all significant."

By the time Young reached Branca, the young pitcher was insisting he had only talked contract with Rickey, not signed. Young refused to believe him and then wrote in the *News*:

> The righteous Mr. Rickey is contributing to the delinquency of a nice young man like Branca by ordering him to lie.
>
> Branca followed instructions by stating that he had not signed, but that he expected to do so when he met Mr. Rickey again.

Young was asserting that two prominent Dodger people, Rickey and Branca, were outright liars. His anger continued to burn and the next day Young wrote:

> This morning Ralph Branca will enter the gas chamber for a second exposure to Branch Rickey's oratorical fumes. This afternoon the Dodger front office will be able to announce that its star right-hander has signed his '48 contract for something less than $14,000—one of the most miserly documents ever offered a 20-game winner.

Rickey called a press conference that was convened in his office and read aloud much of Young's story and concluding comments: "Branca, after wiping the blood off his ears, was more than willing to escape with his life."

Rickey shook his head and said to the assembled press, "That's supposed to be clever writing, I guess."

Rickey pressed a button on his intercom. A side door opened and in walked a hulking, hawk-nosed nervous youngster. Ralph Branca.

"Sit down, Branca," Rickey said. "Have we been holding conversations?"

"Yes, sir."

"About what?"

"You feel I should get married," Branca said. "You said if I don't get married I'll be nothing more than a matrimonial coward."

"Correct, Branca," Rickey said. "Have you signed your 1948 contract?"

"Not yet, Mr. Rickey."

Rickey pointed a stubby index finger directly at Dick Young. "I demand an apology from you right now and I want one with a retraction in your newspaper tomorrow." Everyone in the room turned to stare at Young. "I apologize," the newspaperman said.

Rickey decisively won the skirmish, but knowingly or not he was starting a war. He had made a lifetime enemy of Young.

Dick Young's cauldron continued bubbling with spleen, although his primary target would change from the Dodger general manager to the Dodger field manager. After Chandler suspended Durocher in 1947, Rickey wanted to replace Leo the Lip with somber, hard-drinking "Marse" Joe McCarthy, who had won four consecutive pennants while running the Yankees. But McCarthy, highly allergic to sportswriters, considered the Brooklyn situation and decided to stay retired in Buffalo, New York. Then Clyde Sukeforth declined the job. Rickey reached back into his past and brought in Burt Shotton, a grumpy 62-year-old baseball veteran whom Rickey had known in St. Louis 40 years earlier. Never afraid of the dramatic, Rickey wired Shotton at his Florida home: "Be in Brooklyn in the morning. Call nobody. See no one."

Shotton told Rickey that at his age he no longer wanted to climb into uniform. He would manage in street clothes. Under the rules that meant he could not leave the dugout. He could not go face-to-face with umpires, nor, in an on-field blowup, could he rush to Robinson's aid. Rickey accepted the terms. He announced at a press conference that Shotton "has always been my idea of a number one pilot. I believe he'll prove to be the greatest manager hereabouts since John McGraw." This was pure Rickey hyperbole.

Obviously a manager determines the lineup, rotates the pitchers and calls the plays. Less recognized, but just about equally important is a manager's handling and, if necessary, pacifying the media. Three of the most successful managers of my experience, Whitey Herzog, Joe Torre and Casey Stengel, were masters of media relations. They knew baseball, of course, but they also formed close, even affectionate relationships with important journalists. Stengel, cold to writers he did not know, became a wonderful dugout host for Red Smith of the *Trib* and Arthur Daley, Smith's genial but prosaic bookend at the *Times*.

Today baseball rules control the media's access to clubhouses. Ball clubs set time restraints so that, at least in theory, players can focus their concentration before each game and establish their composure afterwards. The trainers' quarters are off-limits, on the grounds of privacy. The media is completely barred from players' private lounges within dressing rooms. Some of the reasoning here is questionable. Ball club officials are manipulative about injuries. Open trainers' rooms would assist honest reporting. Private lounges? An invention of haughty ballplayers and their haughty union, who would prefer absolutely no dealing with the press. But during the 1940s, particularly in Brooklyn, the clubhouses were open and constantly alive with friends, cousins, visitors, journalists and chirping children. Privacy was not then seen as an issue. Ballplayers were public figures. Leave privacy to dental hygienists and librarians.

Young walked about the Dodger clubhouse with a swagger and when he wanted to interview a player he began by ordering, "Sit down." Young was short, perhaps five foot six. When asking questions, he preferred to tower over his subject.

His manner annoyed Shotton. Far from courting Young, Shotton tried to ignore him. Young rode the team hard, questioning the courage of certain players and in time informing his readers that Shotton was a fraud. "Behind the phony, grandfatherly manner," Young wrote, "there lurks a mean old man." With heavy sarcasm Young began referring to Shotton in the *Daily News* as KOBS, an acronym for Kindly

Old Burt Shotton. If the Dodgers lost, usually it was because of mismanaging by KOBS. If they won, usually it was in spite of KOBS.

Shotton did not get along with Harold Rosenthal of the *Trib* either, and took to addressing him as "Rosenberg." Rosenthal then told all who would listen, "The son of a bitch is not only mean. He's an anti-Semite."

Where was Rickey amid these disruptive events detonating about his ball club? I'm afraid the answer is that for the time being at least, Mr. Rickey was out to lunch.

Finally one late summer day—the specific precipitant is lost to history—a few minutes before game time Burt Shotton exploded on the bench. He stood up in his street clothes and shouted, "I hate you, Young. Everybody on this team hates you, Young. You are barred from our clubhouse."

"Hey, Dick," Harold Rosenthal shouted. "I'll give you my clubhouse notes every day."

Shotton yelled: "You stay out of this, Rosenberg."

The entire team sat in silent shock. Then Pee Wee Reese got up and threw an arm around Young's shoulders. "I don't hate you, Dick," Reese said.

Here, in retrospect, was a Rickey mistake. Instead of putting up with Shotton and the veteran's mangling of Dodgers press relations, it seems to me that Rickey should have dumped KOBS and hired Pee Wee Reese to manage. Reese was smart, humorous, poised, knew the game and had the affection and respect of the entire team and all the sportswriters who were covering the team, including the feral Dick Young.

Was Reese too young to manage? After Bill Veeck appointed the Cleveland shortstop Lou Boudreau as player–manager, the Indians swept to a pennant and won the 1948 World Series from the Boston Braves. Lou Boudreau was all of one year older than Pee Wee Reese.

Not that Rickey was entirely passive. He organized a task force in the Dodger offices to gather negative information about his tormentors on the *Daily News*. In 1949, Arthur Mann reported, someone, never identified, sent Rickey a copy of a letter Jimmy Powers had written during World War II to an official of the corporation that owned the *News*. The specific suggestion was an allegation that Powers was sympathetic to Adolf Hitler.

"I talked to the captain [publisher Joseph Medill Patterson] last night," Powers began, "and he told me not to worry over latrine gossip picked up by the FBI, that if Winchell and the rest of the Jews had their way America would be a vast concentration camp from Maine to California. There wouldn't be enough barbed wire to hold back all the decent Christians maligned by the Jews and those who run with them. In short I was in pretty good company with Col. McCormick [the isolationist publisher of the *Chicago Tribune*], Joe Kennedy [the isolationist father of the future president] and several other decent family men. [Joe Kennedy's philandering with the actress Gloria Swanson was widely known.] How in hell can I be termed 'pro-Nazi' simply because I don't like certain crackpot politicians and Jews."

This appalling letter, thought Rickey, the old Michigan Law School graduate, was just what he needed to bring a suit against Powers and the *News* for libel and defamation of character. When Powers's simmering anti-Semitism came to light, Rickey reasoned, it would surely cost him his job. The El Cheapo slurs would then become history. But the Dodgers' lawyer advised against litigating. He said, "Laugh it off. A suit will mean that every newspaper turns against you. They hang together like pack rats." The club lawyer, Walter Francis O'Malley, hardly a disinterested party, was staying up late nights and getting up early mornings, plotting to throw Rickey out of Brooklyn. Then the Big Oom would seize the Dodgers for himself.

Was Byzantium itself ever so byzantine?

I doubt it.

NINE

BRANCH AND MR. ROBINSON

ONE COULD NOT WORK OR PLAY FOR LONG with Jackie Robinson without hearing him mention the name of Branch Rickey. Robinson's admiration for his loquacious, heavy-browed benefactor was unqualified and unalloyed to such an extent that it made some observers uncomfortable. Although their association lasted a quarter century, Robinson never addressed or referred to Rickey as "Branch." It was always and pointedly *Mister* Rickey. Robinson intended this as a dignified expression of respect, but repeated often enough, the word "mister" seemed to suggest subservience, notably to more radical blacks such as Malcolm X. "I'd expect," Malcolm told me during a telephone interview shortly before he was assassinated in 1965, "that sooner or later Jackie will start calling Rickey 'Massa.'"

Robinson never used "mister" in referring to anyone else in the generally informal world of baseball. Not to his teammates, not to opponents, not to umpires, nor even to other prominent officials who influenced his career. Bavasi, the Dodgers' general manager after Rickey, was simply Buzzie. Ford Frick, who as National League president heroically put down a planned redneck strike against Robinson, was simply Frick.

When Robinson organized the monthly magazine *Our Sports,* which was directed primarily at black fans, he hired me to write articles, suggest story ideas and help him compose a monthly column. It would not take much time, I knew, before Mister Rickey would be the subject of a column. But it surprised me when Robinson in a very inventive way made sure his Rickey piece drew wide attention from the mainstream media.

Robinson telephoned me in January 1953 and asked if I could join him for lunch and a meeting in the Flatiron Building, a venerable, steel-framed skyscraper in lower Manhattan. "It will be worth your while," he said. "There's something in it for you." We had become close during the season of 1952, when Robinson put in a characteristically solid year, batting .309, hitting 19 home runs and making the all-star team at second base. As I've indicated, I came to my Dodger assignment predisposed to supporting Robinson because I was supportive of baseball integration.

Jack was innately proud, and after six major-league seasons, he had become increasingly confrontational. He needled umpires. He taunted opponents. He corrected reporters when he thought their stories went off the tracks. These qualities in a white baseball man, say Leo Durocher or Eddie Stanky, drew acceptance and even approval from the general run of reporters, who described both as aggressive fighters. But to most reporters around at the time, these same qualities made Robinson "uppity." They liked their Negroes docile, subservient and saying if and when they spoke, "Yowsah, boss." These newspapermen were not robed night riders. They just felt that Negroes should know their place, and remain several paces back of the whites. No mainstream New York newspaper—not one—employed a black sportswriter until the *New York Times* hired Bob Teague in 1959, a full 13 years after Robinson broke into organized ball. All the sportswriters reporting on the Dodgers in the 1950s were white men. Robinson had the keen eyes of a .300 hitter. He noticed.

Among the various estates in which Robinson sought acceptance—playing field, clubhouse and press box—he believed that the press, the fourth estate, was by far the most acutely bigoted. That is one reason why he started his own magazine.

◆ ◆ ◆ ◆ ◆

AN UMPIRE NAMED FRANK Dascoli called a close pitch against Carl Erskine one summer day at Braves Field in Boston. From second base Robinson shouted, "Do the best you can, Dascoli."

Another close pitch. Ball two. Again, "Do the best you can." After two more close pitches, the runner walked. "Do the worst you can, Dascoli," Robinson yelled, his strong tenor carrying toward Bangor, Maine. "We've seen your best."

I laughed. Dascoli threw Robinson out of the game.

Did this smack of prejudice? I asked Robinson over dinner at the Kenmore Hotel. "I don't think so," Robinson said. "Just the case of a lousy umpire. Bad eyes and rabbit ears."

At least until his betrayal at the chubby hands of Walter O'Malley in 1956, Robinson accepted the Dodger management that followed Rickey without much complaint. Neither Bavasi nor O'Malley offered anything approaching Rickey's admiration for Robinson, but Jack accepted that as the way things were. This is not to say that O'Malley and Bavasi were bigoted men. They were not. But neither possessed Rickey's flaming social conscience.

During the 1953 season, Robinson telephoned me at the Chase Hotel in St. Louis and reported that during the previous night's game Eddie Stanky, then managing the Cardinals, held up shoes when Robinson came to bat. "Hey, boy!" Stanky called. "Shine these!" That was followed by some name-calling, "black bastard." Robinson said to me, "I've been in the league for six years and I don't think I should have to put up with this shit anymore." Stanky dismissed Robinson's charges at first, but then backed down. He was competitive, he said, not racist, and he would bother Robinson any way he could.

I wrote the story, which ran in the early edition of the *Herald Tribune*. Then the racist sports editor, Bob Cooke, read my piece and ordered it killed. He wired me angrily, "We will not be Jackie Robinson's sounding board. Write baseball, not race relations."

Perhaps I should have quit and gone public right then, but that was beyond what I knew how to do. I was only 25 years old. (I did have the sense and gumption to quit the following year.) When the Western trip ended, O'Malley invited me for "a friendly visit" in his office at 215 Montague Street.

He began with the obligatory reference to the Brooklyn prep school I had attended and he had served as a trustee. "I'm surprised," he said, "that a Froebel Academy boy would be so easily taken in."

"Who?" I said. "What? I don't understand what you're getting at."

"I'm getting at Jackie Robinson, who got at you." O'Malley had seen the one-edition story and he said it was "a waste of valuable newspaper space. I've known Robinson longer than you and I can assure you that he is first and foremost an inveterate seeker of personal publicity."

"But, Walter. What I wrote actually happened."

"I have no doubt that it did, but it was of no consequence. By playing up these remarks you make them become more important than they were and, as I have suggested, you give Robinson personal publicity over trivialities."

"Walter. The manager of the St. Louis Cardinals called Jack a shoeshine boy. I'd hardly call that trivial."

"But it is. It most definitely is. When I was practicing law, I spent hours around the Kings County courthouse. You heard ethnic comments all the time. 'Look they've appointed another Jewish judge.' A comment like that is absolutely meaningless."

"I'd say it is absolutely offensive."

O'Malley's face briefly showed unhappiness. He bit off the end of a cigar, then lit it. "I'm simply suggesting that you focus on the positive," he said. "We won that game in St. Louis. But now it seems that you and I have a difference of opinion."

"My father says that's what makes horse racing."

"How is your dad?" O'Malley said with real warmth. "If he wants to come to the game tonight, I'll have two box-seat tickets waiting for him at the press gate with my compliments."

For me it was just about impossible to dislike Walter Francis O'Malley. But the larger issue here became brilliantly clear in remarks Branch Rickey made on September 22, 1957, the 95th anniversary of the preliminary Emancipation Proclamation.

"Once Negroes organize effectively in certain areas of the country," Rickey began, referring to the southern states, "we must be prepared to see political control pass locally to colored citizens. If that day comes, it would be too much to expect all Negroes to forgive and forget the record of the past 100 years. I am afraid the white man will justly reap as he has sown.

"How long will the white citizens of this country go on ignoring the agony of the Negro? They call you an extremist if you want integration now—which is the only morally defensible position. To advise moderation is like going to a stickup man and saying to him, 'Don't use a gun. That's violent. Why not be a pickpocket instead?'

"A moderate is a moral pickpocket."

Here we encounter two remarkable characters, both agreed on the integration of baseball and in time the country, both agreed that bigotry is wrong. But what a difference in each man's ethical compass.

◆ ◆ ◆ ◆ ◆

STORY IDEAS FOR *OUR SPORTS* came in a great rush, partly because Robinson and I had been thinking through racial issues from our different viewpoints across several seasons. I write "partly" here because another reason that story ideas sprouted was nothing less than the mainstream press itself. The *New York Times,* Bob Cooke's bigoted *Herald Tribune, Newsweek* magazine and the *New Yorker,* to cite just a few samples, all lacked the conscience or the courage to cover racism in sport, let alone in the country at large. The field of socially conscious sportswriting was wide open.

I remember an enlightened few: the great sports editor Stanley Woodward, who was fired by the *Tribune*; Jimmy Cannon, composer of passionate columns for the *New York Post*; Shirley Povich, the Maine gardener's gentle son who wrote for the *Washington Post*; and the irascible Dave Egan, a Harvard man who worked for the *Boston Record*. There may have been others who dared to take on racism, but not many.

When I first traveled with the Dodgers in 1952, the team was working through a spring-training stretch in Miami, where I was struck at once by the dazzling skills of major-league ballplayers. Then I noticed the comfortable interracial relationship between Robinson and Pee Wee Reese, between Roy Campanella and Carl Furillo and so on through the lineup. I asked the manager, Charlie Dressen, about color as an issue and he snapped back, "It ain't an issue. Robinson is the best ballplayer I ever managed and if you want to know about prejudice, let me tell you this. I don't go to church but my family was Catholic. I grew up in Decatur, Illinois. The Klan was big there and the Klan hated Catholics. One night when I was about eight, there was a big commotion and a son of a bitch was burning a cross out on our front lawn. That's all you got to know about them bigots. They burn crosses at night to scare eight-year-old kids."

As I say, there was no visible racism in the Dodger clubhouse, but after the ballgames blacks and whites had to go separate ways. The white players and the sportswriters, all of whom were white, stayed at the McAllister Hotel on Biscayne Boulevard in Miami. The

McAllister rose across the street from a pleasant bayside park with walkways shaded from the Florida sun by stands of palm. No black dared walk in the bayside park. No blacks were allowed to register at the McAllister.

After a few days I wondered about accommodations for the black Dodgers, Robinson, Campanella and Joe Black. That led me to drive a rented Chevrolet to a motel in a northern quarter of Miami Beach. This place was called the Sir John, and as I recall it was two or three blocks distant from the ocean. The sandy shores of Miami Beach were restricted to whites.

Black Dodgers stayed at the Sir John, and so did musicians and other entertainers working the nearby resort hotels, the Algiers, the Roney Plaza and later the Fontainebleau. The Sir John was an undistinguished two-story concrete structure built around a pool. When I got there of an early evening, the scene was dreamlike. In dim light thrown off by Chinese lanterns people sat about on lounges, sipping tropical drinks. Nearby a saxophone player was running off jazz riffs. Except for me, everyone inside the Sir John Motel was black.

Robinson, wearing gray slacks and a dark polo shirt, walked toward me and we sat at a small table under a folded beach umbrella. "Too quiet for you at the McAllister?" Robinson said.

"I wanted to see what this place was like."

"You're the first," Robinson said. "You've broken a color line. You're the first white reporter to come to the Sir John." He offered a pleasant smile.

"I also wanted to get your feelings on the state of integration. I think there could be a story there."

"You might get in trouble trying to do that. Anyway your paper won't be interested in what I have to say."

"I don't know just how much I can get into the *Trib,* but I'll never know if I don't try."

To begin with, Robinson said, I ought to understand that barriers were coming down "not just because of me. It isn't even right to say I broke the color line. Mr. Rickey did. I played ball. Mr. Rickey made it possible for me to play." The brisk (for the time) pace of major-league integration was a pleasant surprise. "It's been what, six years since I came to Brooklyn and something like half the big-league clubs now will pick up a Negro if he has the ability."

"The Yankees—" I started.

"The Yankees are not in that half. Or the Red Sox. Or the Cubs."

"I've read that in the beginning you took fierce abuse."

"There was a core of 'antis.'" He pronounced the word "an-ties," rhyming with "neckties," and it was Robinson's own personal term for bigots. "But then there were guys who were supportive. Lee Handley and Hank Greenberg in Pittsburgh. Stan Musial in St. Louis. And on our club, lots of guys. Gene Hermanski, [Gil] Hodges, little Al Gionfriddo. He was the first guy who told me to come on in and shower with the white guys. And, of course, Pee Wee [Reese]. I've never had a better friend in sports."

"How about the fans?" I said.

"When I first came up," Robinson said, "there was organized opposition coming at me. I could tell it was organized because one fan would yell something from one part of the stands, and another would yell the same thing from somewhere else. It became like a chain; it sounded like it had been planned beforehand. It was that way the first time we played an exhibition at Fort Worth, Texas. Now it's nothing at all in Fort Worth. Only a few yell at you and it's not organized.

"The hardest damn thing has been you guys, the press. Dick Young from the *News* makes things up. Others take shots."

I raised a final topic. Rickey had been forced out of Brooklyn after the 1950 season. "Do you miss him in the front office?" I said.

Before Robinson spoke, he looked at me very hard. "Just say that I'm not Walter O'Malley's kind of Negro."

"Are you saying O'Malley is prejudiced?"

"No. But I guess I'm saying that O'Malley is not my kind of white man."

I shaped Robinson's comments into a Sunday feature for the *Trib* and sent it north by Western Union, night press rate collect. The *Trib*'s editors were always after me for Sunday features, specifically to fill columns of the early edition while waiting for later hard-news stories to break. Sometimes there was nothing to send but fluff. This piece, however, was more than a filler, much more. It contained facts and comments that were fresh and new. I was proud of the story that I called "Jackie Robinson on Integration."

It never ran. The most important sports story of the time was the integration of baseball and the *Tribune,* so admirable in many ways, would have none of it. Just describe ground balls, the editors were telling me. That's the sort of stuff we really want.

"I appreciate your trying," Robinson said, "and look at the bright side."

"There is no bright side, Jack. I just got censored."

"Oh yes there is," he said. He started to laugh. "They didn't make you pay the Western Union bill."

But immediately and ultimately this was no laughing matter. Suddenly I recognized the crippling limitations imposed on my assignment. Write about the first integrated major-league baseball team, but be careful. Never, ever mention integration. When I persisted in writing about race, Bob Cooke, the sports editor, pulled me off the Dodgers and sent me into the Arizona desert to cover the Giants. That was in late winter of 1954. Like the Dodgers, the Giants were becoming integrated, but the team had no firebrand like Robinson. Willie Mays was the brightest Giant star but rather than protest against racism—the Hotel Adams, the Giants' base in Phoenix, refused to accept blacks—Mays affected docility, saying more than once, "Why make a bad fellow of myself?" In his later years, anger exploded within Mays and contributed to his difficult demeanor. But at the time Willie, at 23, was somewhat childlike, except when he was playing ball.

After a nasty spat with Leo Durocher I left the *Trib* during the summer of '54. Durocher accused me of misquoting him and demanded that I apologize. Bob Cooke, the sports editor, said the paper's relations with Durocher required me to do so. Red Smith later wrote that the *Herald Tribune* fired me for quoting Durocher accurately.

By then I was willing, even anxious to move on. Indeed, the story that launched my subsequent writing career was a straightforward, uncensored piece for *Sport* magazine called "The Ten Years of Jackie Robinson." In memory I cherish the *Tribune* and my gifted, cultured colleagues in the sports department. Al Laney, once an assistant to James Joyce. Ed Gilligan, who led me to the novels of Thomas Hardy. The warm, delightful Red Smith, who liked to call his widely popular column "my daily spelling lesson." The *Trib* was more than just a newspaper I worked for. It was my university. But accepting censorship, even genteel censorship from a charming, handsome Yale man named Bob Cooke, poisons a writer's soul.

For his part, Robinson followed our meetings with a quiet quest to find backers for a magazine that would cover what the mainstream press did not. That was what led to his phone call the following winter asking me to help develop *Our Sports*.

I joined him in a suite at the Flatiron Building. Robinson had been conducting a weekly radio show on WNBC and I thought he might want me to help him prepare the scripts. But instead, seated behind a desk in a bare office—there were just two chairs and a desk—he began to outline the magazine that would be called *Our Sports*.

Reading from notes, he said that in the days following World War II Negro athletes had reached the top in most major spectator sports. "*Our Sports* aims to corral all the activities of Negroes in sports into one interpretive medium for the vast Negro audience." His manner was alive with excitement and enthusiasm. "I'm going to write a column every month. I want you to help me there. I'm a lousy typist. Then I want you to write a story for us under your own byline every other month. And meet with our editors from time to time. We need as many ideas as we can get." Most of the editors were white. Robinson then mentioned a fee: $150 a month. Since my *Tribune* salary was only $120 a week, Robinson's offer was a fine supplement. (When I decided to leave the paper a year later, the editor, Whitelaw Reid, offered me a then staggering $10,000 a year to remain.)

Robinson's enthusiasm was understandable. He would finally be able to get his words and ideas into print, and on a regular basis. My enthusiasm matched his; I was excited to start working closely with a complex, brilliant and heroic man.

But the magazine was doomed from the start. Major advertisers—General Motors, Campbell's Soup, Philip Morris—discounted the Negro market in those days, and without major advertising a mass-market magazine cannot survive. Jack and I talked that through, and we convinced ourselves that if we published enough powerful stuff we would break that barrier. "I have experience breaking barriers," Robinson said. We published powerful stuff. The barriers remained.

We ran a piece called "Will There Ever Be a Negro Manager?" The writer, earnest, intense Milton Gross of the *New York Post,* thought Monte Irvin of the Giants and Roy Campanella were excellent candidates. Neither became a manager, although Irvin later signed on as executive assistant to the late commissioner Bowie Kuhn. (Frank Robinson became the first black big-league manager at Cleveland in 1975.) We marched fearlessly into hot-button issues. Was the Yankee organization bigoted? We thought so. They discarded an excellent black Puerto Rican first baseman named Vic Power because a scout reported that Power liked white women. Power played with other American League teams for 12 seasons and recorded a lifetime batting average of .284. When I encountered Vic in Arecibo, Puerto Rico, in 1973, he was coaching the island's national amateur team and was happily married to a pretty blonde.

We proposed Satchel Paige for the then all-white baseball Hall of Fame. He made it—18 years later. We challenged the unwritten rule that barred blacks from being jockeys and relegated them to the lesser role of "exercise boys." That changed during the 1980s.

For the second issue, Robinson urged me to write an article under the title "What White Big Leaguers *Really* Think of Negro Players." I must have interviewed 50 baseball people. Eddie Stanky, the shoeshine-boy needler, presented quite a different aspect. "My relationship with all the Negroes I've played with and managed has been 100 percent pleasant," he said.

"I would not call asking a big leaguer for a shoeshine notably pleasant."

"Don't mind what I say during a game. I want to win and sometimes I get tough. But Robinson does, too, you know. It's part of baseball."

Walter O'Malley was particularly interesting. I caught up with him during spring training and he suggested we walk about Dodgertown in Vero Beach. "There's the dining room," he said. "Our Negro players and our white players eat side by side. This is Florida, but here you couldn't tell it is.

"In our barracks here Negro boys and white boys sleep under the same roof. The other day we had some electricians in to fix the lights in our new stadium. They worked a long day. When they were through it was late and I asked them if they wanted to sleep over because Melbourne is a 45-mile drive. They asked me if they'd have to sleep under the same roof as Negro players and I told them, 'Of course.' They said they couldn't. What did I say to that? It doesn't matter. You couldn't print it, anyway."

Although the staff at *Our Sports* dispatched hundreds of copies of press releases, nobody picked up that story. Nobody at all. It was as if Stanky and O'Malley had spoken in a vacuum. Jack's column that month, "My Feud with Leo Durocher Is Over," exploded with vitality and inside stuff. Nobody seemed to notice that story either, except for Durocher, who wrote a thank-you letter to Robinson.

Now we come to the column about Branch Rickey. Here it is exactly as Robinson and I presented it in the June 1953 issue of *Our Sports.* The column was called "The Branch Rickey They Don't Write About." It ran under the line "*By Jackie Robinson.*"

> "Prejudice" is a word that usually sticks in my throat. But don't be shocked when I admit to a prejudice of my own.
>
> I'm prejudiced in favor of Branch Rickey, the man who gave me a chance to destroy baseball's color line. And that's one prejudice built on more than emotion. It stands on dozens of hard, but pleasant facts.
>
> Emotion enters into it, of course. Admiration and gratitude and a lot of other feelings that are hard to express. Perhaps the best way to explain is to go back to October 1, 1952—the day the Dodgers opened the World Series against the Yankees.
>
> Come back to Ebbets Field with me and look at the 35,000 spectators who filled every seat in the ballpark and every inch of standing room. If you study the countless faces through my eyes, you'll know just what I mean.
>
> To me there were only two people in Ebbets Field that day who really mattered—my wife, Rae, and Mr. Rickey. It was for Rae and Rickey that I wanted to win the series so badly. The Yankees won, but I've been a Dodger for seven years and I know how to take a loss philosophically.
>
> "Wait till next year." Isn't that what the philosophy book says? I have a hunch the Dodgers will write a new chapter this October. But I'm getting a little ahead of myself.
>
> Perhaps it seems strange for a Dodger infielder to want to win a World Series from the Yankees for the general manager

of the Pittsburgh Pirates. When you think about it, though, it isn't strange at all.

In the first place, Rickey's ties to Brooklyn didn't end when he went to Pittsburgh at the close of the 1950 season. Most of the Dodgers who played in last year's series came into their own under Mr. Rickey. Fellows like Roy Campanella and Duke Snider entered the game through his help. Others, like Preacher Roe and Billy Cox, came to Brooklyn and reached their primes under him. Still others, like Pee Wee Reese, were boosted to greatness by an assist from Rickey. The 1952 Dodgers were pretty much his club—certainly more so than the 1952 Pirates. We were his boys and I know he was pulling for us. That's one reason I didn't want to let him down.

In the second place, without Branch Rickey there probably would have been no Jackie Robinson in baseball, nor a Monte Irvin or a Larry Doby. At a time in life when most men settle down in rocking chairs, Rickey launched a crusade. He battled until the crusade was a universally recognized success. He succeeded because he had something called "guts"—and even eloquent Rickey couldn't find a better word for it.

Mr. Rickey, as you know, is a great man with words. Baseball writers who make a living by turning phrases can't touch him. The first time I met Branch I knew he was a spellbinder. I knew he was sincere too.

In Chicago, summer of 1945, someone said, "There's a man outside the clubhouse who wants to see you."

I went over to see "the man."

"My name's Clyde Sukeforth," he said. "I'm with the Brooklyn Dodgers. How are you feeling?"

"Pretty well, thanks. My arm's a little sore from a fall on the base paths, but I'm okay."

"I've been watching you for a while. Would you mind going out to the infield and throwing a few from short to first?"

"I don't think I can. My arm is so sore I can't play."

"Never mind then," Sukeforth said.

Then he asked me something I'll never forget. "Can you

come to New York with me to see Branch Rickey, the Dodger president?"

"Sure," I said. "Sure."

I was thinking much more than that one word. I was thinking that this might be a gag, a cruel gag. I didn't dare think of becoming a Dodger. Hundreds of other things entered my mind, and I was still thinking when we got off the train in New York.

The first time I saw Branch Rickey he was setting up a smokescreen with his cigar. Behind the smoke was a face revealing sincerity.

"Do you think you are capable enough to play baseball in the major leagues?" Mr. Rickey began.

"I don't know. I've only played professional baseball for one year. I don't know how the Negro Leagues stack up against the minors, let alone the majors."

Mr. Rickey did not wait to deliver his punch line. "I am willing to offer you a contract in organized baseball. Are you willing to sign it?"

Now I was the one who did not hesitate.

"Certainly," I said.

Then Mr. Rickey began to speak. He spoke of barriers to be broken and how to break them. He spoke of bigotry and hate and how to fight them. He spoke of great things to be done and how to do them.

He spoke of himself and how his own family had advised him against signing a Negro because at his age the bitterness he'd have to face might make him sick, or even kill him.

He spoke of my future in baseball and of the taunts and insults that would be hurled in my face and the dusters that would be hurled at my head.

He spoke of others who would wait for me to slip so they could say that Branch Rickey had been wrong and that baseball was no place for Negroes.

All this he hurled at me like thunder. And then he asked me if I still wanted to sign.

"Certainly," I said again.

Looking back now, I think Branch Rickey had a vision of what was to be. What he said would happen did and the method—his method—to progress was the right way and the only way.

"Above all," he warned me, "do not fight. No matter how vile the abuse, ignore it. You are carrying the reputation of a race upon your shoulders. Bear it well and a day will come when every team in baseball will open its doors to Negroes. The alternative is not pleasant."

A few months after our first meeting, Rickey announced my signing to the press. In a few more months I was on the Montreal squad.

It was in the International League that I first came to know Rickey's ability to do the right thing at the right time. He called me just before we went to Syracuse for a series there.

"Someone has informed me," he said, "that you're in for a considerable amount of abuse at Syracuse. They intend to bring you to a boil so you can hardly play. The way to beat them is to ignore them."

I was abused in Syracuse during the following days but I didn't come to a boil. I had been forewarned so I ignored the remarks and played my game. There were other similar incidents that year. Each time Mr. Rickey called the turn.

The next year—1947—when I was promoted to the Dodgers, Rickey did more than call the turns. I know now—I didn't know then—that a lot of club-owners ganged up on him and tried to run me out of baseball. He received crackpot letters and a dozen different pressures were put on him. He didn't yield an inch.

And he did more than that. He spoke to Negro leaders, civic groups and churchmen in every National League city. We both knew that just as we were carrying a great responsibility, so were the Negro fans who came to see me play. Their actions would be watched just as mine were and the I-told-you-so guys were looking for slips. Disorder in the stands was as deadly as disorder on the field. Working hand-in-hand with leaders of our race, Mr. Rickey did all that any man could have done to let the fans know the importance of their role.

"There will be race riots in half the ballparks," the know-it-alls were saying. "You mix all those Negroes and whites in the stands when Robinson plays and there's going to be a blow-up."

Negroes and whites have been watching me in the majors for seven years but Mr. Rickey laid so careful a groundwork that nothing has blown up on my account. Except, of course, a few ballgames, but that's the way I earn my money.

I've mentioned money and Mr. Rickey in the same paragraph and I guess that prompts a question.

"Is Branch Rickey a tightwad?" I've been asked time and again. A writer on one New York paper invented a nickname—"El Cheapo"—for Mr. Rickey and almost every day the sports pages ran stories about his stinginess.

That's hard for me to understand. With the help of a newspaperman, I did a little research and I learned that the Ebbets Field press club was always well-stocked. Anytime any sportswriter wanted to he could enjoy some fine old Scotch whisky with the compliments of "El Cheapo." And the liquor wasn't there to keep Rickey's throat moist when he was talking at press conferences either. Mr. Rickey does not drink.

In my own financial dealings with Mr. Rickey, I learned he was as fair a man to work for as a ballplayer could ask. My first year with Brooklyn I was paid $5,000, the minimum. Almost all rookies get that. The next year Rickey nearly tripled my salary—jumped it to $14,000. I got periodic boosts after that and when Mr. Rickey left Brooklyn I was well up in the $30,000 class.

President Walter O'Malley and the rest of the current Dodger management are a fine group of men—but they aren't paying me a cent more than Mr. Rickey did in his last year at Brooklyn. I'm as good now as I was then and I'm older. As a rule, if a player doesn't slump, he gets raises as he gets older.

Maybe you think my prejudice for Mr. Rickey is influenced by the way he handles money. Pee Wee Reese isn't prejudiced and he agrees with me.

"They never accuse Larry MacPhail of being cheap," Pee Wee once told me, "but until I played for Mr. Rickey I never got much of a break in my contract. Larry never made me rich; Mr. Rickey fixed it so I had real income tax worries for the first time."

Other players second Pee Wee's opinion. Dodger salaries as a whole are no higher than they were when Mr. Rickey left. In the meantime we've won a pennant and the cost of living has gone up.

Along with "tightwad," "fraud" is another charge I've heard hurled at Rickey by people who don't know any better. Was he a fraud when he stood alone in organized baseball and signed me?

"He did it for attendance," you hear people say.

I've never met a club-owner who didn't want larger attendance and every one had the same chance as Rickey to attract Negro fans. The thing is that Rickey did it—he took the step no one else had the courage to take.

Certainly crowds increased with my arrival, but I believe what motivated Branch Rickey to sign me was his sincere belief in the brotherhood of man. Mr. Rickey is a student of the Bible—a serious student.

"But he's a pompous windbag," others object. You can judge for yourself when you check a few more facts.

I've always admired the way he handles the language but the one time we had to make sure that every word was the right word, Rickey was humble enough to seek assistance from others.

That was in 1949 when I was asked to testify in Congress as a loyalty witness. They wanted me to voice my feelings—as an American Negro—about my country. Between us, Rickey and I must have spoken to fifty people as we tried to frame my beliefs in the best possible phrases. The words weren't quite right until

> Rickey remembered Lester Granger, whom he'd met at a dinner of the Urban League. Mr. Granger is one of the finest men we have in our race and possibly one of the smartest men in the whole country.
>
> Among the three of us we worked out a speech that perfectly expressed my views. What impressed me so much was Rickey's insistence on getting another Negro to help. He did not trust his own ability alone to aid in explaining the viewpoint of a Negro.
>
> Because of the speech, I came in for a lot of praise and delivering it was as important a step as any in my life outside of baseball.
>
> But with every forward step I made, Branch Rickey was at my side. Today I think baseball has reached the point where Negroes are accepted by every real fan and soon will be accepted by every team.
>
> Baseball has advanced—and with baseball the country—because of Mr. Rickey.
>
> Vicious men may insult him, foolish men may make fun of him and petty men may not understand him. But when the vicious, the foolish and the petty men are forgotten, Mr. Rickey will be remembered. And all decent men—whether Negro or white—will respect the memory and the blow Branch Rickey struck in the cause of human progress.

This column did draw a response, but one that was less than positive. When Robinson told me that he was not earning more in 1953 than he had in 1950, I stopped taking notes. "That isn't what you hear in the Dodger front office, Jack."

Robinson's answer was curt. "Just write what I told you."

The June issue of *Our Sports* appeared when the Dodgers were playing at Pittsburgh. Two newspapermen called my room in the Hotel Schenley to ask about Robinson's assertion that his salary had not increased. Now it was my answer that was curt. "I just typed what he told me."

At Forbes Field during pregame warm-ups, perhaps 20 reporters were gathered around Robinson. Among all of his observations on Rickey, the reporters focused only on Robinson's assertion that his salary had not increased under Walter O'Malley. The lead questioners, Al Abrams of the *Pittsburgh Post-Gazette* and Bill Roeder of the *New York World-Telegram,* pressed him again and again. How could he say his salary was frozen when the Dodgers announced salary increases for him in 1951, '52 and '53? Was he charging that Walter O'Malley and Buzzie Bavasi were liars? Listening in, I had a nervous moment. Several Dodgers, notably Roy Campanella, tended to issue controversial quotes and then, when the controversy flared, deny that they had said any such thing. Doublespeak still is common in baseball. I worried that Robinson would say that in preparing the column it was I, not he, who had messed up.

Doublespeak was not Robinson's way. As the rapid-fire questioning crackled around him, he said without flinching, "Sure they've announced raises for me and sure I've gotten them. But as my salary has gone up, so has the cost of living. So in a real sense my salary is not a penny higher than it was when Mr. Rickey left Brooklyn." Abrams and Roeder then wrote sour pieces, saying Robinson was at the least guilty of misleading readers. I suppose in a limited way they were right, but Robinson, also in a limited way, was right as well.

Aside from money, the press ignored all the issues the Rickey column raised. No probing into Robinson's trials during his epochal rookie season with Montreal. No reconsidering his testimony before the House of Representatives. No review of Rickey's solidarity with Robinson. Jack and I were dedicated to the ideology of integration. The mainstream press was not. Their interest seemed to be money, only money.

The silence of the mainstream press proved fatal. *Our Sports* did not survive the season. Today few copies can be found. The Library of Congress issues an imposing purpose statement:

> *The Library's mission is to support the Congress in fulfilling its constitutional duties and to further the progress of knowledge and creativity for the benefit of the American people.*

I could find no copies, not one, of any issue of *Our Sports* in all the files and warehouses of knowledge and creativity that constitute America's national library. Until now it was almost as if Jackie Robinson and I wrote the *Our Sports* stories between midnight and 4:00 a.m., then put them into a bottle and shipped them out before the sun rose into a dark and endless sea of silence.

TEN

NORTH OF THE BORDER

"Do you really think a nigger is a human being, Mr. Rickey?"

—CLAY HOPPER, Montreal manager, during spring training 1946

"Robinson must go to the majors. He's a big-league ballplayer, a good team hustler and a real gentleman."

—CLAY HOPPER at the conclusion of the 1946 season

GLENN HALL, THE GREAT HOCKEY GOALIE WHO grew up in Manitoba, succinctly described Canadian attitudes on black and white. "We are nice to our Negroes in Canada," Hall told me. "Both of them." (It is a touch ironic that the first Canadian inducted into the American Baseball Hall of Fame was the fine right-handed pitcher Ferguson Jenkins. An Ontario native, he made Cooperstown in 1991. Fergie Jenkins is black.)

Actually, the Anglo-Canadian Establishment discriminated against both Eskimos and Native Americans and was constantly at odds with the proud French-speaking minority that was clustered mostly in the province of Quebec. But the kind of sweeping antiblack segregation that infested the United States was unknown.

On the afternoon of October 23, 1945, a cadre of 15 Canadian sportswriters gathered at the offices of the Royeaux de Montréal, the

Montreal Royals, of the Triple A International League. They had promised "a major announcement." Dink Carroll of the *Montreal Gazette* told me, "We'd heard that the Royals were going to announce that they'd hired Babe Ruth to manage. That would have been one helluva story. What awaited us was one helluva different story."

At the appointed hour Hector Racine, the portly president of the Royals, entered a conference room followed by Branch Rickey Jr., now director of the Brooklyn Dodgers' superb 22-team minor-league farm system. The Montreal press corps had previously encountered both men. But the third entrant was a surprise, even a shock. He was a muscular, athletic-looking black man named Jack Roosevelt Robinson. "Here is the newest member of the Brooklyn Dodger organization," Racine said. "Last year he was the star shortstop for the Kansas City Monarchs. He will have every opportunity to make the Royals for the upcoming season, 1946."

"There was no applause," Al Parsley of the *Montreal Herald* told me, "and neither were there hostile outbursts. I'd sum up the reporters' approach in two words: belligerent neutrality."

Rickey Jr. read a prepared statement: "Mr. Racine and my father undoubtedly will be criticized in some sections of the United States where racial prejudice is rampant. We are not inviting trouble, but we will not try to avoid it if it comes. Jack Robinson is a fine type of young man, intelligent and college-bred. And I think he can take it, too. Some players may protest. A few may even quit. But they'll be back in baseball after they work a year or two in a cotton mill." Then, in a long-distance howitzer shot at Jimmy Powers and the nickname "El Cheapo," Branch Jr. said, "We believe that Jackie Robinson is the right man for this mission and we have spared no expense in trying to make sure of that. The cost of scouting Negro players has run to over $25,000."

Next Robinson stood up. "Of course I can't tell you how happy I am that I am the first member of my race in organized baseball," he began. "I realize how much this means to me, my race and baseball. I can only say I'll do my best to come through in every manner." He smiled a disarming smile. "I guess I'm just a guinea pig in a noble experiment."

A reporter called out, "Are you going to try and take Stan Breard's job?" Stanislaus Breard, a Montreal native, was expected to be the Royals starting shortstop.

"I'm not trying to take anybody's job. I'm just going to do the best I can."

Summing up, Dink Carroll commented, "I wouldn't say that he turned all the pagans into Christians right there and then. Lloyd McGowan of the *Star* said there was no need for him in baseball. But Robinson made a more than decent start. I know some were impressed just by the clarity of his diction."

Jack was only beginning his long assault on the stereotypical Negro, exemplified by the comic actor Stepin Fetchit, who on the screen was invariably wide-eyed and afraid of ghosts and answered questions by saying, "Yowsah, boss." (Fetchit's real name was Lincoln Theodore Monroe Andrew Perry. He is said to have been the first black actor to become a millionaire.)

The response to the Robinson announcement was volcanic and, to put this charitably, mixed. Jimmy Powers wrote in the New York *Daily News,* "Robinson will not make the grade this year or next. . . . Robinson is a 1,000-to-one shot to make the grade."

Bob Feller, the great right-hander, had pitched against Robinson in barnstorming games. "He won't hit," Feller said. "He has too much upper-body muscle. He isn't supple enough to get around on high inside fastballs."

"This move," said Clark Griffith, longtime owner of the Washington Senators, "is a bad one. It's going to kill the Negro Leagues." (Griffith, whose teams were seldom contenders, made important money renting the Washington ballpark to teams in the Negro Leagues.)

Alvin Gardner, president of the Texas League, said, "You'll never see any Negro players on any teams in the South as long as the Jim Crow laws are in force. And that may be forever."

The president of the National Association, the umbrella group covering the minor leagues, was one William Bramham, a former Rickey protégé and a Carolina native. "Father Divine will now have to look to his laurels," Bramham told reporters, referring to a popular, oddball black evangelical minister who claimed to be no one less than God. "Soon we can expect to see a Rickey Temple erected in Harlem."

"This whole thing is okay with me," said Herb Pennock, the general manager of the Phillies, "as long as Rickey doesn't bring the nigger to Philadelphia. We're not ready for him here [in the City of Brotherly Love]."

"I have no problem with this," said Dixie Walker, the Dodgers skilled and popular right fielder, "just so long as I am not asked to play on the same team as Robinson."

Commissioner Happy Chandler claimed in later years that he championed integration. But on this day, when the issue was hot and words were so very important, Chandler had no comment.

Billy Werber, a scrappy big-league infielder for more than a decade, was a graduate of Duke University and a man of strong opinions. He telephoned Rickey Sr. in Brooklyn and spoke in controlled anger. "A large segment of the ballplayers who contribute to the success of major-league baseball are of Southern ancestry or actually live in the South," Werber said. "To attempt to force them to accept socially and to play with a Negro or Negroes is highly distasteful. You are for some unaccountable reason discriminating against the majority." Rickey controlled his own anger and thanked Werber for the call.

On November 1, 1945, the *Sporting News* printed a harsh editorial.

MONTREAL PUTS NEGRO PLAYER ON SPOT

In signing John Roosevelt Robinson, 26-year-old Negro native of Georgia, and former all-round athletic star at UCLA, the Montreal club of the International League, through Branch Rickey, president of the parent organization in Brooklyn, touched off a powder keg in the South, unstinted praise in Negro circles, and a Northern conviction that the racial problem in baseball is as far from a satisfactory solution as ever.

In New York, there is a feeling that the engagement of Robinson is, in the main, a legalistic move. Last July 1, there became effective in the state of New York what is known as the Anti-Discrimination Law. This has to do, in part, with the barring of Negroes from jobs and professions.

Rickey virtually admitted the legal facet of the Robinson signing when he said that, before long, every professional baseball club operating in the state of New York would be forced to engage Negroes.

But how? Col. Larry MacPhail of the Yankees, who some time ago wrote a long report on the Negro-in-baseball question to the Mayor's Committee in New York and Rickey himself, admits there is not a single Negro player with major-league possibilities for 1946. Satchel Paige, of course, is barred by his age. Nor could he afford to accept a major contract, even if he were 10 years younger. Robinson, at 26, is reported to possess baseball abilities which, were he white, would make him eligible for a trial with, let us say, the Brooklyn Dodgers' Class B farm at Newport News, if he were six years younger.

Here, then, is the picture which confronts the first Negro signed in Organized Baseball as a Negro:

(1) He is thrown into the postwar reconstruction of baseball, and placed in competition with a vast number of younger, more skilled and more experienced players. (2) He is six years too old for a chance with a club two classifications below the Double A rating of Montreal. (3) He is confronted with the

sweat and tears of toil, with the social rebuffs and the competitive heartaches which are inevitable for a Negro trailblazer in Organized Baseball. (4) He is thrown into the spotlight, the one man of his race in any league under the jurisdiction of Commissioner Albert B. Chandler, and will be expected to demonstrate skills far beyond those he is reported to possess, or to be able to develop.

Granted that Robinson can "take it," insofar as points 2, 3 and 4 are concerned, the first factor alone appears likely to beat him down.

The war is over. Hundreds of fine players are rushing out of service and back into the roster of Organized Baseball. Robinson conceivably will discover that as a 26-year-old shortstop just off the sandlots, the waters of competition in the International League will flood far over his head. One year ago, with baseball suffering from manpower stringencies, Robinson would have faced a better chance on the technical side of the game.

The Sporting News believes that the attention which the signing of Robinson elicited in the press around the country was out of proportion to the actual vitality of the story.

The Sporting News also is convinced that those players of southern descent who gave out interviews blasting the hiring of a Negro would have done a lot better by themselves and baseball if they had refused to comment.

"It's all right with me, just so long as Robinson isn't on our club"—the standard reply—is unsportsmanlike, and, above all else, un-American.

Meanwhile it would be well for the players to keep their opinions to themselves and let the club owners work out this perplexing problem.

Years later some *Sporting News* staffers denied to me that this editorial actually appeared. Others, better informed, simply were embarrassed.

Although I have not found editorials in any major newspapers acclaiming Rickey and Robinson, there was no shortage of positive comments. Bill Corum, an affable Missouri-born columnist for Hearst's *New York Journal-American,* wrote, "Good luck to Rickey! Good luck to Robinson! Good luck to Baseball, which may be a little slow on the uptake, but which usually gets around to doing the sensible thing in the long run."

Al Laney of the *Herald Tribune* discussed the move with Jimmy Odoms, a retired Pullman car porter who supplemented his pension by sweeping the floor of the *Tribune*'s fifth-floor newsroom. He was the closest available Negro. "Pick out just one good boy," said Odoms, a passionate baseball fan. "Put him in the minors and let him come up. He's gonna make it and when he does the stars ain't gonna fall. They'll be plenty kids ready to try it after Robinson makes good."

Writing in the Baltimore *Afro-American,* Sam Lacy made a powerful and ultimately accurate prognostication. "Alone, Robinson represents a weapon far more potent than the combined forces of all our liberal legislation."

Red Smith, then working for the long dead *Philadelphia Record,* presented a thoughtful overview in his gentle and eloquent way. "It has become apparent that not everybody who prattles of tolerance and racial equality has precisely the same understanding of the terms."

◆ ◆ ◆ ◆ ◆

WHY WASN'T BRANCH RICKEY himself, the Baseball Liberator, presiding at Robinson's titanic press conference or at least present there to work his polysyllabic spells? "As you know, I have never run from appropriate publicity," he told me, "nor have I consciously sought it. I was experienced enough to realize that, had I attended, flurries of questions would have been hurled in my direction, placing me, so to speak, in the public glare. But October 23, 1945, was not a day that belonged to me.

"That day belonged to Jackie Robinson."

Now in his mid-60s, Rickey, far from slowing down, was taking on the challenge of a lifetime. Many years earlier he had contracted tuberculosis, recovering slowly at a sanitarium in the Adirondack Mountains. But otherwise his health had been excellent and his energy seemed to be unlimited. Except for Sundays, he reached the Dodger offices on Montague Street at 8:00 a.m. and worked long into the night. Like his interests, his circle of friends extended beyond baseball, and included Frank Tannenbaum, an Austrian-born professor at Columbia University whose historic study, *Slave and Citizen,* won Rickey's profound admiration. "That book," Rickey told Arthur Mann, "is a wonder. We would all do well to memorize a passage."

> Physical proximity, slow cultural intertwining, work their way against all seemingly absolute systems of values and prejudice. . . . Time will draw a veil over the black and white, the record of strife, and future generations will look back with wonder and incredulity. For they will not understand the issues that the quarrel was about.

(Important as this approach was to the Jackie Robinson experience—proximity did indeed break down walls—it completely collapses when considering the prejudices underlying the Holocaust. The physical proximity between German Jews and German gentiles never modified in any way the Nazis' murderous systems. In Rickey's later years, this, and the Holocaust itself, greatly troubled him.)

Lowell Thomas, an immensely popular network newscaster, was another good friend, and on Sundays Rickey often drove north where Thomas lived in the manicured Quaker Hill section of Pawling, New York. Other Quaker Hill residents included Edward R. Murrow, Norman Vincent Peale, Thomas E. Dewey and Pherbia and Raymond "Pinky" Thornburg, world travelers and fellow graduates of Ohio Wesleyan. Rickey relaxed with conversation or by playing bridge and chess. His favorite parlor trick delighted the children of Quaker Hill.

Somehow he could balance three baseballs, one on top of another on top of another. He was so good at checkers that no one would take him on. "Here's a valuable rule," Rickey said. "Never play checkers with a man who carries his own board."

According to the Rickey papers in the Library of Congress, he traveled incessantly after the Robinson signing. The Dodgers bought a plane, a twin-engine Beechcraft, and Rickey flew about St. Paul, Fort Worth, Cincinnati, pursuing prospects and reviewing outposts of the Dodgers' great minor-league system. His quest for talent was relentless. On one occasion, when he was trying to fly into Dubuque, Iowa, the pilot said, "I'm sorry, Mr. Rickey. There's a bad squall line ahead. I'm going to set her down. We'll have to wait to reach Dubuque until tomorrow."

Rickey had an appointment with the prospect. "Look," he told the pilot. "You fly us through that squall line. I'll take the responsibility."

Attending the winter baseball meetings in Chicago that December, Rickey suddenly was overcome with vertigo. He returned to New York and went by ambulance first to the Brooklyn Jewish Hospital and then to Peck Memorial Hospital nearby. The dizziness persisted. Rickey decided that he was suffering from a brain tumor. But after a number of workups doctors diagnosed the ailment as Ménière's disease, an affliction of the inner ear. It causes ringing in the ear and varying degrees of dizziness. There is no cure, but a number of medications palliate the condition.

"I was relieved, of course," Rickey told me, "but even with medication the darn thing kept coming back. I had just left my office on Montague Street one night when a wave of dizziness hit me as I was on the sidewalk. I clutched a lamppost to keep from falling. I held on, swaying until the attack passed.

"Numbers of people walked by. Nobody offered to help. I heard one woman say to her companion, 'Be careful. Stay away from that old drunk.'"

A doctor told Rickey that stress appeared to worsen the disease. "I'd suggest you cut down on your workload," the doctor said.

The Robinson adventure was underway. Rickey looked at the doctor and said, "Impossible."

Before Rickey established the remarkable self-contained spring-training base called Dodgertown on the western edge of Vero Beach, Florida, Brooklyn's minor-league affiliates trained at an east-central Florida town situated in a rural agricultural belt. As a tribute to the prime local crop, Sanford bore the nickname of Celery City, USA. It also, coincidentally, was the community in which the noted Dodger broadcaster Walter "Red" Barber spent his boyhood.

In the South, "rural" meant racist, passionately racist, and Rickey concerned himself with the living and dining arrangements for Robinson in Florida. With Rickey's enthusiastic support, Jack had decided to marry Rachel Odom, a bright and attractive nursing student he met at UCLA. "I knew organized baseball was going to be rough," Robinson told me, "but I felt sure that I was going to make it. I told Rae that if she married me and stayed by my side during the tough early going, when I had it made down the road, I'd build her a home with everything a woman could want." (So he did in North Stamford, Connecticut, a handsome mansion of stone and timber. But at the time of his death in 1972, Jack was several months behind in his mortgage payments.)

Rachel found the honeymoon with the handsome groom "decidedly disappointing." First the newlyweds drove to San Jose to live in a home owned by one of Rachel's aunts. "I had something less than a great time there," she told me. "Some of Jack's cronies showed up and reminded him that the Harlem Globetrotters were in town. We spent two nights watching them. Then some of Jack's other friends invited us to join them in Oakland. What do you know? The Globetrotters now were coming to Oakland. So we went to see more basketball again. We had some delightful honeymoons in later years, but the first one . . . well we just goofed and bungled our way through."

Rickey meanwhile wrote to one of his deputies, Bob Finch, "It might be well for you very quietly to find out about [the Robinsons' Florida] living accommodations. I don't believe I would take it up with white folks to begin with. No use to stir around them unnecessarily. It seems that the first approach would be to some leading colored citizen who could be trusted with an inquiry."

Rickey assumed, as most Northerners would have assumed, that the Robinsons' journey from California to Florida would be uneventful. "But," Robinson told me, "it turned out to be a passage through hell."

The Dodgers made reservations on American Airlines from Los Angeles to Daytona Beach with a change of planes scheduled in New Orleans. Rachel packed a shoebox full of chicken and hard-boiled eggs and the couple boarded a night flight that arrived in New Orleans at seven in the morning. Their airliner to Florida was scheduled to depart at 11:00. An American Airlines clerk promptly told them that the 11 o'clock was fully booked, but he would try to get something for them later. "That's when we found out that there was no place anywhere in the New Orleans airport for a Negro to take a rest or buy a meal," Robinson told me. "No waiting rooms for Negroes. Nor any chairs. A black cabbie directed us to a Negro hotel that turned out to be dirty and dreadful. We telephoned American several times and finally an airline employee said there would be space on a one-stopper to Daytona Beach, with a layover in Pensacola.

"When we got to Pensacola, American Airlines kicked us off the plane. They said something about weight. With all the fuel, the plane would be too heavy with us aboard. We got off. A few minutes later two white men took our seats. I said pretty loudly, 'I'm never going to fly American Airlines again.'

"Nobody gave a damn."

The Robinsons found a bus terminal and finished their nightmare journey on a cramped and rattly bus, jammed into an overcrowded back row. Their food had run out. They were tired, harassed and hungry. At length Rachel, a strong, proud woman, began to cry. "I couldn't help it. I cried as quietly as I could. I was trying not to upset Jack."

As the Robinsons began settling in with a black family in a two-story house at 612 South Sanford Avenue, Rickey suddenly ordered the entire Royals squad moved to Daytona Beach. He had heard—he never specified from whom—that local men in Sanford, many of them members of the Ku Klux Klan, were planning a midnight march on the house where the Robinsons were staying. At the very least they intended to burn a cross on the front lawn.

According to reliable histories, a mob of white men in 1946 shot and killed two young African American couples near Moore's Ford Bridge in Walton County, Georgia, 60 miles east of Atlanta. This murder of four young sharecroppers, one a World War II veteran, shocked most of the nation, but went unpunished. It was a key factor in President Harry Truman's decision to push civil rights legislation. But for decades a thick cotton curtain—white Southern senators—blocked the way.

I later asked Rickey directly if he thought that in 1946 a mob of night riders in Sanford, Florida, Celery City, USA, might have lynched Jackie and Rachel Robinson. Rickey took in the question carefully and paused before he responded. "From reports that reached me," he said, slowly, "that was not entirely beyond the realm of possibility."

Although Daytona Beach was relatively safe, Robinson's problems with violent Floridians persisted. When the Royals traveled 20 miles to DeLand for a game against Indianapolis, Robinson singled in the first inning, stole second and slid home on another single. As he was dusting himself off, a local policeman burst onto the playing field and said, "Get off the field right now, or I'm putting you in jail."

Robinson told me his first reaction was to laugh. "Ridiculous," he said. "I thought the cop was just ridiculous." But the crowd in the stands rose to its feet. The Indianapolis players on the field stood stock-still. Clay Hopper, the Montreal manager, said to the policeman, "What's wrong?"

The cop responded with a speech. "We ain't having niggers mix with white boys in this town. You can't change our way of livin'. Niggers and whites, they can't sit together and they can't play together and you know damn well they can't get married together."

Hopper had no answer.

"Tell your nigger to git," the policeman said. He put one hand on his Colt .45. Robinson left silently. He spent the next few hours sitting alone on the team bus. DeLand city officials ordered the next Montreal–Indianapolis game canceled because "the ballpark lights are out of order." The canceled game was scheduled for an afternoon.

◆ ◆ ◆ ◆ ◆

ROBERT CLAY HOPPER, A NATIVE of Porterville, Mississippi, a longtime successful minor-league manager, was undergoing a crisis of his own. When he heard Robinson had signed with Montreal he sought out Rickey. "Please don't do this to me, Mr. Rickey," Hopper said. "I'm a white man, been living in Mississippi all my life. I got a fine plantation there. If you do this to me, Mr. Rickey, you're gonna force me to move out of Mississippi."

"Clay," Rickey said, "this is the greatest opportunity of your life. We're giving the colored boy a fighting chance to show what he can do. We aren't moving him into your home. We're just giving him an opportunity on the ball field. Managing him, winning with him can turn out to be a great accomplishment for you. I believe you are up to it, Clay. Indeed I do."

Hopper nodded. He liked being a manager. A few days later Robinson was playing second base in an intersquad game, with a runner on first. Someone smoked a low drive into the hole between first and second. Robinson hurled himself through the air and stabbed the ball on one fierce hop. Then, on his knees, he whirled and threw out the runner at second base.

"What a play!" Rickey said to Hopper in the dugout. "There's coordination and agility and adventure all at once. Clay, no other human being in the world could have made that play!"

Hopper scratched his jaw. "Mr. Rickey," he said, "do you really think a nigger is a human being?" At that point Clay Hopper quite suddenly began to weep.

Rickey said his first response was rage. "But then I saw that this Mississippi-born man, ignorant as he had remained, was sincere. His tears told me this: Regarding a Negro as subhuman was part of his heritage. Here was a man who had practically nursed racial prejudice from his mother's breast. So I decided to ignore the comment.

"About a month later, after he had gotten to know Robinson, Hopper sought me out and told me, 'Mr. Rickey, those words I said in Florida about Robinson not being human. Mr. Rickey, sir, right here and now I want to apologize.'"

Telling me about Hopper, Rickey said, "His remarkable adjustment certainly bears out Professor Tannenbaum's theory about physical proximity destroying prejudice. And that's not theory. That's a fact."

One Royals game against the Jersey City Giants in Jacksonville was canceled. A municipal law there forbade blacks and whites from competing against each other.

"It was just one grueling spring," Robinson told me. "The scouts reported that I did not have a big-league shortstop's arm. I began putting everything I had into every throw. Inside a week, I had a very sore arm. My wife applied cold compresses. Didn't help. I went to a local doctor. He applied hot compresses. Didn't help either. I played as best I could through all that pain. On top of which I simply was not hitting. Pressure? Maybe. Whatever. I specialized in pop flies to shortstop.

"It was Mr. Rickey who kept me going. He pretty much deserted the Dodger camp to cheer me on with the Royals. He'd get a seat near first base and shout to me over and over again, 'Be daring. Run it out. Take a bigger lead. Worry that pitcher into a sweat. Adventure! Adventure!'

"A white newspaperman, I forget his name, wrote in one of the Florida papers: 'It's do-gooders like Rickey who hurt the Negro. They try to force inferior Negroes on whites and everybody loses. Take this guy Robinson. If he was white the Royals would long ago have booted him out of camp.'

"'Try not to be perturbed, Jack,' Mr. Rickey said. 'We have scouted you most carefully. We know you're going to make a great success.'

"I did my best to tune out the hate. Mr. Rickey's words kept me going.

"What a spring."

◆ ◆ ◆ ◆ ◆

LIBERATION DAY, THURSDAY, APRIL 18, 1946, broke cool with a dusting of snow and then turned sunny in Jersey City, New Jersey, less than half an hour distant from the towers of New York. By game time the sky had cleared and the temperature had reached the 60s.

Jersey City then was the private preserve and cash machine of one Frank Hague, a Democratic Party leader universally known as "Boss" Hague. He was mayor of Jersey City from 1917 to 1947 and on a salary of $8,500 a year he managed to amass a personal fortune of $10 million. Hague's desk, which survives to this day, included a specially designed lap drawer that could be pushed outward toward a visitor. This allowed Hague's guests to deliver—quite literally under the table—envelopes bulging with cash.

Boss Hague was a solid baseball fan and each year he closed his city's schools for the opening game of the Jersey City Giants in the Class Triple A International League. That was a sound franchise; future New York Giant stars who played for Jersey City on the way to the major leagues included Whitey Lockman and Bobby Thomson. Boss Hague also required all city employees to buy tickets for the opener. A sellout, he felt, was a demonstration of municipal pride. The Jersey Giants sold 51,872 tickets for Jackie Robinson's debut game. Roosevelt Stadium, the team's art deco ballpark, seated only 25,000 people. On Robinson's first day fans crouched in the aisles, sat on the fences and hung from girders. The best figure for the boisterous, cramped assemblage on hand remains vague: "in excess of 25,000."

Doug Kennedy, a wartime PT boat commander turned peacetime sportswriter, covered the game for the *Herald Tribune,* which ran his story under an imposing eight-column banner headline that began: "Robinson Leads Montreal."

"Jackie Roosevelt Robinson," Kennedy wrote, "first Negro to sign in modern organized baseball, making his debut in the sixty-third season of International League competition, completely stole the show and the hearts of more than 25,000 fans as he led Montreal to a 14-to-1 conquest of Jersey City.

"After the game in Haguetown it took Robinson fully five minutes to reach the dressing room as he was mobbed trying to leave the field by fans of assorted ages, sizes and colors."

Jackie used to say to me, "I never had it made." But on that one day, April 18, 1946, he surely did. He had it made because on that golden afternoon in spring he took an overwhelming challenge and—with bat and glove and legs—he made a triumph.

He would always remember that day. "The crowd," he said, "and the marching band and the jugglers on the field and the bunting flying everywhere. When I stood, we all stood, for 'The Star-Spangled Banner,'

I knew it was really happening. Integration. That gave me a lump in my throat. I thought, I honestly thought, *This is a day of destiny.*"

Hopper gathered the Royals into a semicircle. "All right, boys. Let's get off to a flying start. The game you lose on the first day of the season hurts just as much as the game you lose in the pennant stretch drive. So let's go out there and win this one and pile up such a big lead that nobody can catch us. You know the lineup. Breard at shortstop. Robinson at second base. . . . " "And then," Robinson told me, "I finally knew that it was real. Some said that this project was a phony attempt to please Negroes, I wasn't really a ballplayer, just window dressing. The hell with that. Right then in Jersey City I knew I was within reach of the dream of every boy who ever went to a sandlot carrying a ball glove. The major leagues."

Leading off for Montreal, Stan Breard bounced out. Robinson stepped in. His palms were wet. The count went full. Then he hit a weak grounder to shortstop and Jaime Almendro, a white Puerto Rican, threw him out by four steps. Robinson said when he went back to the dugout he felt more relief than disappointment.

Montreal put runners on first and second with nobody out before Robinson came to bat in the third inning. This was a bunt situation and word was out that Robinson was an excellent bunter. A sacrifice here would advance the runners to scoring position with nobody out. Robinson looked at Clay Hopper who was coaching third. Hopper flashed three signals and then, with a downward swipe of his right hand, wiped them out. Robinson was free to swing.

Warren Sandell, pitching for the Jersey Giants, suspected a bunt and kept his first pitch high, a high fastball, that soon went higher and faster. Robinson swung hard and lined the pitch about 350 feet into the left-field stands for a three-run homer. "A brilliant personal triumph," wrote Joe Sheehan in the *New York Times.*

When Robinson reached home plate, the on-deck hitter, George

"Shotgun" Shuba, stood waiting with a wide smile and his right hand outstretched. Several photographers caught the instant of the handshake. "A great moment for me," Shuba says, "for Jackie, for baseball and for the country." A large framed photograph of that handshake today graces a wall of the Shuba home in Youngstown, Ohio. Shuba adds, "I call it 'the handshake of the century.'"

Robinson said that the homer "burst the dam between me and my teammates. Northerners, Southerners both let me know they appreciated the way I had come through. I began really to believe one of Mr. Rickey's predictions: Color won't matter if the black man is a winner."

As I mentioned, the Royals went on and defeated Jersey City, 14 to 1. Perhaps the only positive note for the junior Giants was the batting of their young center fielder, who would later play a dramatic role in baseball history. Bobby Thomson went 2 for 4.

Robinson proceeded from his splendid beginning to a season of great success amid great stress. When the Royals moved on to play in Baltimore, Rachel Robinson found herself seated among foul-mouthed white spectators. "More than once," she says, "I heard my husband called a nigger son of a bitch." After that she seldom traveled with the team. Ball clubs generally discourage wives from making trips. Simplistically, but reasonably accurately, the hometown belongs to the wives. The road belongs to the sometimes merry, sometimes sorry band of women called camp followers.

Jimmy Powers of the *Daily News* had written that "Robinson will never hit." At Montreal in 1946 Robinson won the International League batting championship. He batted .349. "Never" seldom has had a shorter life. Robinson also stole 40 bases and led the league in runs scored. One Eddie Robinson, a powerful left-hand-hitting first baseman from Texas who hit 34 home runs for the then Triple A Baltimore Orioles, was voted most valuable player, despite committing 24 errors. Jackie Robinson was named rookie of the year.

Had Rickey summoned Robinson to Brooklyn during the 1946

season, and had Jack converted one lost game into a victory—a wholly reasonable expectation—the Dodgers would have won the 1946 pennant. Rickey maintained that bringing up Robinson "would have been unfair to the fans of Montreal." But what about the fans of Brooklyn who were coming to Ebbets Field in unprecedented numbers and underwriting the entire Rickey operation with their dollar bills and quarters? Rickey had no answer to that question, or none that he cared to utter. Actually, I suspect, Rickey was not yet emotionally ready for the great and challenging task, integrating the major leagues. Although his hesitation can be justified on psychological and sociological grounds, it probably cost the Dodgers a pennant.

The population of Montreal in 1946 was less than 2 percent black. There were no black neighborhoods as such and the Robinsons felt apprehensive about apartment hunting. The Royals front office supplied leads—ball clubs customarily do that for their players—and full of trepidation, Rachel knocked at the door of a private home that included a modest duplex apartment. The landlady opened the door, smiled and invited the Robinsons in for a cup of tea.

"The apartment was lovely," Rachel says. "Clean and sunny." The landlady spoke French and the Robinsons did not. A bilingual neighbor appeared and communicated good news. The landlady would be happy to rent to the Robinsons. Further she would leave them her utensils, linens, towels, dishes and flatware.

Rachel felt overjoyed. She said quietly to Jack, "How can a few miles, a mere border, make that much difference in people?" Before long Jack became a celebrity in his new neighborhood. Children greeted Rachel at the general store and helped her carry home packages. She kept a bowl of fresh fruit on her kitchen table inside a screen door. Youngsters poked their noses against the screen waiting to be offered pieces of fruit. Rachel says, "It didn't take these French-speaking kids long to learn to ask *in English* for the fruit that was their favorite.

"Jack and I both fell in love with Montreal. Where the housing situation in Florida had been simply a nightmare, up in Montreal it was a delight."

In February 2011, the United States government unveiled a plaque at 8232 de Gaspé Avenue, where the Robinsons lived in Montreal. "On behalf of the president of the United States and on behalf of the American people," said David Jacobson, ambassador to Canada, "I want to thank the people of Montreal not only for what you did for the Robinsons and all baseball, but for what you did for the great American journey from Jim Crow to Barack Obama."

The Robinsons' daughter, Sharon, attended the ceremony on a raw, wet day. Rachel, then 88, sent a message. "That place in Montreal was so warm and loving it was really our honeymoon cottage."

The Royals would run off with the '46 pennant, finishing 18½ games ahead of the field. Stan Breard didn't make it at shortstop. Al Campanis replaced him and batted .294. Years afterward Campanis told me more than once that he had taught Robinson the footwork a second baseman needs to master the pivot and complete a double play. "Jack had the greatest natural aptitude of any player I've ever seen," Campanis, an NYU graduate, said. "In one-half hour he learned to make the pivot correctly. He had some deficiencies including arm strength and going to his left, but he overcame both because he was such a great athlete and he applied himself to the game with such intensity." Years after that, as general manager of the Los Angeles Dodgers, Campanis lost his job for making rock-headed racial comments on network television. But he showed no bigotry whatsoever at Montreal. (Robinson himself did not mention help from Campanis. Instead, he said one Lou Rochelli, a reserve infielder from Illinois, was the man who took the time and effort to teach him double-play footwork. Louis Joseph Rochelli died in 1992 and few in baseball remember him today. Robinson never forgot him.)

Robinson's season, Montreal, 1946, can well be said to have been the greatest performance turned in by any baseball player ever up to that time, including:

1. Christy Mathewson of the New York Giants pitching three shutouts over six days during the 1905 World Series. In 27 innings, he walked one batter.
2. Ty Cobb of the Detroit Tigers hitting .420 and stealing 83 bases in 1911. He led the American League in everything but smiles.
3. Babe Ruth of the New York Yankees hitting 60 home runs in 1927 and burying the dead ball behind and beneath his considerable bulk.

Although the historic numbers I cite are meaningful, they don't present Mathewson's magisterial presence, Cobb's jungle ferocity or Ruth's swaggering intimidation. The numbers game is a nasty gambling racket. Baseball is a game of people.

Statistics are significant, but not nearly as important or revelatory as suggested by many earnest Figure Filberts. The Oakland Athletics, the model statistical team in *Moneyball,* finished 22 games out of first place in 2011. Attendance at the Oakland Coliseum was the poorest in the 14-team American League. That same year the Boston Red Sox, another *Moneyball* bunch, lost their field manager, their general manager and, if the *Boston Globe* is to be believed, their self-respect.

Robinson's numbers in Montreal were strong. He led the International League in batting at .349 and in runs scored, 113 in 124 games. He stole 40 bases; his teammate Marv "Rabbit" Rackley, from a South Carolina mill town, stole 65. But Robinson was caught stealing 15 times, roughly 1 out of every 4 tries, which suggests he was still learning the art of baserunning. Although these numbers are interesting, they cannot begin to suggest the revolutionary nature of Robinson's presence.

John "Spider" Jorgensen, the Montreal third baseman in 1946, recalled that he was civil to Robinson, but not close. "I didn't go over to his house for dinner or anything like that. If I had, there were guys on the team who would have called me 'nigger lover.'" Jorgensen said he was focused on his own career—he and Robinson would make their Dodger debuts on the same April day in 1947—and didn't recognize the historic nature of Robinson's role until it was pointed out to him by Rackley. "People are always going to remember this team," Rackley said, "because we're playing the first Negro in the history of baseball." Rackley said he had no trouble adjusting to Robinson as a teammate. "A lot of that, probably, was because he was such a terrific ballplayer. And he was soft-spoken off the field. A real gentleman."

Herman Franks, a Montreal catcher, had played for the Dodgers and would go on to manage the San Francisco Giants and the Chicago Cubs. Franks didn't hit in Brooklyn—his lifetime batting average was .199—and the fans, echoing the cries of vendors, took to shouting at him, "Get hot, Franks." He eventually became an investment advisor and for several years managed Willie Mays's money.

"That Montreal team," Franks told me, "was really well-rounded. We didn't have a 20-game winner, but we had a lot of good hitters and we played good defense and we had plenty of speed. Jackie was a great teammate, but he really had a tough time breaking in. I won't even repeat the garbage that got shouted at him. When we went down to Baltimore early in the season, some of the Baltimore squad wanted to know if we were really going to come on the field with a black player. They said if we did, they didn't want to play the game. We said, 'Well, you don't have to play the game. We're going out there and we'll take a win by forfeit.'"

Homer Elliott "Dixie" Howell, another Montreal catcher, made the Dodgers briefly in 1953 when I was covering the team. He was a personable fellow out of Louisville, Kentucky, and one night after the Dodgers had been caught in a harrowing beanball battle, we had dinner together on a Pullman diner. The fare, it was always the fare on ballplayer dining cars: shrimp cocktail, steak, apple pie à la mode. We started talking about the knockdown pitches and I asked Howell, who had been playing pro ball for 14 years, if this was the worst he had seen. He looked surprised. "No way," he said. "I was with Jackie on Montreal. The way he was thrown at that year was unbelievable. Unbelievable and disgraceful."

Perhaps the single most appalling incident occurred when Montreal was playing a game in Syracuse against the Chiefs. A Syracuse player—his name is lost—threw a black cat out of the dugout and onto the field. Then he shouted, "Hey, Robinson. Here's your cousin." The game stopped while umpires retrieved the frightened animal.

Robinson dug in and doubled to left. The next batter singled. As Robinson rounded third and headed home he shouted at the Syracuse dugout, "I guess my cousin's pretty happy now."

The Royals far outpaced the rest of the International League. By August their lead was substantial; eventually they would clinch the pennant two weeks before the end of the regular season. A headline summed up "Robinson Leads Royals to Title," but the stress, mostly fueled by incessant racism, pushed Robinson to the edge of a nervous breakdown.

Outwardly he seemed to be taking everything in stride, including Rickey's prime directive that he was not to fight back. But in the modest apartment on de Gaspé Avenue, Rachel, who as we have noted trained as a nurse, saw increasing signs and symptoms of stress. Robinson never smoked and did not drink until the last years of his life, when a physician suggested he take a few cocktails daily to improve his circulation. But he was always a big eater, so much so that in time he developed weight problems. Now in Montreal his robust appetite disappeared.

He began suffering periods of nausea. He found it hard to fall asleep and harder still to stay asleep. Clay Hopper thought Jackie looked tense and suggested that he see a doctor. Rachel made the same suggestion. Insisting that he felt fine, Robinson went for a checkup.

The examining physician, a sports fan, had some idea of the pressures his celebrity patient was enduing. At length he reported, "You're a fine physical specimen, Mr. Robinson, but the tension is taking a toll. I want you to get completely away from baseball for at least 10 days. Take a medical leave from the Royals. Don't read the sports pages. Don't listen to the radio. Do you have a favorite pastime?"

"I like driving golf balls."

"Then for 10 days I want you to drive golf balls and picnic with your wife. That's my prescription."

Robinson's medical leave lasted one day. "I was leading the league in hitting with a good chance to win the batting championship. That would be a fine thing, wouldn't it, the first black ballplayer becomes a batting champion? But if I took 10 days off, you know what the 'antis' would say. 'He's goofing off to protect his average. He's only a batting champion by default.'"

Robinson gave me a look that was both hard and vulnerable. "I couldn't have that. I went back to work with my glove and bat."

Montreal swept through the playoffs, defeating Newark, a Yankee farm team, four games to two. In this set Robinson batted .318. Then the Royals defeated the raucous Chiefs, a team in the Cincinnati chain, four games to one. Here Robinson batted .400. These victories set the stage for him to play in a widely popular event called the Little (or Junior) World Series, which flourished from 1905 to 1975. The Little World Series, which was not of course *the Little League World Series,* annually matched the champions of the International League and the American Association. Although dissenting voices sounded from the Pacific Coast, the winner of the Little World Series could claim to be the best of all the teams in the minor leagues.

Louisville—I learned much of this from Pee Wee Reese, who grew up there—was as rigidly racist as any city in the United States. Reese recalled his father, a detective for the Louisville and Nashville Railroad, walking him down a country lane toward a tree with a stout branch extending parallel to the ground about 10 feet high. "When a nigger gets uppity," the elder Reese said, "that's the branch we lynch him from." (Reese's evolution from his apartheid boyhood to his championing of Robinson became one of the wonders of American sport and indeed the American experience.)

The Louisville stadium, Parkway Field, was one of the most notable of the old minor-league arenas. It opened on May 1, 1923, complete with a grandstand that was reported to accommodate 18,000 fans. Several major-league stars played in exhibitions there, most notably Babe Ruth. During an exhibition on June 2, 1924, Ruth, according to Bruce Dudley, then sports editor of the *Courier-Journal,* "socked the gosh-awfullest ball that ever has been croaked in the history of the game in Louisville." Though that seventh-inning drive went foul, Dudley wrote, "Louisville never can believe that any foul ever has gone higher or farther. For many moments it seemed that the ball would drop on to the top of the grain elevators across the road beyond the right field barrier. Then in the ninth inning everybody stood, seemingly in a salute to a national hero, and Babe Ruth, the hero, merited that mark of homage by crashing the ball over the Louisville Provision Company's sign in right center field." (But that day the Louisville Colonels defeated the Yankees of Ruth and Lou Gehrig, 7 to 6. Even the magnificent Yankees could lose to a good minor-league team, *at least in an exhibition game.*)

A less inspiring aspect of Parkway Field tradition was segregation. "I remember going to games there when I was in high school," Reese told me, "and it was pretty much whites only. Blacks had to use a separate entrance way down near the outfield and they were restricted to the worst seats in the place. And of course before Jackie, all the ballplayers were white."

With his farm system mastery, Rickey maintained contacts throughout the minor leagues and private sources now informed him that Robinson's appearance at Parkway Field would stir bitter opposition. "We were going to defy one of the fundamental Kentucky traditions," he told me. "An obnoxious tradition, but one that many Southerners held sacred. Putting a black second baseman on the field side by side with whites seemed to them nothing short of sacrilege."

The Brown Hotel in Louisville became famous as a gathering place for sporting types each spring around Kentucky Derby time. The white Royals would bunk in there during the Little World Series, but Robinson was barred. Montreal officials placed him in the home of a prosperous black lawyer. "The family welcomed me," Robinson said, "but away from my teammates I felt isolated."

Rumblings of another sort emanated from Brooklyn. In a poll taken before the 1946 season, 119 sportswriters were asked to predict the National League pennant winner. A total of 115 journalists picked the Cardinals, a team powered by Stan Musial and Enos Slaughter. None chose the Dodgers. But the Brooklyn team broke fast and kept going and at one time built a seven-game first-place lead. "What's keeping the Dodgers up?" asked the confused editors of *Time* magazine in a lengthy feature on Musial. In point of fact, few editors at *Time* had any feel for the grit and gut of baseball; croquet was more up their alley.

Certainly one factor was fan support. Despite the limited capacity of Ebbets Field, the 1946 Dodgers drew 1,796,824 fans, or roughly 25,000 a game. No other team in the league even came close, and these numbers supported the claims of Brooklyn people that theirs was the greatest baseball town on earth. (The idea that in the next decade a buccaneering lawyer would hijack the Dodgers and dump them into the Los Angeles Coliseum was beyond imagination and beyond nightmares.)

Dan Parker, a crackling good columnist for Hearst's *Daily Mirror,* now made an interesting point. Montreal had won its pennant. Robinson had led his league in hitting. The so-called noble experiment so far was a huge success. But the Dodgers suddenly were stumbling. The Cardinals caught them and at the end of the regular National League season the teams were tied for first place, each with 96 victories and 58 defeats. Ford Frick, the National League president, ordered a playoff series, best two out of three. "What better way to crown Robinson's breakthrough season than to bring him up to the Dodgers so he could join and possibly lead the team through an historic playoff?"

"What about the fans in Montreal?" Rickey said.

"My paper," Parker said, "publishes in New York."

In later years Rickey went to some lengths to explain his thinking to me. He did not want to promote Robinson until the other Brooklyn players were ready to accept him. That, he said, could only happen after they had seen how good he was. "Which they will in spring training the following season." That was as misguided a call as any Rickey ever made.

By the time the Dodger playoff began in St. Louis on October 1, the Royals and Robinson were having their troubles in Louisville. But the national focus was directed at the major-league scramble. There had only been one pennant playoff in big-league history and that was the single game between the Giants and the Chicago Cubs in 1908. Christy Mathewson, who won 37 games for the Giants that year, said that his arm felt tired. He had already pitched more than 380 innings. But John McGraw chose to start him and Matty did not walk away from challenges. "I had to start," he said, "to meet my own idea of courage."

Frank Chance, who managed Chicago, played a hunch and started Jack "the Giant Killer" Pfiester. But Chance quickly had to relieve Pfiester with his own ace, Mordecai Peter Centennial "Three Finger"

Brown. That season Brown had won 29. Had you combed the entire cosmos back then, you could not have found two finer pitchers than Matty and "Miner" Brown. In a classic ballgame Brown bested Mathewson, 4 to 2, with Chance contributing a key double. Now, almost 40 years later, a pennant playoff had come again to baseball.

Mathewson was long dead. Poison gas damaged his lungs when he was serving in the Chemical Corps during World War I. He never fully recovered and perished in an Adirondack sanitarium at the age of 45. McGraw had to organize a charity exhibition game to pay Mathewson's final medical bills.

Brown was alive, but quite forgotten. Baseball nostalgia had not yet begun to flood America. Plagued by diabetes, Brown was running a filling station in Terre Haute, Indiana, and telling his baseball stories to anyone who would listen. No one thought to invite a venerable hero to this later playoff. Two years afterward this great pitcher died. His induction into the Hall of Fame, long overdue, was posthumous.

Rickey told me that his ideal ball club would consist of young position players and veteran pitchers. "The position players will have speed. The veteran pitchers will have poise." Unaccountably Rickey and Dodger manager Leo Durocher chose Ralph Branca to start the playoff in St. Louis. Branca was only 20 years old and on the record he would become the most unfortunate pitcher in the history of playoff baseball. He had a fine fastball, a big sweeping curve and a tendency to wilt under pressure. The Cardinals started a tall, elegant left-hander, Howie Pollet, five years older than Branca, who was coming off a 20-game-winning season. Branca did not finish the third inning and in the end the Dodgers had to use five pitchers. Pollet never lost command. He won, 4 to 2.

After a travel day, the teams met again before a noisy sellout crowd at Ebbets Field. The Cards went with right-hander Murry Dickson, who threw curves, changeups, sliders and knucklers. The

Dodgers started a journeyman left-hander, Joe Hatten. The Dodgers reached Dickson for a run in the first inning, but the Cards came back with 2 in the second and 3 more in the fifth. They won handily, 8 to 4 (and would go on to defeat the Boston Red Sox in the World Series).

The Dodgers' performance in the playoff was not terrible. It was simply flat. Suppose Rickey had promoted Jackie Robinson and brought into the major-league playoff series this arrow of dark fire. Would Jack have ignited the dormant Dodgers? I like to think so. Rickey did not like to think so. In truth, no one can say.

> *What might have been is an abstraction*
> *Remaining a perpetual possibility*
> *Only in a world of speculation.*

That is not Branch Rickey I am quoting, but someone else prominent in the annals of St. Louis history.

T. S. Eliot, who was born there in 1888.

By all accounts the crowd that assembled in Parkway Field in Louisville on September 28, 1946, was ugly. Some were surprised there was any crowd at all.

When it became increasingly likely that the Royals, including Robinson, were coming south to play the Colonels in the Little World Series, a vocal group plainly demanded that the series be canceled. Twenty years before, Jack Dempsey had been forced to terminate a series of exhibition bouts in the South because his sparring partner, Big Bill Tate, was a black man. One Southern newspaperman wrote: "Should Dempsey slip, the crowd would see a nigra standing over a white man. That plainly is intolerable."

Bruce Dudley, the president of the Colonels, had opposed Montreal's signing of Robinson, but now he kept his opposition in check. Robinson's contract had the tacit approval of commissioner Happy Chandler, himself, as we have noted, a Kentuckian. Chandler later claimed he sent a message to Dudley saying, "The colored boy has every right to play." No sane minor-league executive who wanted to stay employed would dare to defy the commissioner of baseball.

A second consideration for Dudley was simply practical. The first three games were scheduled for Parkway Field and total attendance would run to at least 50,000 customers, paying for tickets, then buying ballpark hot dogs and swilling ballpark beer. In the battle, racism versus receipts, cash triumphed. As Calvin Coolidge remarked, "The business of America is business."

The Negro section of the stands at Parkway Field had room for only 466 people. A good estimate is that 20,000 Louisville blacks wanted to buy tickets to see Robinson. Dudley refused to increase the number of seats available to blacks. He said he was afraid a large crowd of blacks inside Parkway Field would lead to a race riot.

"I knew I was going to catch hell," Robinson said. "This was a trying time. I was segregated away from my teammates and Rachel couldn't be with me. She developed some problems with her pregnancy and flew home to California where her mother, Zellee Isum, could help look after her. As for me, I was pretty much alone that afternoon."

As soon as Robinson jogged onto the field, the whites booed. A number of fans chanted, "Get your black ass back to Canada." Others shouted "watermelon eater," "shoeshine boy" and, inevitably, "nigger." Otey Clark, a veteran Colonels pitcher from Boscobel, Wisconsin, said, "Everything he did, they booed him. I remember our starting pitcher that day, Jim Wilson, knocked him down, and the fans cheered. Robinson didn't seem to pay any attention to any of it, but if you cared about fair play, and I did, it made for one miserable afternoon." That day Robinson went 0 for 5, but the Royals won, 7 to 5. The jeering continued in harsh crescendos for the next two days and the Colonels won both games. Robinson came to bat 10 times in Louisville. He made out 9 times.

Although racism was popular in Louisville, it was not universal. The *Courier-Journal* published an editorial saying that "a blight" had descended on the baseball season. "The blight," an editorial writer observed, "was inflicted partly by demonstrations of prejudice against Montreal's fine second baseman. A more deeply bitter taste, which may last a long time, came of the management's policies toward Negro patrons." The paper also ran a letter signed by "A Group of Fort Knox GIs." They wrote, with more passion than clarity, "Louisville has now emerged as a city of obnoxious futility."

One for 10 or 10 for 10, Robinson was changing the times.

◆ ◆ ◆ ◆ ◆

IT HAD BEEN SNOWING in the province of Quebec. That happens in Montreal, a great winter carnival of a town, in September and it also happens in April. According to one of my Canadian friends, "The sort of storm that totally shuts down Washington, DC, is what up here we call a dusting."

The Royals returned to their home ballpark, Delorimier Downs on East Ontario Street, and found it choked under seven inches of snow. It had also been laid out for football. Plows cleared the playing area, but with football yard markers chalked along the base paths, the place had a schizophrenic split-sport appearance. Baseball, however, is decidedly malleable. You can play on cement, dirt, plastic grass and even in an arena marked for football. (To give old Delorimier Downs its due, before it was demolished in 1971—11 years after the wrecker's ball destroyed Ebbets Field—Delorimier had been the home field for several baseball Hall of Famers, including Roberto Clemente, Roy Campanella, Duke Snider and Don Drysdale.)

Montreal sportswriters had described the unfortunate behavior of Louisville fans in both English and French newspapers. "By this time," the late columnist Dink Carroll told me, "Robinson was established as a genuine local hero. People felt that if you insulted Jack you were insulting Montreal. That was one point on which the Québécois and the Anglos stood together. And the Jewish fans of Montreal felt the same way." Someone summed up the general feeling accurately if inelegantly: "Southern hospitality, my ass. The bums in Louisville showed our guy only Southern hostility."

Despite the snow and cold, a goodly crowd, 14,685 fans, paid their way into Delorimier on the night of October 2. They came to cheer Robinson and to hoot the Louisville Colonels. "It was something," Al Campanis remembered. "When the announcer read off the Louisville lineup, the fans booed every single name. And face it, there were actually some pretty good fellers like Sam Mele [a Queens native] on that Louisville squad. But the fans hooted each and every one, and cheered for all of us. Jackie got a standing ovation."

Louisville broke well and moved out, 4 to 0. Going into the ninth inning Louisville held a 5-to-3 lead. But the Royals scrambled back, playing a waiting game as right-hander Otey Clark lost his touch and walked three men. Two scored. The second and game-tying run came home in the person of Jackie Robinson.

In the bottom of the 10th inning the Royals rallied against relief pitcher Mel Deutsch. With two men on base, Nemo Leibold, the 54-year-old manager of the Colonels, chose deliberately to walk Marv Rackley and pitch to Robinson. Rackley was a decent minor-league hitter, but in retrospect Leibold's decision suggests he was a candidate for a brain transplant. Cheered by his fans, challenged by his opponents, Robinson cracked a sharp line single into left that scored the winning run. Montreal, 6. Louisville, 5. The Little World Series was tied.

The weather moderated the next night and the crowd for Game 5 reached 17,758 on a Canadian evening that belonged to Jackie Robinson. He doubled in the first inning and scored on Tom Tatum's single. He tripled in the seventh and scored when Lew Riggs doubled. In the eighth, with Campanis on third, Robinson dropped a bunt along the line for a run-scoring single. The Royals won, 5 to 3, and stood within a game of the championship of the minor leagues. "I'm beginning to believe," Dink Carroll said, "that if Robinson bunted every time he came to bat, he'd still hit .300. Is there anything that Jackie can't do?"

Old Curt Davis was lean and long. He came from Greenfield, a small town in rural Missouri, and he long retained his backwoods manner. Some nicknamed him "Coonskin Curt." He threw sidearm, low stuff, breaking balls and sinkers, and his forte was control. He owned the outside two inches of home plate. When you watched Curt Davis pitch, as I did many times, you saw an artist.

Because his stuff was not overpowering, Davis did not break into the major leagues until he was 30 years old. But once there he stayed around for 13 seasons and forged a distinguished career. He broke in with the Phillies, moved on to the Cubs and the Cardinals before coming to the Dodgers on June 12, 1940, in a memorable trade. The dealers were those two masters, Larry MacPhail in Brooklyn and Branch Rickey in St. Louis. The Dodgers acquired Davis and Joe Medwick, one of the great right-handed hitters of the time, in exchange for four lesser players. MacPhail tapped the Brooklyn Trust Company and clinched the deal by throwing in $125,000 borrowed from the bank. Rickey was pleased to get the cash. Most of Brooklyn was thrilled to get Medwick. "He's the meanest, roughest guy you can imagine," said mean, rough Leo Durocher. "He just stands up there and whales the ball—doubles, triples, homers, all over every park."

Just six days after the trade the Cardinals came to Ebbets Field, and Bob Bowman, a rangy right-hander from West Virginia, beaned Medwick. There were no batting helmets back then and as the barely conscious Medwick was carried from the field on a stretcher, the Brooklyn crowd erupted. Billy Southworth, the Cards' manager, pulled Bowman from the game "to avert a riot." As Bowman walked off the field toward the visitors' clubhouse, MacPhail jumped out of his box and punched Bowman, knocking off the pitcher's red Cardinal cap. Two Dodgers, coach Charlie Dressen and catcher Babe Phelps, then restrained MacPhail, who subsequently demanded that Bowman be arrested and charged with attempted murder. Authorities declined. They said that they lacked conclusive evidence. Medwick recovered quickly and returned to the lineup within three days. But he was not again quite the fearsome hitter he had been. (Within four years Bob Bowman dropped back to the minors.)

Coonskin Curt was as quiet a character as Ducky Medwick was flamboyant. During a World War II drive to donate blood to the armed services, one Dodger remarked, "Davis will give a pint of blood, if he has a pint of blood." But he proved a durable pitcher for the Dodgers, starting as many as 32 games in a season. He twice was chosen to pitch on Opening Day and in 1941 he pitched the first game of Brooklyn's World Series against the Yankees. Davis worked reasonably well but lost, 3 to 2.

By 1946 Davis had reached the age of 43. Time had taken its toll on his strong arm and the Dodgers sent him down to Montreal. Baseball salaries were modest back then and pitchers kept playing ball as long as they could "to keep the pork chops coming to the table."

Clay Hopper knew Rickey's credo—young position players and veteran pitchers—and he sent old Coonskin Curt to pitch Game 6. The largest crowd in the history of Delorimier, 19,171, piled in and the middle-aged hillbilly did not disappoint. Robinson cracked out two hits and scored the final run and Davis shut out the Colonels, 2 to 0. In the ninth, with Louisville threatening, Robinson ranged far to his right to start a game-saving double play.

Champions now, the Royals fled to the safety of their dressing room. A joyous crowd overran police and ushers and crowded onto the field. They chanted and they sang, *Il a gagné ses épaulettes* ("He won his bars").

When Clay Hopper appeared in a dugout, the crowd lifted him shoulder high and carted him around the field. Davis appeared. The crowd carted him around as well. Robinson, happy but uncertain, remained in the locker room. The fans chanted his name over and over. *Roh-been-son Roh-been-son.* Finally a delegation of ushers came into the clubhouse and asked Jack please to make an appearance. "People won't leave until they see you and until they leave we can't close up the ballpark. The season's over. We want to go home."

Finally Robinson emerged. "There came a demonstration seldom seen here," wrote Sam Maltin. "The crowd was hugging Jack and kissing him. He tried to explain he had to catch a plane. They wouldn't listen. They refused to hear him."

Finally Jack was able to burst free. He ran through an exit and down a street to a car that would carry him off. The crowd ran after him, shouting and cheering breathlessly.

As Robinson ran, he began to weep. "I'll tell you what made me cry," he told me. "I realized here was a big white crowd chasing after a lone Negro, not with lynching in their hearts, but love."

Has there ever been a finer moment in sport?

ELEVEN

IT HAPPENED IN BROOKLYN

RED BARBER, THE GREATEST OF DODGER broadcasters, was a formal, churchy man who seldom used profanity. But Barber summed up 1947 with expletive force. It was, he said, "the year all hell broke loose in Brooklyn."

Back then the black community in Brooklyn was confined to an east-central section called Bedford Stuyvesant. My great-grandmother, Lillie Lazar Weill, owned a formidable four-story brownstone in "Bed Stuy," at 702 Greene Avenue. For years I was lugged there every Thursday afternoon, when the housekeeper was off, and Nana Lillie peppered me with advice. At the age of six, was I self-occupied. Nana Lillie said, "You ain't the only pebble on the beach." Was I rejecting family discipline? "You dasn't do that," Nana Lillie warned. "Gawd will punish you."

Unlike certain other members of my family, she was not intellectual. Her favorite song was no Schubert Lieder, but "On the Trail of the Lonesome Pine." The book she loved most dearly was *Mrs. Wiggs of the Cabbage Patch,* a lightweight bestseller first published in 1901. But she was practical, living modestly, guarding her inheritance, and as she stared down at me through her pince-nez, a formidable grand dame.

Nana Lillie died at a great age in 1936 and the family put the brownstone up for sale. Ten years later, it was no longer an imposing single-family home. Like most of the other brownstones in rapidly changing Bedford Stuyvesant, it was broken into a warren of single-room-occupancy apartments. My family was long gone. Now poor blacks lived and died there. Slumlords ruled.

During the tormented 1930s a migration of blacks from the rural South to Bedford Stuyvesant coincided with the movement of whites to Long Island suburbs, made possible by the age of the automobile. This change of populace was sudden and dramatic.

Depression times were hard for many and indeed for New York City itself. Industrial jobs were disappearing. Old trolley lines were being abandoned. Only the tracks remained as iron skeletons. Blacks from the Carolina countryside moving into Bed Stuy had few skills to meet such urban needs as existed. There were no fields to plow, no cotton to chop in central Brooklyn. Poverty surged and as it did, there came a sharp increase in poverty's ancient handmaiden, violent crime. The streets, Gates and Throop avenues, once mostly languid, evolved into a battleground with muggers and drug dealers waging combat against others, including other blacks. Studies indicate that middle-class blacks were the main victims of black crime.

The police presence became minimal. White policemen routinely were assigned to the 79th Precinct in Bedford Stuyvesant as punishment. Northern segregation was prevailing and in time the only whites to be seen on the byways of old Bed Stuy were brave social workers and angry cops. All this tumult broke within two miles of Ebbets Field.

A concern heard in the cabinets of major-league baseball was the imagined behavior of black fans. Would blacks, attracted and turned hyperactive by the appearance of Jackie Robinson, show up drunk and bellicose, shoot craps in the bleacher aisles, get into knife fights and generally misbehave? Would they then intimidate white customers? This concern, publicly voiced by Larry MacPhail, who seldom had an unexpressed thought, was held privately by Rickey himself. He now sought help from religious leaders, mostly Baptists or followers of the African Methodist Episcopal faith. (The teetotaling Black Muslim movement was at the time insignificant in Brooklyn.)

Carlton Avenue is an undistinguished urban street, running roughly north–south on the western edge of Bedford Stuyvesant. It was the setting for the modest but functional Carlton Branch of the Brooklyn YMCA. In later years I caught Joe Black there as he kept his arm loose during the winter months and I helped coach a young and fiery all-black basketball team called the Sugar Rays. The great boxer Sugar Ray Robinson had bought the squad uniforms and warm-up jackets. These were attractive in shades of white and blue. Dodger blue. This was Brooklyn.

Blacks were welcome at the Carlton Y, as they were not at other Ys elsewhere in the borough, and Rickey chose the building as the setting for an unusual and contentious meeting on February 5, 1946. "I felt that if integration were to succeed," Rickey told me, "the black fans would have to follow a code of discipline. I was, frankly, more concerned about them than I was about Robinson."

Crowd behavior is always an issue at sports events. I have sat beside drunks at Shea Stadium and heard them curse out visiting ballplayers for nine innings. I've seen fistfights in ball club parking lots and angry and violent shoving around concession stands. Police security details are essential and sometimes, as with the tragic beating of a Giant fan outside Dodger Stadium in 2011, they are overmatched. But Rickey's mistake—and like so much about Rickey it was outsized—was to focus entirely on the behavior of those people in the crowd who were black. Some of his notes, and those of his deputy, Arthur Mann, survive in the Library of Congress and provide a vivid reading of a night gone wildly wrong.

The Dodger organization had invited what it regarded as a

representative black leadership group: teachers, lawyers, merchants, judges, dentists, doctors, morticians. No blue-collar workers were invited, nor were student groups. This was in a sense the elite addressing the elite. Rickey seldom stumbled through as bad an evening.

Crowd control was and is a significant issue at ballparks. Many ballgames are exiting, pumping up energy. Fans drink beer. Some behave badly. Off-duty policemen, armed with authority and side-arms, are as much a part of ballpark crowds as hot dog salesmen. The invitation, formally issued by the Carlton Y, stated that Rickey would address "the things which are on his mind as well as ours, in connection with the projection of what seems to be inevitable." Robinson remained on the Montreal roster. For questionable reasons, Rickey was holding back on the announcement that Robinson would join the Dodgers.

After a chicken dinner paid for by the Brooklyn organization, Rickey rose to speak to an audience of blacks. He had prepared a speech, which does not survive. However, he departed from that text. Arthur Mann reported what Rickey actually said.

Rickey declined specifically to predict that Robinson would be promoted to the Dodgers. In retrospect it seems unthinkable that Montreal's brightest star would be sentenced to another season in the minor leagues. But Rickey had a particular strategy in mind, which later proved to be shaky. "If Robinson does become the first Negro major leaguer," he said at the Carlton Y, "the biggest threat to his success is the Negro people themselves." He went on, "Every one of you will go out and form parades and welcoming committees. You'll strut. You'll wear badges. You'll hold Jackie Robinson Days and Jackie Robinson Nights. You'll get drunk. You'll fight. You'll be arrested. You'll wine and dine the player until he is fat and futile. You'll symbolize [*sic*] his importance into a national comedy and an ultimate tragedy. To prevent this, the black community must police itself."

In essence Rickey was telling a crowd of hardworking upper-middle-class blacks not to shoot craps in the aisles at Ebbets Field and, outside of the restrooms, to keep their trouser flies firmly zipped at all times. A similar talk to black leaders today would prompt hoots, jeering and walkouts. The reality in that long-ago winter of 1946–47 was that the biggest threat to Robinson's success was not the community of black baseball fans, raucous or silent, drunk or sober. It was the pervasive collection of white bigots, the Klansmen of Sportworld, who wore not bedsheets but stylish uniforms marked "Cardinals" and "Phillies" and "Reds."

Joe Bostic of the short-lived black newspaper the *People's Voice* subsequently wrote, "I've never forgiven any of these guys [Rickey's audience] for not showing resentment and indignation at Rickey's effrontery. They were adults. They were educated and intelligent people. And someone, a white man at that, is going to tell them how to act in a public place!"

But as Rickey expanded on his theme, he carried the black leaders along with his patronizing approach. Mann wrote that Rickey's words prompted "deafening applause." Before the evening was done, the blacks had agreed to create a "Master Committee" charged with controlling the enthusiasm of black fans. In time almost the entire black community of Brooklyn was involved, including bartenders who were advised to tell their patrons, "If you want to drink John Barleycorn, then stay away from the ballpark." The black sportswriter Dan Burley, who was raised in Fort Worth, warned his readers against transforming "our Yankee Stadium routines, at Negro League games, to Ebbets Field." Burley went on, "You know the Stadium routines, don't you? They are staged with beer and pop bottles. Knives sometimes. Once in a while they use blackjacks for props. The variations come when two big fat ugly women get to wrestling with each other in the grandstands, sweating and cussing like sailor-trained parrots."

I have not found a comparably appalling description of black baseball fans anywhere in the mainstream white press. Nonetheless Jackie

Robinson in Brooklyn was an idea whose time had come. It was safe even beyond a bit of after-dinner blundering by Branch Rickey and a misguided polemic typed by one Dan Burley.

◆ ◆ ◆ ◆ ◆

JACKIE HIMSELF WAS WINTERING in California. November brought the birth of Jackie Robinson Jr., a star-crossed child whose turbulent life ended in the wreckage of a sleek English sports car before he reached his 25th birthday. As a husband and now a father, Robinson faced a problem common to all young ballplayers in the employ of Rickey: money. Or rather the absence thereof. Rickey paid Robinson a $3,500 signing bonus, and $600 a month during the season. By his standards, these figures were generous. (He refused to pay anything to the Kansas City Monarchs for Robinson's contract on the grounds that the Monarchs "are not a legitimate business.")

Some forgotten black promoters out of Pittsburgh organized a barnstorming tour for the Jackie Robinson All-Stars to play exhibitions in October and November. "I came back to California with the promoters' checks amounting to about $3,500," he told me. "That would have gotten us through the winter in decent shape. But the damn checks bounced. Every one." Robinson took his case to the famous black lawyer (and later Supreme Court justice) Thurgood Marshall. This produced promises but no cash. Robinson then signed to play with a semi-pro basketball team, the Los Angeles Red Devils, for $50 a game. But at Rickey's insistence he quit after a few weeks. "He was afraid," Robinson said, "that I'd get hurt."

All but 1 of the 10 leading batsmen from the International League's season of 1946 quickly were promoted to the major leagues. The exception was the batting champion, Robinson. As hot-stove league conversations rose and fell, questions about Rickey's intent drew only stony silence from the normally loquacious executive. Jackie himself, who never criticized Rickey, told reporters, "I guess he wants to make sure my good season with the Royals was no fluke. And I can't say that I blame him."

Years later, in a number of conversations, Rickey carefully explained to me his thinking during the winter of 1946–47. The concept that Robinson's great season was a fluke, he said, "never crossed my mind. Just take one aspect of his play. Bunting. Jackie was an even better bunter than the old standard bearer, Ty Cobb. There was no question in my mind that Jackie would become a star." But Rickey himself was feeling isolated. Almost to the man, the other club presidents opposed bringing Robinson into the major leagues. The commissioner, Happy Chandler, was not overly opposed to integration, as his predecessor, the sharp-faced Kensesaw Landis, had been, but Chandler offered no public words of support. The press was mixed. For every Jimmy Cannon whose heart and prose reached out to support integration, there was a Jimmy Powers dismissing Rickey as a cheap, self-promoting bum. So it was not as if when 1947 dawned Rickey was riding a mighty tide of approval for the long overdue integration of baseball. He was not.

"Even at home," he said, "I faced opposition. My wife, Jane, a fine Christian woman, enthusiastically supported baseball integration but very firmly maintained that I should stay out of it. I was 67 years old. Jane thought the strains associated with integration would lay me underground."

Looking for support, Rickey said, he turned to the ballplayers. "The Cardinals had just beaten the Dodgers in a pennant playoff. I thought, or anyway hoped, that when the Brooklyn placers saw Robinson, saw what he could do, they would rally round and demand that I call him up. I thought they would see not only a black star but also a World Series share, perhaps $7,500 in those days, essentially doubling the annual pay of many players." As Rickey later conceded, this was a complete miscalculation. To once more cite Sartre on anti-Semitism, "bigotry is a passion." As such it can be totally dominating, like lust.

The 1947 Brooklyn Dodgers would not undergo spring training amid the stubby palmetto trees and racist cops of southern Florida. Rickey moved the Dodgers and the Montreal Royals clear out of the country to a solid, if steamy, baseball town, Havana, Cuba. Broadly, this was a land dominated by a brilliant, charming and totally corrupt former Cuban army sergeant named Fulgencio Batista.

I was invited to lunch at Batista's villa at another time. He proudly displayed a library of at least 1,000 books, all leather-bound and neatly inscribed in white ink *F. Batista*. "I have read every one," he told me. His English was excellent and he said with some pride that he came from a poor working-class family and had been a laborer in the fields, on the docks and for the railroads. "I peddled fruit," he said, "and I was a tailor and a mechanic. All this before I joined the army." He advanced to sergeant and then, through the force of his charisma and his intelligence, he became the union leader of Cuba's noncommissioned soldiers. In 1933 he led an uprising known as the Revolt of the Sergeants, and from that time forward he remained the Cuban Strongman. His absolute power endured until 1959, when Fidel Castro's revolution forced him into exile in Spain. I remember thinking once or twice during a long and genial conversation with this stocky, loquacious character that he could have me liquidated in an instant in the manner of Josef Stalin.

I did ask him about some revolutionary rumblings, explosions in public places throughout Havana. "Hah," he said. "In New York you have the Bomber Mad. Here we have *12* bombers mad."

I thought that was an amusing and harmless response and published it in *Newsweek,* where I had been working as sports editor. The Cuban authorities dissented from my viewpoint. The next issue of the magazine was censored by scissors. The Mad Bomber item was carefully cut out of every copy of *Newsweek* that entered Cuba.

The established white upper class in Cuba, wealthy from fields of sugarcane and tobacco farms, looked down on Batista as a boisterous multiracial character who was dangerous but could be bribed. Batista was of mixed European, Chinese, African and Amerindian descent. Initially he promised the Cuban people democratic socialism, but in a long and dismaying epoch, he sold out to big American industrial interests and then entered into horrific dealings with such American hoodlums as Lucky Luciano and Meyer Lansky. In time Batista ceded to the hoods control of Cuba's two preeminent tourist attractions, casino gambling and prostitution.

An American journalist named David Detzer, visiting Batista's Havana back then, wrote an unsparing description.

> Brothels flourished. A major industry grew up around them: government officials received bribes, policemen collected protection money. . . . Prostitutes could be seen standing in doorways, strolling the streets, or leaning from windows. . . . One report estimated that 11,500 of them worked their trade in Havana. . . . Beyond the outskirts of the capital, beyond the slot machines and the prostitutes, was one of the poorest—and most beautiful—countries in the Western world.

I remember walking the streets of Batista's Havana at night and being constantly solicited by big-bottomed hookers or by their acned, adolescent pimps. "Seestair," one boy called to me. *"Cinco pesos."* He then made a sucking sound. But there was no violence, none at all. American tourists were a significant asset to Cuba, and Batista's police guarded them as though they were vestal virgins.

It is an interesting irony that Rickey, the moralist, seeking to avoid American racism, put his young ballplayers into the hooker (and gonorrhea) capital of the Western world. Some, surely not all, of the ballplayers behaved like churchwardens.

Rickey divided his playing personnel into three categories: major league, minor league and black. He booked the Dodgers into the famous Hotel Nacional de Cuba, a glittering eight-story resort towering over the Malecón, Havana's great roadway overlooking the Gulf Stream and the sea. Winston Churchill had favored the Nacional, as had the movie Tarzan, Johnny Weissmuller, and the Duke of Windsor. Its elegance confused some of the ballplayers, whose customary off-the-field attire consisted of dungarees and T-shirts. Preoccupied with other matters, Rickey never did impose a dress code.

"Let me tell you about the Nacional," said Mike Gavin of Hearst's *New York Journal-American*. "The steaks were so thick you could barely cut them. Rickey picked up the basic tab for most of the writers, but there was another problem. At the Nacional I couldn't afford the tips. . . . "

Rickey booked the white Montreal Royals into the barracks at a nearby upscale military academy. The blacks, Robinson and now Don Newcombe and Roy Campanella, were dispatched to a small, drab hotel called the Boston.

"I was enraged," Robinson told me. "We quit Florida and we get segregated by the dictator of a banana republic. When I calmed down Mr. Rickey told me it was he, not Batista, who did the segregating. He said it was absolutely essential that there be no black–white conflict at this point in time within the Dodger organization. I ended up accepting his approach. I pretty much accepted all of Mr. Rickey's approaches in those days."

Ernest Hemingway's villa, Finca Vigía, was located just outside Havana. Boxing was Hemingway's favorite sport, but he followed baseball closely, and now he invited a dozen Dodgers to party at the villa. Whiskey flowed freely and after a while Hemingway began boasting of his skill with his fists. Although he was 20 years older than the ballplayers, and probably out of shape, he offered to take on any of them, one-on-one. Hugh Casey, the hulking relief pitcher from Georgia, stepped forward and within a minute knocked Hemingway clean through a glass cocktail table. Hearing the clatter and the thud, Mary Hemingway ran downstairs, helped her husband to his feet and banished the Dodgers into the tropic night. "We are never inviting ballplayers here ever again," she said to friends.

"But we were innocent," Pee Wee Reese told me. "No one lifted a finger until Hemingway started throwing punches at Big Hughie." (Curiously the lives of Hemingway and Casey ended in similar ways: suicide, a self-inflicted shotgun blast to the head. Casey died in 1951 at the age of 37 following a broken romance. Hemingway's death came a decade later when he was 61, after extended episodes of mental illness.)

Jackie Robinson underwent a difficult spring. As I've noted, he neither drank nor smoked, but Robinson was a serious major-league eater. Steak, shrimp cocktail, french fries, apple pie topped with two baseball-sized lumps of vanilla ice cream. Jack loved them all. It was said he never saw a meal he didn't like. Except in Cuba. "The food at the Boston," he said, "was so bad it actually made me sick. Everything was fried. Everything was greasy. I suffered a couple of bouts of dysentery. That didn't help my ball playing."

Nor did a decision from the Dodger general staff. Eddie Stanky was the established Brooklyn second baseman of whom it was said, "He can't run, he can't hit, he can't throw. All he can do is beat you." Pee Wee Reese was securely established at shortstop. The Dodgers put a rookie at third, John "Spider" Jorgenson, whose hustling style pleased manager Leo Durocher. But first base? Well, there was Howie Schultz, tall and strikeout prone, and "Big Ed" Stevens, who had some power but essentially was a .250 hitter. "First base," Durocher told Rickey, "is where we most need help." Rickey dispatched one of his assistants to a Cuban sporting goods store where, for $14.50, he bought a new first baseman's mitt. Rickey presented the glove to Robinson, who had never before played an inning at first base in organized ball.

"I wasn't pleased," Robinson told me. "Now, in addition to everything else, I was going to have to learn a new position." First base is different from the other infield spots in that most of the time you move not toward the ball but to the bag. Catching throws properly involves a stretch toward the ball and deft footwork. Robinson never became really comfortable at first.

For all Rickey's expertise at scouting, he was unaware that the organization already included an athlete who would become an all-star first baseman. That was 23-year-old Gil Hodges, who came up as a catcher. The Dodgers summarily assigned Hodges to Newport News of the Piedmont League for 1947, where he caught 120 games and hit .276 with good power. It was not until 1948 that Hodges became the Dodger first baseman. Robinson then moved to second (Stanky moved to the Boston Braves, charging, "I've been stabbed in the back.") When Rickey acquired third baseman Billy Cox in a trade with Pittsburgh, the Dodgers fielded one of the great defensive infields of all time: Gil Hodges, Jackie Robinson, Pee Wee Reese and Billy Cox. "Those fellers can really pluck 'em," Joe Black said in his understating way.

Reviewing this period with Robinson, I thought of Job. Jack was segregated from the white players, stuck in a third-rate hotel, fed brutal cooking and now to crack the major leagues he had to learn a strange position. "At least," I said, "Rickey neglected to ask you to sweep the clubhouse." Robinson did not crack a smile.

Attendance at Havana's Gran Stadium was disappointing, running to only about 3,500 a game. Robinson's color—and gate appeal—were not distinctive in a Caribbean setting. The Cuban Baseball League traced back to the 1870s and began including black ballplayers in 1900. All the great Negro League stars, Satchel Paige, Josh Gibson, Cool Papa Bell, played Cuban winter ball without controversy. "Negro League salaries were terrible," Joe Black said. "We had to play winter ball in Cuba to make a living."

After Rickey's athletes rounded into shape, he organized a seven-game trip across the Panama Canal Zone, where the Royals took on the Dodgers every day. Rickey met privately with Robinson and issued marching orders. "Jackie, you can forget about what you did at Montreal last year. That's ancient history so far as these men [the Dodgers] are concerned. Your minor-league record doesn't mean a thing. You'll have to make the grade on the field against major-league pitching and major-league defense, so I want you to be a whirling demon against the Dodgers. I want you to concentrate, to hit that ball, to bunt, to get on base by any and every means, I want you to run wild, to steal the pants off the Dodgers, to be the most conspicuous player on the field—but conspicuous only because of the kind of baseball that you're displaying. Not only will you impress the Dodger players, but the stories that the newspapermen send back to Brooklyn and New York will create demand on the part of the fans that you be brought up—*now*!" In an uncertain time, Rickey looked everywhere for support.

Robinson thought briefly. "I'll do my best" was all he said. Robinson then played superlative baseball and the Dodgers responded by circulating a petition to bar him from the team. Glory and infamy were marching side by side.

The story of the anti-Robinson petition has been told and mistold several times, most recently in a 2010 book called *Dixie Walker of the Dodgers: The People's Choice,* composed by Dixie's daughter, Susan, and the late, prolific Maurice Allen Rosenberg, who wrote under the name of Maury Allen for a variety of publications. Allen/Rosenberg was energetic at the keyboard but a tireless self-promoter who was often a stranger to truth. He claimed, for example, to have covered the Dodgers in their late years in Brooklyn, but during that period he was a lowly fact-checker working within the Manhattan offices of *Sports Illustrated*. Allen and Susan Walker insist in their book that Dixie did not originate the petition, which is not the story that Walker told me.

Not only did he originate the petition, he typed a letter to Rickey on March 26, 1947, requesting a trade. I found that memorable letter in one of the many bins in one of the many warehouses of the Library of Congress. Rickey had donated it to the library.

"Recently," Walker wrote in that long-ago spring, "the thought has occurred to me that a change of ball clubs would benefit both the Brooklyn baseball club and myself. Therefore I would like to be traded as soon as a deal can be arranged. For reasons I don't care to go into, I feel my decision is best for all concerned."

In those old reserve-clause days, ballplayers were given no control of their careers—highly paid peons, some called them—and Walker's letter infuriated Rickey. At a staff meeting Rickey said, "No players on the Dodgers will have anything to say about who plays or who does not play on the club. I will decide who is on it and Durocher will decide who of those who are on it does the playing."

He did not deal Walker until December. Then he shipped him with two journeymen pitchers, Hal Gregg and Vic Lombardi, to Pittsburgh. In return Rickey acquired the great left-hander Preacher Roe and Billy Cox, at his peak arguably the best defensive third baseman of all time. Trade? This was more like grand larceny.

Dixie Walker was a marvelous ballplayer, a fine defensive right fielder with a strong arm and, when it came time to bat, a picture swing. He thrived on clutch situations and, as Brooklyn fans warmed to him, he won the National League batting championship in 1943, hitting .357.

Dixie and I met in 1976 at Dodger Stadium in Los Angeles, where he was working as batting coach and had just finished giving tips to Dusty Baker, later a prominent manager, and Steve Yeager, later a convert to Judaism. Baker was black and Yeager was white. Coach Walker did not seem to notice any difference.

Walker approached me and asked if we could drink some wine together after that night's game. Baseball is a world of beer and the wine suggestion surprised and pleased me. Walker turned out to be an oenophile and we sipped a marvelous Margaux. He told me of a recent trip to England, where he had journeyed to seek out family roots, and he spoke vividly of the Salisbury Cathedral and the flowering gardens of Devonshire. Not, clearly, basic baseball talk. Then Walker got to the point of our meeting. "I organized that petition in 1947 not because I had anything against Robinson personally or against Negroes generally. I had a wholesale hardware business in Birmingham and people told me I'd lose my business if I played ball with a black man. That's why I started the petition. It was the dumbest thing I did in all my life and if you ever get a chance sometime, write that I am deeply sorry."

I used Walker's remarks in my 1993 book, *The Era,* but the *New York Times* (and others) ignored my Walker reporting and didn't get around to covering this vital story for another 17 years. I am surely not the only soul who misses the *New York Herald Tribune.*

Times columnist Harvey Araton did a workmanlike job with Maury Allen's book on Walker, but followed up with a tendentious blog under the headline: "Does Dixie Walker Deserve Scorn or Sympathy?" Of course he deserves both, but the point of his experience is more complex than Araton understood. Ol' Dixie changed and grew, moving from segregationist outfielder to integrationist batting coach. As he aged, Walker grew in understanding and compassion. During a lifetime a man can indeed be modified. (I recall here Robert Frost's witty observation: "I never dared be radical when young, for fear it would make me conservative when old.") Shakespeare's commentary was matchless. "One man in his time plays many parts."

Robinson never grew close to Walker. "I think in 1947," he told me, "I was on base three times when Walker hit a home run. But I never stopped at home plate and offered a hand. Why not? I thought Walker would not take my hand. Then we would have had the beginnings of an incident."

Again not getting the point, Araton wrote in the *Times* that Robinson refused to shake Walker's hand as a protest against bigotry. The *Times* error here misses many things, including the fact that for all his fiery nature, Jack never was a vengeful man.

◆ ◆ ◆ ◆ ◆

RICKEY SCHEDULED EXHIBITION GAMES between the Dodgers and Montreal at Ebbets Field on April 9 and 10. "My plan," Rickey told me, "was to have Durocher say to the newspapermen that all he needed to win the pennant was a good first baseman and that Jackie Robinson was the best first baseman in sight."

As pointed out earlier, on April 9, Commissioner Chandler arbitrarily suspended Durocher for the remainder of the year "for conduct detrimental to baseball." Chandler never explained his decision. Durocher had some friends who were gambling men. He was himself a high-stakes poker player. His adulterous affair with the Mormon actress Laraine Day created a sex scandal that delighted the tabloids. The Brooklyn Catholic Youth Organization threatened to boycott Dodger games if the libidinous Durocher continued to manage. "The Catholic Church," someone remarked, "never boycotted Mussolini or Hitler. Just Leo Durocher."

It is impossible to paint Durocher in soft colors, but the sheer arrogance of Chandler's decision and his czarist refusal to discuss his reasoning would cost him his job. In 1951, after one term as commissioner, he was dismissed and replaced by Ford Frick. He reacted with rage. "It was really those New York drinking bastards from Toots Shor's that did me in," Chandler wrote me. "Like those friends of yours, Red Whiskeyhead Smith and Frank Whiskeyhead Graham."

In Brooklyn, Rickey had to find a manager. On April 19, while a search was under way, Arthur Mann, Rickey's deputy, walked through the Ebbets Field press box distributing a news release. It read: "Brooklyn announces the purchase of the contract of Jack Roosevelt Robinson from Montreal. He will report immediately. [Signed] Branch Rickey."

Jimmy Cannon of the *New York Post* stood up and slowly walked to a seat occupied by Lester Rodney of the Communist *Daily Worker*. Intensely and sincerely Cannon said, "Congratulations."

TWELVE

RECESSIONAL

The tumult and the shouting dies;
The Captains and the Kings depart. . . .
—RUDYARD KIPLING

THE LAST-MINUTE PROMOTION, AND RICKEY'S unbending frugality, created an immediate housing problem for Robinson. As soon as Jack joined the Dodgers, Rachel and the baby, now four months old, flew from Los Angeles to Idlewild (now JFK) Airport, where Jack met them and took them to his quarters. These were a single room in a commercial hotel called the McAlpin that rose 25 stories tall at Herald Square, Broadway and 34th Street, a neighborhood dominated by the Empire State Building and Macy's department store. "It was basically a miserable setup," Robinson told me.

The three were crammed into a single hotel room, no kitchen. Rachel bought a hot plate to warm the baby's formula. She set up a makeshift clothesline in the bathroom where the baby's diapers could dry. "There was room service," Robinson said, "but I couldn't afford it; Rachel and I had to take turns getting our meals in a cafeteria down back of the hotel. She brought little Jackie to Opening Day at

Ebbets Field and he caught cold. Then the switch in water from California to New York upset his stomach. So there we were trying to make do in a single room with very little money and a sick baby."

"What was Rickey paying you?" I asked.

"The minimum. All rookies got the minimum. Five thousand for the season. That did not go very far in New York City.

"We liked to take the baby outside in his carriage, for fresh air, but this wasn't one of those easy walks in a park. Thirty-Fourth Street. Busses. Trucks. Noise. Exhaust fumes. All part of my family's welcome to the major leagues."

As we have noted, Robinson's Opening Day in Jersey City had been a glittering triumph. That was not the case on April 15, when the 1947 season began in Brooklyn. The Dodgers took on the Boston Braves, who led with their ace, Johnny Sain, a master of the breaking ball and a 20-game winner that year. Newspapers reported "a sprinkling of black fans" in the stands, but the game did not sell out. The paid attendance was announced at 25,623, which meant there were about 6,500 empty seats. (The all-white Yankees, playing that same date in the stadium, drew more than 39,000 fans, and Aqueduct Racetrack, with an undistinguished card, attracted 27,306. Historic though Robinson's Brooklyn debut was, it was no better than the third most popular sporting event in New York City that chilly April day.)

Nor did the newspapers respond appropriately. Their big baseball story continued to be the banishing of Leo Durocher. Arthur Daley's column in the *New York Times* was typical. "The little man who wasn't there would have been proud of his Dodgers yesterday," Daley began. "Leo Durocher was missing." Daley did not get around to mentioning Robinson until his eighth paragraph and the reference was less than flattering. "The debut of Jackie Robinson was quite uneventful, even though he had the unenviable distinction of snuffing out a rally by hitting into a double play. His dribbler through the box in the fifth might have though gone for a safety, but shortstop Dick Culler, playing in on the grass, made a diving stop, threw to second for a force while prostrate on the ground and Connie Ryan nailed the swift Robbie at first for a dazzling twin killing."

Hitless though Robinson was, he still played an important role in the game, which Brooklyn won, 6 to 3. With a man on first and Brooklyn losing by a run in the seventh inning, Robinson deftly bunted toward first base. Earl Torgeson, the Braves' lanky first baseman, fielded the bunt. Then his hurried throw toward first base hit Robinson on a shoulder and carried into right field. This could have been scored a base hit, but was not. Whatever, the error placed Dodgers at second and third. When "Pistol Pete" Reiser lined a double to left, both runners scored, Robinson with the run that put the Dodges into the lead.

Afterward a reporter asked Robinson if tension explained his failure to hit safely.

"Not at all," Jack said.

"What was it then?"

"Try Johnny Sain's curveball."

The next day Robinson dragged a bunt against a left-handed pitcher named Glenn Elliott. That became his first major-league hit. His batting picked up markedly when the Dodgers moved to the Polo Grounds in Manhattan for a weekend series against their traditional uptown antagonists, the New York Giants.

In Durocher's absence, Rickey appointed the crafty Maine man Clyde Sukeforth as Dodger manager pro tem. But Sukeforth preferred life as a scout and coach and troubleshooter to the heavy day-to-day responsibility of managing. He turned down the permanent appointment. Rickey next contacted Joe McCarthy, who had enjoyed great success managing the mighty Yankee teams of the 1930s. McCarthy was also famous for his Ten Commandments of Baseball Success. These were:

1. Nobody ever became a ballplayer by walking after a ball.
2. You will never become a .300 hitter unless you take the bat off your shoulder.
3. An outfielder who throws in back of a runner is locking the barn after the horse is stolen.
4. Keep your head up and you may not have to keep it down.
5. When you start to slide, SLIDE. He who changes his mind may have to change a good leg for a bad one.
6. Do not alibi on bad hops. Anyone can field the good ones.
7. Always run them out. You never can tell.
8. Do not quit.
9. Try not to find too much fault with the umpires. You cannot expect them to be as perfect as you are.
10. A pitcher who hasn't control hasn't anything.

Now almost 70 years old, retired in Buffalo and fighting alcoholism, McCarthy also declined the Brooklyn job. In California Casey Stengel, then managing the Oakland Oaks of the Pacific Coast League, told reporters that he really didn't want to go back to Brooklyn, where he had broken in as an outfielder 36 years before. But was Stengel actually asked to return to Flatbush? Rickey would neither confirm nor deny that rumor. A plus would have been Stengel's popularity with the press. A minus was his attitude toward Negroes. He was managing the Yankees in 1955 when the gifted black catcher Elston Howard joined the team. After a while Stengel complained, "With all the fast jigaboos there are in the world, why do I get stuck with a slow one." To make a point that may already be obvious, Stengel would not have been an ideal manager for Jackie Robinson.

Rickey felt increasingly discomfited. He had a strong team with a pioneering black man but here in the first week of this dramatic season the strong team and the pioneering black were playing without a permanent manager. That way could lead to chaos. Approaching desperation, Rickey wired a crony, 62-year-old Burt "Barney" Shotton, in Lake Wales, Florida. "Come to Brooklyn at once. Tell nobody. Say nothing."

Shotton had played outfield for the Cardinals and the Browns during Rickey's St. Louis days. In the early 1920s, when Rickey was field manager of the Cardinals, his own bristling religiosity let him suit up only six days a week. Barney Shotton stepped in on the Christian Sabbath. He became known as Rickey's "Sunday manager." Shotton later managed seven days a week but without notable success in Philadelphia and Cincinnati.

Surprised when Rickey offered him a golden apple, Shotton quickly accepted with one proviso. At his age he would not be comfortable getting into uniform. He would manage wearing street clothes and a Dodger cap. Under the rules of baseball, this limited his range to clubhouse and dugout. Once a game started, he could not walk onto the playing field to talk to a pitcher or to argue with an umpire. Agitated, Rickey accepted Shotton's condition and the new man, a virtual unknown in the New York area, began to settle in. Over the next four years the Dodgers won two pennants and Shotton is widely regarded as a success. "His calm demeanor," someone has written, "provided the quiet leadership the Dodgers needed." But, particularly in his effect on Rickey's career, Old Barney Shotton was a nothing less than a disaster.

Dealing with the press, now the media, is a significant aspect of major-league managing. There are daily press conferences before and after games, as well as individual interviews. No fewer than 10 newspapermen covered the 1947 Dodgers every day. Keeping this journalistic gumbo soup below the boiling point was difficult.

Like Rickey, Shotton had been an Ohio farm boy, but he lacked his boss's education and sophistication. He thought it was funny to address Harold Rosenthal of the *Herald Tribune* as "Rosenberg." Harold was not amused. He took to calling Shotton "that Jew-hating old son of a bitch."

Dick Young was increasingly powerful at the *Daily News,* which had amassed that staggering circulation, more than two million copies a day. Young demanded special treatment in many ways, including being slipped exclusive news leaks. Shotton offered Young no deference or any leaks. Without realizing it, the new manager faced a crouching tiger.

After Dodger pitching had folded, costing the team a game, Young began his story with that brilliant angry lead: "The tree that grows in Brooklyn is an apple tree and the apples are in the throats of the Dodgers." Young told me he meant not everybody, but the pitchers, specifically Ralph Branca, were choking. Open warfare now existed between the *Daily News* and the Brooklyn Dodger management. Calculating, ambitious Walter O'Malley began using the conflict as a hammer to weaken Rickey's position with the other Dodger trustees. "This fellow Young is damaging our investment," O'Malley said many times. "How long can we allow this to go on?"

Why then didn't Rickey arrange a private meeting with Young? A man-to-man talk and some flattery might have softened a reporter whose ego stretched from Borough Hall at least to Canarsie. But Rickey regarded Young as a vulgar, uneducated lout, certainly not his equal in any way. "To meet with Young," he told me, "I would have had to go down in the gutter with him and I'm not good at that, going down in the gutter." As Rickey spoke, his face turned harsh. His eyes showed hatred.

The tabloid warfare persisted until the scheming O'Malley gained control of the team in 1950 and drove Shotton and Rickey out of town. ("O'Malley," Rickey pronounced subsequently, "is the most devious man I ever met.") As the new overall boss, O'Malley made a shrewd deputy, Emil "Buzzie" Bavasi, vice president in charge of the Dodgers. The other vice president, Fresco Thompson, would run the farm system, which numbered as many as 22 teams.

Buzzie Bavasi had a prime directive: Mollify the *Daily News* and Rowdy Richard Young.

Bavasi took Young shopping and bought him sportswear. He found Young a rent-controlled apartment within walking distance of Ebbets Field. He offered a variety of news leaks. When not axe grinding, Young was a very good reporter. The news leaks made him seem even better than he was.

Bavasi's crowning accomplishment was setting up Young with a pretty, bucolic woman in Vero Beach, the shapely star of a local bowling team. Young was married, but the Vero Beach beauty quickly became his mistress. Soon she was making trips with the team, all expenses paid by the Dodgers. In a highly emotional episode Young said to me, "I've played around a lot in my time and now God is getting even. He's made me fall in love. But I can't marry her, now or ever. My wife is Catholic and she won't give me a divorce." While taking the mistress to bars and bed, and spending happy nights in hotel rooms, Young never again criticized Dodger management until that startling day in 1957 when a team spokesman announced that the ball club was being moved to Los Angeles.

For the most part Robinson kept clear of the tabloid feud. Young never became his champion. "He is too swelled-headed for me," said Young, who himself obviously was no exemplar of modesty. Rather than the press, a first focus for Robinson was the establishment of relationships with his white teammates. He said, "I don't anticipate trouble. I've been on teams with whites before." But his overall reception was not enthusiastic. Spider Jorgensen, the rookie third baseman, had played with Robinson in Montreal and became friendly. Reese at first was courteous but distant. Eddie Stanky greeted Robinson warmly because, he said, "We all gotta pull together as a team." But Carl Furillo would not speak to Robinson. He told Lester Rodney, "I just don't like playing with no niggers." Others, such as Dixie Walker and the veteran pitcher Hal Gregg, tried to ignore Robinson's presence. In the locker room and in the dugout there was zero small talk between Jack and other members of the team.

The shower room at Ebbets Field had no individual stalls. After the games, the players stripped naked and stood under individual nozzles soaping themselves. At first Robinson did not enter the shower room until the last white player had left. Then one day in late April, Al Gionfriddo, a stumpy reserve outfielder from Pennsylvania, said, "Hey, Robinson. You're as good as anybody else. Come on and take a shower with me." With that simple, forceful statement from an obscure backup player, the shower-room color line in Brooklyn vanished.

Hugh Casey, the big relief pitcher from Georgia, was a curious case. He spent some time with Robinson, offering pointers on covering first base, but he went absolutely wild during a poker game. The Dodgers were traveling to Boston by train and Reese made it a point to invite Robinson into Pullman car cards. Casey lost repeatedly and began muttering. Then suddenly he reached across the table, placed a large white hand on Robinson's head and rubbed. "Jackie, man," Casey said. "Am I in lousy luck today! Got to change my luck, boy. Back home in Georgia when my poker luck ran bad, I'd jes' go out and rub me the tits of the biggest, blackest nigger woman I could find. You're the closest thing around here to a nigger lady, even though you got no tits."

The table fell silent. Robinson told me that Casey's words so shocked him that for a moment he could not see. Quite suddenly his throat went dry. Then, under tremendous control, he said to Casey, "Just deal, man. Just deal." And the game resumed.

Robinson's bat had come to life at the Polo Grounds, where

Shotton made his debut, managing in a topcoat and a pearl gray fedora. Starting on April 18, the Dodgers played a short set there against the Giants, and now large crowds began turning out. Many black fans made the relatively short walk down from Harlem into Coogan's Hollow.

During the 1940s, a number of academics, including William Shockley, who later won a Nobel Prize in physics, were investigating the success of blacks in sport. Joe Louis, the Brown Bomber, had been heavyweight champion for 11 years. Jesse Owens's performance in the 1936 Nazi Olympics established him as the greatest sprinter ever. Other blacks were almost as successful. The academics were working in an uncertain field known as eugenics. At length Shockley and others maintained they discovered that among certain West African tribes the heel bones of males were exceptionally long. This, Shockley said, explained blacks' speed afoot and general athletic success.

On that April day, his Polo Grounds debut, Jackie Robinson came up in the third inning against a smallish left-hander named Dave Koslo. He lined the third pitch deep into the upper stands in left—his first major-league home run. A number of Dodgers lined up near home plate to shake Robinson's hand. The crowd, particularly the blacks in an assemblage of 37,000 fans, cheered mightily. In the press box the witty sportswriter Heywood Hale Broun made a home run notation in his score book. Then deadpan Woodie Broun said, "That's because their heels are longer."

Afterward Red Smith wrote in his *Herald Tribune* column, View of Sport:

> Burt Shotton saw for himself that Jackie Robinson isn't exactly bad. Robinson hit a fierce line drive for a home run, hit a fiercer one that became a double play through the splendid offices of the Giants rookie Lucky Lohrke, and finally dropped a single in short right. Even before this, alert souvenir hawkers were offering lapel pins, which read, "I'm for Jackie Robinson."

On April 22 the Dodgers began a three-game series against the Philadelphia Phillies at Ebbets Field. "Ben Chapman, our manager, was one forceful character," the late Robin Roberts told me over drinks three years ago at the Otesaga Hotel in Cooperstown. Roberts, one of the best right-handers in the annals, was a 20-game winner in Philadelphia for six consecutive seasons. "Before that first game against Robinson and the Dodgers," he said, "Chapman ordered all of us, the whole team, to get on Robinson in any damn way we could. Anybody who failed to get on Robinson would be fined $50, serious money back then."

Robinson later recounted to me some of the slurs that came bellowing out of the Philadelphia dugout.

"They're waiting for you in the jungles, black boy."

"Back to the cotton fields, nigger."

"How did your mother like fucking that ape?"

During the series Robinson went only 3 for 12. He said he was unprepared for the onslaught because he thought the Phillies as a northern team would give him no particular trouble. But here they were defiling him and in his own home ballpark, Ebbets Field. Robinson remembered Eddie Stanky shouting at the Phillies, "Fucking cowards. Why don't you yell at somebody who can answer back!" He also remembered to the end of his days a trim Phillie infielder, Lee "Jeep" Handley, apologizing to him.

A few newspapermen learned of the Phillies' behavior. Typically the *New York Times* ignored the issue but Dan Parker, who wrote trenchant columns for the tabloid *Daily Mirror,* cheered Robinson as "the only gentleman in the entire incident." Walter Winchell, the country's preeminent gossip columnist, heard about Chapman and in his lair at the Cub Room of the Stork Club Winchell said of Chapman, "I'm gonna make a big *hit* on that bigot." Alarmed, commissioner Happy Chandler stepped in, offering admonishments. He then ordered Chapman to pose for a picture with Robinson. The photograph survives. The two are holding the ends of a Louisville Slugger. Neither appears happy. Each man is looking away from the other. A year later the Phillies fired Chapman and he never managed in the major leagues again. (He did resurface as a coach with Cincinnati in 1952. That season the Reds finished sixth.)

Afterward Rickey cited the Philadelphia story as critical to Robinson's acceptance by the Dodgers. "Chapman did more than anyone else to unite the team," he said. "When Chapman poured out that string of objectionable abuse, he solidified and united 30 men." (Not quite. Dixie Walker and Bobby Bragan still demanded to be traded away from Robinson and Carl Furillo continued to grumble about playing with him.)

At the Otesaga Hotel years later Robin Roberts concluded his Philadelphia memories in an interesting way. "After a while," he said, "Chapman came to realize that Robinson usually played his best when he felt the heat was on. So then Chapman issued a new directive. The $50 fine stuck. But now it went against anyone who *did* get on Robinson.

"'Don't stir up the jungle boy,' Chapman would say.

"I never liked Robinson myself, but I have to give you this. He was one hell of a competitor."

◆ ◆ ◆ ◆ ◆

THE UNCHALLENGEABLE TRIUMPH OF baseball integration was assured soon afterward during a period of roughly seven days in May. One factor was the failure of a massive racist movement. The other was a simple touch of friendship.

I have previously published some details of the great anti-Robinson strike, but the murky tide of revisionist history has since blurred truth and impels me here to tell the story in full, this time including major facts that I did not earlier have at my command. The strike could well have made the National League, and perhaps all major-league baseball, a disaster area. The piece that saved the game ran on May 9, 1947, as a copyrighted story in the *New York Herald Tribune.*

In an earnestly researched but ultimately plodding book, *Baseball's Great Experiment,* the late Jules Tygiel wrote, "[Stanley] Woodward often receives credit for averting a player rebellion [against integration]. This was not the case." Tygiel, a college professor in Northern California, had never covered major-league baseball on a daily basis, nor was he aware of the workings of big-city newspapers. These shortcomings probably led him to a conclusion that was thumpingly incorrect.

In a more recent book, this one claiming to cover Robinson's first major-league season, a journalist named Jonathan Eig is also dismissive of Woodward, who was the finest sports editor of his time. Eig sometimes writes effectively, but he simply does not understand what went on in 1947, a season that unfolded roughly two decades before he was born.

One man who immediately understood Woodward's achievement was Jimmy Cannon, Woodward's intense, complex contemporary on the *New York Post.* All but forgotten now, Cannon was one of the most eloquent and passionate of all the columnists who reported and typed for newspapers in their heyday.

The idea of a player's strike originated in the busy brain of that exceptional and contradictory character Fred "Dixie" Walker of Brooklyn and the Confederacy. The issue, as Walker rationalized it and later carefully explained it to me, was not about banning blacks from organized baseball. Rather, he said, it was about establishing the right of professional athletes to chose with whom and against whom they would play—and with whom or against whom they would *not* play. At the time I was too startled by Walker's sweeping assertion to put up much of an argument. But no such players' right exists. However lofty their salaries, ballplayers are employees. In a capitalist society the team's owner and management decide who will play, whether the management is brilliant (Larry MacPhail, Branch Rickey in Brooklyn) or blundering (Peter O'Malley, Frank McCourt in Los Angeles). In a communist society, as I learned while traveling through Canada with the great Central Soviet Army hockey team, the choice of players rests with coaches working under commissars. Nowhere do pro players get to pick their teammates or their opponents. That simply is the way things are.

But Walker recognized that a case for players' rights, however implausible, would play better with the press and public than a campaign for a continued ban against blacks. After the dramatic days of World War II, America was becoming a more open community. Besides, the Holocaust had given bigotry a bad name.

Walker's original idea called for a league-wide strike. Working in as much secrecy as possible, he recruited leaders on other National League teams. He found confederates in Ewell Blackwell, a star pitcher with the Reds, and first baseman Phil Cavarretta, who later managed the Chicago Cubs. Neither was a Southerner. Cavarretta was born in Chicago. Blackwell grew up in Fresno, California. But the key people with the St. Louis Cardinals were as Southern as grits. Those included were Enos Slaughter from North Carolina, Marty Marion from South Carolina and the team captain, Terry Moore, a native of Alabama. I have not been able to learn the names of the other Walker allies on other teams. Some surely existed but their secret remains buried in their coffins. (Walker himself died of stomach cancer at the age of 71 on May 17, 1982.)

The story burst forth in the city edition of the *Herald Tribune* dated May 9, 1947. Copies went on sale at about 10:30 the night before. The Associated Press picked up the story crediting the *Herald Tribune* and a brief version, citing the AP—but not the *Trib*—appeared in late editions of the dormant *New York Times*. Editors at the *Times* made a deliberate decision not to credit the *Herald Tribune* as the source of the story. The legal issue here may be somewhat muddy, but the moral issue is clear. The *Times* pilfered and minimized Woodward's scoop. Here is all the *Times,* America's self-proclaimed Paper of Record, published on a movement that could have shattered the National League.

> **FRICK SAYS CARDS' STRIKE PLAN AGAINST NEGRO DROPPED**
>
> Ford Frick, National League president, said last night a threatened strike by the St. Louis Cardinals against the presence of Negro First Baseman Jackie Robinson in a Brooklyn Dodger uniform has been averted, The Associated Press reported.
>
> Frick said that Sam Breadon, owner of the Cardinals, came to New York last week and informed him that he understood there was a movement among the Cardinals to strike in protest during their just-concluded series with the Dodgers if Robinson was in the line-up.
>
> "I didn't have to talk to the players myself. Mr. Breadon did the talking to them. From what Breadon told me afterward the trouble was smoothed over. I don't know what he said to them, who the ringleader was, or any other details," Frick said.
>
> Asked if he intended to take any action, Frick said he would have to investigate further before he could make any decision.
>
> The National League president said he had not conferred with Baseball Commissioner A. B. (Happy) Chandler concerning the matter.

The *Tribune*'s headline and subhead went like this:

NATIONAL LEAGUE AVERTS STRIKE OF CARDINALS AGAINST ROBINSON'S PRESENCE IN BASEBALL

General League Walkout Planned by Instigators

The story carried the byline of the sports editor, Stanley Woodward, and a copyright notice that the *New York Times* chose to ignore. Spectacular as this scoop was, the *Tribune* published it not on page 1, where it would have boosted newsstand sales, but back on page 24, where it was invisible, unless of course you had already bought the paper. The managing editor responsible for this misplay, George Anthony Cornish, was, Woodward pointed out, "a native of the Hookworm Belt." (Actually, a village in Alabama called Demopolis.) Woodward felt that Cornish was so excessively cautious that he nicknamed the editor "Old Double-Rubber." Woodward added, "In this instance, caution and boyhood bigotry combined. Old Double-Rubber couldn't kill my story, but he could keep it the hell off the front page, which is what he did. Obviously that night my story should have led the paper."

Woodward was a large, myopic, powerful man with a strong tenor voice. (I am reminded of other large, powerful tenors, Jack Dempsey and Jackie Robinson.) Woodward's first name, which he never used, was Rufus. Generally he was called Coach. Woodward ran the *Tribune* sports section when I began working there, first as a nighttime copyboy at $26.50 a week. Woodward sometimes sent me downstairs to the storied saloon the Artist and Writers Restaurant to buy him "a couple of packs of Camels." Invariably he handed me two dollars. Back then a pack cost a quarter in a machine and when I returned Woodward said, also invariably, "Keep the change, son." Given the pay scale of a copyboy, the tip was good enough for a modest meal—salisbury steak, a Mrs. Wagner's Home-Baked Apple Pie and muddy coffee—in the *Herald Tribune*'s cafeteria. Although many *Tribune* people sent me on many errands during my copyboy years—executives, clerks, Pulitzer Prize winners—Woodward was the only person kind enough and generous enough to tip.

He encouraged my writing and in time, joined by our love of journalism, poetry, lucid prose and well-played sports, we became close friends. Over the years he told me much of how he came to write the great Robinson strike story.

The *Tribune* employed a debonair Canadian, Cecil Rutherford Rennie, called Rud, as one of its senior baseball writers, and Rennie developed friends, both male and female, all around the major-league circuit, which then ran from New England to Missouri. One such was Dr. Robert Hyland, an orthopedist whom the St. Louis Cardinals used as team physician and the St. Louis Browns engaged as a consulting specialist. Hyland, a prominent figure on the St. Louis sports scene, liked to call himself "the surgeon general of baseball."

Rennie came into St. Louis with the New York Yankees in May 1947. The Yankees were about to play and outclass the St. Louis Browns. Rennie, a highly skilled typist, filed a fast piece and then joined his friend Hyland and some others for an evening of drink and song. "Not opera," Rennie told me, "or even Broadway songs. Just barbershop stuff. 'Sweet Adeline' . . . 'If You Were the Only Girl in the World' . . ."

As the group sang and drank whiskey that long-ago night hard by the Mississippi River, Doc Hyland turned to his friend and said, "Rud, it's a shame you aren't covering the Dodgers. If you were, you'd get one helluva story."

"What might that be?" Rennie said.

"Strike," Hyland said. "The whole [Cardinal] team is going to strike, rather than take the field with that colored boy."

"Robinson?"

"You got it," Hyland said. "And not just the Cardinals. If this thing goes through the way they're planning it, no team in the National League will take the field on May 21. Not one. And no team will take the field again until the Dodgers release Robinson. What I understand is that the men want the basic contracts changed giving them the right to approve or disapprove of the people they play with and play against." Incredibly, Dixie Walker's wild scheme was coming to life.

Rennie was sober enough to think sensibly. Hyland was right. A big-league baseball strike, however insane, would be one helluva story. But Rennie felt he could not be the person to write it. His friendship with Hyland was widely known. If he wrote the piece himself, Rennie feared, Hyland would be suspected as the source. He was the Cardinals' team doctor and here he was, ignoring medical confidentiality, spilling the team's darkest secret. Rennie went to a telephone and quietly passed along Hyland's words to Stanley Woodward, who was relaxing with his wife, Ricie, and a five-to-one martini, in his comfortable apartment on Park Avenue in New York. After Rennie hung up, the Big Coach put down his drink. Then he exploded into action.

Both logic and tradition have made protecting sources the prime commandment in newspaper work. Indeed, newspaper people are forever campaigning—with limited success—to have the confidentiality of sources shielded by law.

Close as we were, Woodward would not tell me much about how he proceeded to confirm Dr. Robert Hyland's astonishing tip. The identities of most of his secondary sources thus are lost. Which is not to say, as some new journalists do, that they did not exist. The *Herald Tribune,* highly reputable and essentially conservative, for decades retained a renowned libel lawyer, E. Douglas Hamilton of New York. The lawyer reviewed Woodward's reporting, in utmost confidence, before recommending that the story be published. Shielded by lawyer–client confidentiality, Woodward disclosed everything he had and did to Doug Hamilton. Without a shield, speaking with me, Woodward later said, "I talked to Ford. I'll tell you that much. And no more."

Ford Christopher Frick, an Indiana native, had been a sportswriter for Hearst newspapers in New York, a baseball publicist and now in 1947 he was president of the National League. Frick confirmed Hyland's tip and gave Woodward the text of a statement he had prepared for delivery to the entire Cardinal squad.

> If you strike, you will be suspended from the League. You will find the friends you think you have in the press box will not support you. You will be outcasts. I do not care if half the league strikes. Those who do will encounter quick retribution. All will be suspended, I don't care if it wrecks the National League for five years. This is the United States of America and one citizen has as much right to play as another. You will find if you go through with your intention that you will have been guilty of complete madness.

Woodward called this statement "the most noble ever made by a baseball man." In another century, few would disagree. But in the excitement of the moment, Woodward made a mistake. Frick did not deliver his powerful message to the insurgent ballplayers. Instead he handed it to Sam Breadon, a tough onetime auto mechanic, later a dealer of luxurious Pierce-Arrows and now a self-made millionaire who owned the Cardinals. "I'd like you to pass this on to your team, Sam," Frick said quietly and very firmly.

Tough old Sam Breadon read quickly. Then he nodded. He did not argue. The Cardinals assembled in a clubhouse at Ebbets Field "to talk about pitching problems." The real topic was hidden in utmost secrecy. There, in the old Brooklyn ballpark, Breadon read to his ballplayers Frick's ringing and threatening words.

(Frick later became baseball commissioner and as such he

allowed the Dodgers and Giants to abandon the New York area after the 1957 season, with no replacement teams in sight. Simply wielding a pen he summarily could have stopped both moves. A rational and orderly expansion to California might have followed. Where Frick truly was a hero in 1947, taking on a lynch mob wearing Cardinal red, to many Dodger and Giant fans 10 years later he became a bum. The evidence is irrefutable. Ford Frick was unwilling or afraid to grapple with the Big Oom, Walter O'Malley, conqueror of Branch Rickey, trader of Jackie Robinson and baseball's all-time ultimate power broker.

Hero to bum, that is a not an atypical career in the mercurial business of sports.)

Woodward's story, in the May 9th *New York Herald Tribune,* began:

> A National League players' strike, instigated by some of the St. Louis Cardinals against the presence in the league of Jackie Robinson, Negro first-baseman, has been averted temporarily and perhaps permanently quashed.
>
> In recent days Ford Frick, president of the National League, and Sam Breadon, president of the St. Louis club, have been conferring with St. Louis players. Mr. Breadon [a native of New York City] flew east when he heard of the projected strike. The story that he came east to consult with Eddie Dyer, manager, about the lowly state of the St. Louis club, was fictitious. He came on a much more serious errand.
>
> The strike, formulated by certain St. Louis players [outfielder Enos Slaughter, shortstop Marty Marion, team captain Terry Moore], was instigated by a member of the Brooklyn Dodgers who has since recanted [our new old friend, that Southern sipper of fine margaux, Fred "Dixie" Walker].
>
> It is understood that the players involved—and the recalcitrants are not all Cardinals—will say that their objective is to gain the right to have a say on who shall be eligible to play in the major leagues. . . .

> This story is factually and thoroughly substantiated. The St. Louis players involved will unquestionably deny it. We doubt, however, if Frick and Breadon will go that far. A return of no comment from either or both will serve.

When "Spike" Claassen, the deputy sports editor of the Associated Press in New York, reached Frick, he drew a somewhat vague reply. "Any player who tries to strike," Frick said, "will leave me no alternative but to suspend him indefinitely. That's all I can tell you."

He was somewhat more assertive with a reporter for the *Sporting News*. Here Frick said, "The National League stands firmly behind Jackie Robinson."

After that Frick retreated into silence. He came from a generation of baseball people who believed that when something nasty happened in the game, hush it up. Tell no one, least of all reporters. Why then did Frick speak with Stanley Woodward? Because the Coach had the goods on baseball and Frick was sensible enough to realize that a roused Woodward could write up a mighty storm.

Highly pleased, Woodward wrote a few days later, "It can now be honestly doubted that the boys from the Hookworm Belt will have the nerve to foist their quaint sectional folklore on the rest of the country." But even as Woodward typed, a powerful disinformation campaign was breaking loose.

Protecting his investment, or so he believed, Sam Breadon told outright lies. Robinson trouble? Tut, tut, my man. Sheer nonsense. "I came to New York only because my team was losing ballgames. I spoke to team leaders, Terry Moore and Marty Marion, about stories of excessive drinking on my club."

Bob Broeg, the preeminent baseball writer in St. Louis and usually a solid reporter, in this instance disgraced himself. There was no strike threat, he said, never was. Woodward? "The son of a bitch is guilty of barnyard journalism. He's written chicken shit." For the rest of his life, Broeg preached this nonsense. Too many people listened.

In 1995, Stan Musial wrote, or lent his name to, a book foreword in which he described baseball's color line as "reprehensible. I can thank Mr. Rickey for making it possible for me to have teammates like Curt Flood and Bill White. You know," Musial went on, "Willie Mays says that when he looks at his wallet he thinks of Jackie Robinson. Well, he should think of Rickey, too!"

But where was Stan the Man, the greatest of Cardinal players, in the contentious spring of 1947? Conflicted by his sense of right and wrong and by his sense of loyalty to fellow Cardinals, Musial was paralyzed into silence. He did not confirm the strike story for the rest of his life. But he did arrange for me to meet with Terry Moore in 1991, and he told Moore that I was "fair-minded." The result was nothing less than a final and conclusive confirmation.

Terry Bluford Moore, called by Joe DiMaggio "the greatest center fielder I ever saw," and a longtime Cardinal team captain, was retired to a modest home in Collinsville, Illinois, across the big river from St. Louis. A painted cardinal adorned Moore's mailbox. He was 71 years old and suffering from prostate cancer.

Moore welcomed me to his porch and fetched me a soft drink. "I gotta get radiation for this thing [the cancer]," he began. "They burn me every few weeks. If you live long enough, you'll get prostate cancer, too."

"I can hardly wait, Terry," I said, and we both made sounds of strained laughter.

He unbent slowly. Yes, the Cardinals were talking about a strike. Bob Hyland, the doctor, said, "You fellers don't have to like Negroes, but a strike is a terrible idea." Sam Breadon read a threat from the league president that everyone would be suspended. Paychecks would stop. "None of us was making a lot of money," Moore said. "A suspension without pay would mean some fellers would lose their homes or the family farm. That killed the strike movement right there.

"Look," the old outfielder said with great earnestness, "Robinson was a great player. The Dodgers beat us out of the pennant in '47. They couldn't have done that without him." I was taking notes in a steno pad. "I'm being honest with you," Moore said, "and now I want you to do something for me. I was raised in a small town called Vernon, Alabama. When you write about the strike thing please point out that I was only acting on what I had been taught to believe as a boy."

We shook hands. I felt we had been men together. When I read that the cancer killed Terry Moore in 1995, I felt a twinge of sorrow. Like Dixie Walker, Terry Moore was a redneck who grew and changed.

The press at large did not do much with Woodward's story. The *New York Times* belligerently ignored it. Rationalizing, the *Times*'s senior baseball writer, a genial sort named John Drebinger, said to me, "The strike didn't actually happen, did it? At the *Times* we don't cover things that don't actually happen."

But there was one luminous exception, the gifted and largely forgotten Jimmy Cannon, who wrote for the *New York Post*. A self-educated Irishman from Greenwich Village, Cannon drew on Thomas Wolfe and Ernest Hemingway—and of course himself—for a style that many, including Hemingway, found overwhelming. I am here reprinting the entire column Cannon wrote following the Woodward scoop. It dazzled me when I first read it 65 years ago. It dazzles me today.

LYNCH MOBS DON'T ALWAYS WEAR HOODS

by Jimmy Cannon
"America's ace sportswriter"
New York Post, May 12, 1947

You don't always lynch a man by hanging him from a tree. There is a great lynch mob among us and they go unhooded and work without rope. They have no leader but their own hatred of humanity. They are quietly degraded, who plot against the helpless with skill and a coward's stealth and without fear of reprisal. Their weapon is as painful as the lash, the hot tar, the noose or the shotgun. They string up a man with the whisper of a lie and they persecute him with ridicule. They require no burning cross as a signal of assembly and need no sheet to identify themselves to each other. They are the night riders who operate 24 hours a day.

They lynch a man with a calculated contempt which no court of law can consider a crime. Such a venomous conspiracy is the one now trying to run Jackie Robinson out of organized baseball. It does not go for all ballplayers and not even all the St. Louis Cards, some of whom are accused of trying to arrange a strike to protest against the presence of a Negro in the big league. But such a state exists and we should all be ashamed of it, not only those connected with the sport, but any one who considers this his country. It is an indication, I believe, that as a people we are a failure and not as good as the laws by which we live.

We are a people guaranteed more freedoms than any other on earth. Yet there are among us some who would refute those documents which pledge us the things that people fight for everywhere and rarely achieve. When such persecutions become the aim of a government it is the record of history that men rise in revolt against the leaders of their state. It was to defeat such persecutions that men fought in the undergrounds of Europe and in every righteous army since man first realized freedom is seldom achieved without struggle. We are a people who consider such privileges as ordinary because they were written down in the book for us to live by long ago. But among us are those who consider these liberties as their own and would take them from the defenseless whom they can afford to torment. They form a lynch mob that is out to avenge a right.

Only the stupidly bold among them collect on mountain sides by the light of torches. You find them wherever you go and their lodge is national although they pay no dues and carry no card. It is only natural that baseball, being our country's sport, should be played by some of them because they are in all trades and professions and they carry an invisible rope with them at all times. It is my belief that such a philosophy of hate does not dominate baseball. If it does, then they should burn up all the bats and balls and turn cattle to graze on the outfield grass. Baseball is not a way of life but an escape from it. It is to the bleachers and the grandstands that the multitudes flee to forget the world beyond the fences. Such a haven should not be corrupted by senseless hate, but once it is, baseball has no reason to exist.

Baseball is supported by the people and I have heard them demand justice for Robinson. If their applause is any indication, they ask that Robinson be accepted as an athlete and is entitled to the right to be judged by the scorer's ledger and not by the prejudices of indecent men. It is my belief that Robinson is a big leaguer of ordinary ability. If he is not, then he should be sent down to the minors because it is the opinion of all of us who consider baseball a sport that skill and honesty are the only qualifications a man should have. It is doubtful if Robinson has yet shown his true worth. He came up as a shortstop, was transformed into a second baseman at Montreal and now is playing first. It is a tribute to his solidness as a man that he hasn't fallen apart as a ballplayer. Less heart has burned better ballplayers out of the big leagues. About him rages the silent uproar of a perpetual commotion. He is the most discussed ballplayer of his time and his judges do not evaluate him for his actions on the field alone. But he has concealed the turmoil within him and when you talk to him there is no indication he regards himself as a special man who faces problems no other big leaguer ever faced before. The times I have spoken to him he has praised all those with whom he plays.

What goes on in the privacy of the hotel rooms where the Dodgers gather I don't know. I have listened to Eddie Stanky praise Robinson for his alertness. Jackie told me himself that Hughie Casey had helped him when he needed practice and advice on making the difficult plays a first baseman must face.

> But in the clubhouse Robinson is a stranger. The Dodgers are polite and courteous with him but it is obvious he is isolated by those with whom he plays. I have never heard remarks made against him or detected any rudeness where he was concerned. But the silence is loud and Robinson never is part of the jovial and aimless banter of the locker room. He is the loneliest man I have ever seen in sports.
>
> We have been involved in a war to guarantee all people the right to a life without fear. The people of the earth are still assailed by the same doubts and terrors. The old men once more talk of violence and only the dead are sure of peace. In such a world it seems a small thing that a man be able to play a game unmolested. In our time such a plea should be unnecessary. But when it happens we must again remember that all this country's enemies are not beyond the frontiers of our homeland.

Everything in this long, eventful history seemed to be coming down to just a few days in May. The Dodgers headed west to Cincinnati, where they would play three games at Crosley Field against a mediocre Reds ball club. Mediocre but loud.

The paths of glory lay beckoning ahead.

AFTERWORD

GRAND LARCENY

JACKIE ROBINSON'S CANDLE BURNED BRIEFLY. BLINDED and partially crippled by diabetes, he died in October 1972, at the age of 53. Branch Rickey lived to be 30 years older. Rickey died in 1965 after suffering a stroke, while orating in Columbia, Missouri. I think it is fair to say that the year of major-league integration, 1947, was the climax of the lives of these two extraordinary Americans.

Walter O'Malley, Rickey's "most devious man," plotted, schemed and insinuated to drive Rickey out of Brooklyn. Rickey had continued to cut himself in on the receipts from player sales, and to make sure that there were plenty of players to be sold he maintained a Dodger farm system including as many as 25 minor-league teams. Most lost money. Rickey started a professional football team, also called the Brooklyn Dodgers, and despite great work by a tailback named Glenn Dobbs, this venture lost money as well. O'Malley told the other trustees that they, and the Dodger organization, would never turn a profit as long as Rickey remained in charge. The O'Malley gang voted out Rickey after the 1950 season, although the Dodgers had finished a close second to the Phillies.

Rickey owned 25 percent of the Dodger stock, which he was now obliged to sell to O'Malley, provided that O'Malley matched the highest outside offer Rickey could find. O'Malley told me that he thought Rickey's stock was worth about $250,000. But Rickey produced a bid from William Zeckendorf, an early version of Donald Trump, for nothing less than a cool million bucks. Furious, O'Malley insisted that the offer was fraudulent. But without proof, he had to pay Rickey $1,000,050 (which he borrowed from the Brooklyn Trust Company). After that O'Malley, as the new Dodger president, issued a directive: Anyone mentioning the name of Branch Rickey in the Dodger offices at 215 Montague Street was to be fined $1. "Walter wanted to make Rickey a non-person," says Frank Graham Jr., the Dodgers' publicity director at the time. "Shades of Josef Stalin. But since Rickey had signed Duke Snider, Carl Erskine, Jackie Robinson and the rest, you could never make him a non-person in Brooklyn."

Soon afterward John Galbreath, a multimillionaire real estate developer who was principal owner of the Pirates, brought Rickey to Pittsburgh as de facto general manager. The great performer Bing Crosby, a minority Pirate shareholder, came visiting and spent a few hours in a private conversation with Rickey. "Amazing ideas. Amazing vocabulary," Crosby told me later. "I thought I'd seen and heard just about everything. But I've never met anyone even close to Rickey in Hollywood."

Unfortunately for Rickey, his Pittsburgh team was slow to develop. He was forced to resign in 1959. But in 1960 the Pirates, with such Rickey stars as Roberto Clemente and Dick Groat, won the World Series from the New York Yankees.

With no National League teams in the New York area, talk began to rise about starting a third major circuit, the Continental League. Rickey now emerged as founding president. He sought backers for franchises from New York to Denver, but the start-up costs were monumental. (Think constructing, all at once, six or eight new big-league ballparks.)

Harold Rosenthal of the *Herald Tribune* asked at a press conference,

"Don't you think the odds are strong against the Continental League actually getting into operation?"

"Harold," Rickey said. "My father died at the age of 86, planting fruit trees in unpromising soil."

Frank Chance, first baseman and manager for the Chicago Cubs early in the 20th century, was widely known as "the peerless leader." Considering Rickey and his latest venture, John Lardner, the gifted columnist, called him "the peerless leader of the teamless league."

When the major leagues expanded early in the 1960s, the Continental League ceased to exist. It played a role in the baseball expansion and is a sort of forgotten godfather to the New York Mets. But when the billionaire Whitney family created the Mets, they turned not to Rickey but to old Yankee hands to run the business. With George Weiss supervising the front office and Casey Stengel managing the team, the 1962 Mets lost 120 of the 161 games they played.

August Busch of Budweiser, the brewmeister who owned the Cardinals, hired Rickey as a consultant in 1963. Now in his 80s, Rickey could not get along with general manager Vaughan "Bing" Devine. Busch fired Rickey two years later, on December 9, 1965.

The late years of Wesley Branch Rickey, a family member has told me, were weighted by considerations of the Holocaust. Baseball's Great Emancipator shared the common revulsion for Adolf Hitler, but his concern was more subtle than simple horror. He knew Germany as a nation of devout Lutherans and Roman Catholics. How, Rickey wondered, could the Holocaust have been spawned in a country that professed to follow the teachings, real or imagined, of Jesus Christ?

Branch Rickey's final question abides.

The *New York Times* continued its inaccurate and negative reporting on Jackie Robinson into the 21st century. On April 14, 2007, it published a so-called op-ed article asserting that Pee Wee Reese's memorable embrace of Jackie Robinson was "a myth."

That embrace took place at Crosley Field in Cincinnati on the Dodgers' first visit there in 1947. Fans, many from across the Ohio River in segregated Kentucky, began jeering Robinson, who was playing first base during infield practice. A number of Cincinnati ballplayers followed suit. Robinson set his teeth and made no response. At length Pee Wee Reese raised a hand, stopping the drill. Then he walked over from shortstop and put an arm about Robinson's broad shoulders. He said nothing, but simply stared the racists into silence. "After that happened," Robinson told me, "I never felt alone on a ball field again."

The *Times* writer was an obscure journalist named Stuart Miller, who had published a book called *The 100 Greatest Days in New York Sports.* The *Times* headlined the story "Breaking the Truth Barrier." As I say, the Miller article ran on April 14; a week later the *Times* published two corrections. Miller had misplaced Eddie Stanky's birthplace by 1,200 miles and he had misspelled the name of the Boston Braves star first baseman, Earl Torgeson. Miller then argued that Reese's embrace, if it happened at all, occurred in Boston. But Robinson himself told the sportscaster Jack Buck the place was Cincinnati. Reese, as we've seen, expansively confirmed that to me.

At the *Herald Tribune* long ago I was taught "If you didn't write something yourself, then don't deny it." But today the *New York Times* is archived and its reportage can be found in most libraries. To let Miller's sloppy little op-ed story become part of history is unacceptable.

Jackie Robinson played 10 seasons for the Brooklyn Dodgers, and during that time the team won the National League pennant six times. In its entire pre-Robinson history, stretching back to the 19th century, the Brooklyn team previously had finished first on only three occasions: 1916, 1920 and 1941.

Robinson's best single season came in 1949, when he was 30. He led the league in hitting at .349, and stolen bases with 37, including 5 steals of home. Following his rookie season he played second base into the mid-1950s, then moved to third and put in some time as an outfielder. After the Dodgers had clinched the pennant in 1952, I covered a game where Robinson played every position but pitcher. It was a publicity stunt, of course, but interesting. He made no errors anywhere.

One of Robinson's fortes was baserunning (as opposed simply to base stealing). He went from first to third on an infield out at least 10 times. He always took a daring lead off first. "If the pitcher throws and I don't have to dive back," he told me, "then I haven't taken a big enough lead." I saw him pivot on hundreds of double plays, but I never saw a baserunner crash into him. Never. "I'll tell you why," he said. "I'm fast. I get to second before the runner. Then I feint. He slides toward my feint. I move the other way and throw on to first." He was a brilliant student of the art of playing baseball.

After the 1956 season, when age and diabetes were slowing Robinson, O'Malley told Buzzie Bavasi, "Get rid of him." Among other things, this may have been a final jab at Robinson's sponsor and O'Malley's adversary, Branch Rickey.

That December Bavasi dealt Robinson's contract to the New York Giants for $50,000 and rights to a journeyman left-handed pitcher named Dick Littlefield. O'Malley then dictated a remarkably cynical letter.

> *Dear Jackie and Rachel:*
> *I do know how you and your youngsters must have felt.*
> *The roads of life have a habit of re-crossing. There could well be a future intersection. Until then, my best to you both.*
> *With a decade of memories.*
>
> Au revoir,
> Walter O'Malley

Instead of reporting to the Polo Grounds, Robinson quit. He then sold the announcement of his retirement to *Look* magazine for $50,000. In a rare burst of public anger Red Smith attacked Robinson "for peddling his retirement announcement." Jackie responded without raising his voice. "Red Smith doesn't have to send my kids through college. I do."

That is as much of the story as has been reported up to now. But on one of my last meetings with Buzzie Bavasi, in his mansion overlooking the deep and dark blue ocean, Bavasi added significant detail. He and O'Malley joined the Dodgers in Milwaukee during a western trip in 1956. The two executives shared a suite at the Hotel Schroeder.

"We were starting downstairs for breakfast," Bavasi said, "when Robinson came out of a room down the hall with a nice-looking white woman on his arm. It was pretty obvious to us that they had spent the night."

O'Malley elbowed Bavasi and the two retreated into their suite. O'Malley then said the four fateful words. *"Get rid of him."*

I was not on the scene but Bavasi's story rings true. Jackie always had a keen eye for the ladies. "You know," he told me once, "more white women want to take me to bed than I've got time for."

"Congratulations," I said.

"Eat your heart out," said Jackie Robinson.

After baseball Robinson worked for a chain of fast-food restaurants, a bank, an insurance company and campaigned with Nelson Rockefeller. His particular focus was housing. "Everybody talks about integrated schools," he said, "but regardless of the schools, if the housing is bad, children are going to hang out on the streets. And find trouble."

In his last years diabetes left him virtually blind. But he kept going. He was preparing to fly to Washington to lobby for a housing bill on October 24, 1972. Early that morning, in his imposing home on Cascade Road in North Stamford, Connecticut, a heart attack ended his life.

Feeling that the end was coming, Jackie Robinson composed his own epitaph. The words are carved on his stone in Cypress Hills Cemetery, an historic resting place located in Brooklyn. "A life is important only in the impact it has on other lives." Perhaps one final word is appropriate here.

Amen.

CHRONOLOGICAL LIST OF STEALS OF HOME BY JACKIE ROBINSON

DATE	OPPOSING PITCHER	TEAM	HOME	INNING
06-24-47	Ostermueller, Fritz	Pittsburgh Pirates	Pittsburgh	5
07-19-47	Pollet, Howie	St. Louis Cardinals	Brooklyn	1
08-29-47	Beggs, Joe	New York Giants	Brooklyn	6
07-04-48	Hansen, Andy	New York Giants	Brooklyn	7
07-25-48	Lombardi, Vic	Pittsburgh Pirates	Pittsburgh	8
08-04-48	Meyer, Russ	Chicago Cubs	Brooklyn	1
08-22-48	Voiselle, Bill	Boston Braves	Brooklyn	5
09-28-48	Spahn, Warren	Boston Braves	Brooklyn	5
06-02-49	Brecheen, Harry	St. Louis Cardinals	Brooklyn	6
07-16-49	Wehmeier, Herm	Cincinnati Reds	Brooklyn	2

Chronological List of Steals of Home by Jackie Robinson

DATE	OPPOSING PITCHER	TEAM	HOME	INNING
07-18-49	Rush, Bob	Chicago Cubs	Brooklyn	6
08-09-49	Trinkle, Ken	Philadelphia Phillies	Philadelphia	5
09-20-49	Muncrief, Bob	Chicago Cubs	Chicago	8
07-02-50	Meyer, Russ	Philadelphia Phillies	Philadelphia	4
09-26-51	Burdette, Lew	Boston Braves	Boston	8
05-18-52	Ramsdell, Willie	Chicago Cubs	Brooklyn	4
04-23-54	Friend, Bob	Pittsburgh Pirates	Pittsburgh	6
08-29-55	LaPalme, Paul	St. Louis Cardinals	Brooklyn	6
04-25-56	Hearn, Jim	New York Giants	New York	2

THE PIONEERS

FOLLOWING ARE THE FIRST BLACK PLAYERS SIGNED into the major leagues, listed in chronological order by the date of their debut and by team. Daggers indicate eventual election to the Baseball Hall of Fame. I am certain each man has, or would have had, an interesting story to relate. I'd further suggest that for his struggle against bigotry, everyone on this list qualifies as an all-star.

PLAYER	TEAM	DATE
Jackie Robinson †	Brooklyn Dodgers, NL	April 15, 1947
Larry Doby †	Cleveland Indians, AL	July 5, 1947
Hank Thompson	St. Louis Browns, AL	July 17, 1947
Monte Irvin †	New York Giants, NL	July 8, 1949
Hank Thompson	New York Giants, NL	July 8, 1949
Sam Jethroe	Boston Braves, NL	April 18, 1950
Minnie Miñoso	Chicago White Sox, AL	May 1, 1951
Bob Trice	Philadelphia Athletics, AL	September 13, 1953
Ernie Banks †	Chicago Cubs, NL	September 17, 1953
Curt Roberts	Pittsburgh Pirates, NL	April 13, 1954

PLAYER	TEAM	DATE
Tom Alston	St. Louis Cardinals, NL	April 13, 1954
Nino Escalera	Cincinnati Reds, NL	April 17, 1954
Chuck Harmon	Cincinnati Reds, NL	April 17, 1954
Carlos Paula	Washington Senators, AL	September 6, 1954
Elston Howard	New York Yankees, AL	April 14, 1955
John Kennedy	Philadelphia Phillies, NL	April 22, 1957
Ozzie Virgil Sr.	Detroit Tigers, AL	June 6, 1958
Pumpsie Green	Boston Red Sox, AL	July 21, 1959

ACKNOWLEDGMENTS

A LONG TIME AGO, IN 1952, THE LATE *NEW YORK HERALD Tribune* loosed me on the world of organized baseball. Perhaps neither I nor baseball has since been quite the same.

Although in time I covered all three New York teams, I primarily wrote on the Brooklyn Dodgers. They were not the best team of that era. The New York Yankees were. But with Robinson, Rickey and later Walter O'Malley, the old Dodgers were the most interesting of ball clubs.

My friendships with Jackie Robinson and Branch Rickey date from that period. Talk during those friendships was a vital source for this book. But significant fresh research was required. Here I benefited from the help of Joseph Bacchi, a star student at a college near my home, SUNY New Paltz.

Mark Weinstein of Rodale brought vigor and intelligence to his task as editor. He has my gratitude. My literary agent Robert Wilson, now of Orlando, Florida, was supportive and helpful throughout.

On a personal level reliving the integration of baseball was quite an experience. In plain English, it made for one hell of a trip.

RK

ABOUT THE AUTHOR

ROGER KAHN IS WIDELY REGARDED AS THE GREATEST living American sportswriter. The author of 20 books and hundreds of articles for national magazines, he is the only baseball writer to have had three titles appear on the *New York Times* bestseller list. His 1972 classic, *The Boys of Summer*, was named the best baseball book of all time by the editors of *Sports Illustrated*. Kahn joined the staff of the *New York Herald Tribune* as a copy boy in 1948 and rose quickly to the position of baseball writer. He began to cover the Dodgers in 1952, and also traveled with the other New York teams, the Giants and the Yankees. In 1956, Kahn was named sports editor of *Newsweek* magazine and then from 1963 to 1969 served as editor-at-large of *The Saturday Evening Post*. For a decade he wrote a monthly column for *Esquire* magazine. Five times his articles were voted the best in the country and awarded the E.P. Dutton prize. His 1993 book, *The Era*, was nominated for the Pulitzer Prize. Kahn has taught writing at various colleges and lectured at Yale, Princeton and Columbia universities. Mr. Kahn held the distinguished position of Ottaway Professor of Journalism at SUNY New Paltz in the spring of 2004, and in 2006 he was inducted into the National Jewish Sports Hall of Fame. A native of Brooklyn, where he grew up rooting for the Dodgers, he now makes his home in Stone Ridge, New York, with his wife, Katharine.

INDEX

Underscored page references indicate boxed text or tables.

Index

Index

Index